DATE DUE

GAYLORD · PRINTED IN U.S.A

AMERICAN MADONNA

Recent titles in
RELIGION IN AMERICA SERIES
Harry S. Stout, General Editor

AMERICAN MADONNA

Images of the
Divine Woman
in Literary Culture

JOHN GATTA

New York   Oxford • Oxford University Press   1997

Oxford University Press

Oxford   New York

Athens   Auckland   Bangkok   Bogota   Bombay   Buenos Aires
Calcutta   Cape Town   Dar es Salaam   Delhi   Florence   Hong Kong
Istanbul   Karachi   Kuala Lumpur   Madras   Madrid   Melbourne
Mexico City   Nairobi   Paris   Singapore   Taipei   Tokyo   Toronto   Warsaw

and associated companies in
Berlin   Ibadan

Copyright © 1997 by John Gatta

Published by Oxford University Press, Inc.
198 Madison Avenue, New York, New York 10016

Oxford is a registered trademark of Oxford University Press

Library of Congress Cataloging-in-Publication Data
Gatta, John.
American madonna : images of the divine woman in
literary culture / John Gatta
p. cm.
Includes index.
ISBN 0-19-511261-X; ISBN 0-19-511262-8 (pbk.)
1. American literature—19th century—History and criticism.
2. Mary, Blessed Virgin, Saint—In literature. 3. American
literature—Protestant authors—History and criticism. 4. American
literature—20th century—History and criticism. 5. Mary, Blessed
Virgin, Saint—Cult—United States. 6. Christianity and literature—
United States. 7. woman (Christian theology) in literature.
8. Femininity (Psychology) in literature. 9. Women and literature—
United States.   10. Christian saints in literature. I. Title.
PS217.M35G38   1997
810.9'351—dc21   96-48856

1 3 5 7 9 8 6 4 2

Printed in the United States of America
on acid-free paper

For
my wife, Julia,
and
daughter, Mary Lian

PREFACE

IN SEVERAL WAYS, the topic addressed in this book seems to have discovered me rather than vice versa. Marian piety struck me as decidedly embarrassing, if not repugnant, at an earlier phase of my life. Even while completing my undergraduate studies at the University of Notre Dame in the late 1960s, I thought of devotion to the Virgin Mary as unscriptural, superstitious, and too steeped in the sentimentality of popular culture for thinking Christians—not to mention secularists—to take seriously.

Later I became more impressed by the capacity of Christian tradition to baptize for itself worthy elements in "pagan" spirituality or mythology. I also came to appreciate the contemporary case for rediscovering Mary—for understanding her role theologically, for recognizing the enduring psychic and spiritual sources of her appeal. Christian theologians, some feminists, and Jungians have all contributed intellectually to this revival of interest over the past thirty years or so. The cultus of Mary now engages students of gender studies and post-Reformation history as well as literary theorists such as Julia Kristeva and Mary Jacobus. In a British context, its persistent cultural and social relevance is displayed in the title of Helen Hackett's recent book, *Virgin Mother, Maiden Queen: Elizabeth I and the Cult of the Virgin Mary*. And some of the new curiosity about Christianity's Virgin Mother falls somewhere within the larger swell of current popular interest in a resurgent Mother Goddess.

Even so, it did not occur to me that American literary culture or Protestant culture held any commerce with the matter of Mary. In the ever-expanding reach of United States literary scholarship since World War II, publications charted the topoi not only of an American Adam and an American dream but also of an American apocalypse, typology, savagery, hieroglyphics, pastoral, incarnation, and Eve. But what of the second or new Eve? Had *she* ever claimed a distinctive presence in New World imaginations outside Canada and Latin America? I assumed not. Nor had my previous studies of the New England Puritan tradition led me to suspect otherwise. It was only when I happened to visit the Stowe house on Forest Street in nearby Hartford, and was struck by the Raphael Madonna so boldly displayed in this household of a retired Protestant clergyman and renowned Protestant author, that I began to reconsider. I started to reread familiar texts such as "The Virgin and the Dynamo" and *The Marble Faun,* and then found other texts germane to an emerging pattern. All the rest followed. That the version of early American literature lately presented by *The Heath Anthology* should include the Aztec "History of the Miraculous Apparition of the Virgin of Guadalupe in 1531" no longer strikes me as so oddly irrelevant to the larger course of our literary history.

I do not claim that the crosscurrent highlighted in this book ever becomes an altogether mainstream force in canonical American literature. But it does figure in many more writers than the few I have elected to discuss. If one wished, for example, to look beyond Eliot to other twentieth-century poets, variant developments of the theme could be found in H. D., Robert Lowell, Wallace Stevens, Charles Olson, and Luci Shaw. It figures also in Emily Dickinson and, with further mythic permutations, in fictionalists as otherwise dissimilar as Harriet Prescott Spofford, Edith Wharton, Thomas Pynchon, and Toni Morrison. Colleagues keep proposing to me the names of more and more candidates. In this opening investigation, though, it seemed to me preferable to work at some depth with six figures rather than more superficially with many. And except for Harold Frederic, who was exposed in childhood to Methodism in upstate New York, all of the writers considered in the following pages shared a New England heritage once shaped by Puritan sensibilities.

Storrs, Connecticut   J.G.
August 1996

ACKNOWLEDGMENTS

AS I TRUST THE documentation throughout this study will show, I am much indebted to scholarship that has been published over the years on the six writers I address and on topics related to my central theme. Closer to home, my greatest debt is to the University of Connecticut Research Foundation and to Dean Thomas Giolas and Associate Dean James Henkel for allowing me use of office space—blessedly free of telephone—in which to conduct research and writing for this project. Without the chance to escape my administrative duties occasionally by retreating to this office, I could not have written the book.

For a variety of archival services, I am grateful to library personnel at the Houghton Library, Harvard; the Beinecke, Yale; the Stowe-Day Library, Hartford; the Massachusetts Historical Society, Boston; the Utica Public Library; and the Homer Babbidge Library and Dodd Research Center at the University of Connecticut. For permission to present in chapter 4 the revised expansion of an essay first published in *Connotations: A Journal for Critical Debate* 5 (1995–96): 147–66, I am grateful to the editors of that journal. It is a special pleasure to acknowledge the contributions of graduate students—particularly Monica Hatzberger, Kurt Heidinger, and Susana Martins—who took the seminar in which I tried out ideas later developed in the book. Kurt Heidinger also helped me set the manuscript and accompanying illustrations in final form for submission.

Among the others who supplied encouragement or help of various sorts along the way, I would like to name Lynn Bloom, Michael Colacurcio, Robert Daly, William O'Brien, Milton Stern, and my wife, Julia. Finally, I want to thank one I cannot name: an anonymous reader for Oxford University Press. Several valuable suggestions in this reader's report have been imperfectly incorporated into the argument that follows.

CONTENTS

AMERICAN MADONNA

INTRODUCTION

FOR SEVERAL REASONS, one would scarcely predict a substantial role for the medieval cultus of Mary in the land of the Pilgrim Fathers. Most obviously, the United States remained a largely Protestant country before the mass immigration movements of the late nineteenth century. Within a climate of Reformation animosity toward suspected pagan and mythic accretions to Scripture, one does not expect Marian piety to flourish or to find expression in imaginative literature. Then, too, the fin de siècle cult of Teddy Roosevelt's "strenuous life," with its rigorous masculinity and code of mercantile exertion, must be deemed inimical to the values of spiritual receptivity, intuitionism, and psychic femininity commonly associated with the Virgin Mother. Nor was there much to favor Mary's reputation in the demythologizing, technocratic temper of the emerging twentieth century or in the aura of disjunctive skepticism surrounding modernism, to say nothing of postmodernism.

Yet a notable undercurrent of interest in Mary as mythical Madonna *has* persisted in American life and letters from fairly early in the nineteenth century into the later twentieth. In these latter days, for feminist writers such as Starhawk, it has shifted toward fascination with the Great Goddess of matriarchal prehistory.[1] This imaginative involvement with the Divine Woman—verging, at times, on devotional homage—becomes all the more intriguing as manifested in the Protestant writers who are the exclusive focus of this study. My concern, then, is to delineate a countercultural pattern of mythic assertion that has yet to be acknowledged in standard surveys of American cultural or literary history.

The argument here is that flirtation with the Marian cultus offered certain Protestant writers symbolic compensation for what might be culturally diagnosed as a deficiency of psychic femininity, or of anima, in America. For these writers, the Christian Magna Mater and her pagan precursors embodied a principle of creativ-

3

ity distinct from factory models of production or from the actively competitive ideals of Victorian manhood. Especially for writers like Hawthorne and Stowe, figures of divine maternity also challenged the predominantly masculine symbol-system inherited from Puritan forebears. Dwelling mainly on nineteenth-century texts, I hope to show how literary configurations of the mythical Madonna express a subsurface cultural resistance to the prevailing rationalism and pragmatism of the American mind in an age of entrepreneurial conquest.

This engagement with Christianity's figurative relative of the primordial Mother Goddess surfaces in a wide range of literary forms. Likewise from the standpoint of authorial imagination, the following treatment of selected fiction, nonfictional prose, and poetry plays through several distinct variations on the theme of divine womanhood. Yet of the writers I have chosen to consider closely, Henry Adams is the only one whose involvement with the Marian mythology has already been clearly recognized, if not fully discussed. Just as Adams's Marian reflections claim a predictable prominence in *Mont-Saint-Michel and Chartres,* so also his exposition on "The Virgin and the Dynamo" is commonly appreciated as the emotional and symbolic centerpiece of *The Education.* Still, the cultural ramifications of this tormented skeptic's attraction to the Virgin cannot be fully appreciated apart from the antecedent tradition—at once American, Protestant, and literary—in which he stands and which this book exists to explore.

As complementary exemplars of that tradition, the cases of Nathaniel Hawthorne and Harriet Beecher Stowe are illuminating. Often portrayed as a child of Puritanism, Hawthorne's shaping religious environment in Salem was more nearly Unitarian. Yet the Romantic, or perhaps Christian-Romantic, spirituality of his fictive imagination ultimately runs counter to the demythologizing rationalism of both Puritan and liberal Protestant influences. Hawthorne's figurative involvement with the Marian typology, which antedates his European sojourn, gives revealing expression to this dissenting impulse. Besides enriching our understanding of problematic attitudes toward contemporary womanhood reflected in Hawthorne's fiction, study of the Madonna theme brings to light new literary dimensions and psychocultural subtexts in such familiar works as *The Scarlet Letter, The Blithedale Romance,* and, above all, *The Marble Faun.*

Harriet Beecher Stowe's little-known but even more pronounced Marian interest was likewise implicated in her movement away from a Calvinist orthodoxy that shaped her early personal identity much more decisively than it did Hawthorne's. Delineated fully and explicitly in nonfictional prose writings, Stowe's Marianism likewise illuminates the peculiar character of her domestic and matriarchal feminism, which must be reckoned with as a central force in fictions such as *Uncle Tom's Cabin* and *The Minister's Wooing.* This revalorization of the Madonna stressed the Virgin's conjunctive relation to a singularly "feminine" and maternal Christ. In Stowe, of course, as in Margaret Fuller, one also has occasion to observe the variant reactions of a female writer to questions of cultural femininity that might otherwise be construed from the exclusive—hence, misleading—perspective of male authorship.

At the same time, it would be impossible to identify a monolithic "woman's response" to these issues. Thus, whereas Stowe developed her own domestic vision of Mary as paradigmatic mother, Margaret Fuller inclined toward a radical social conception of Mary as virgin-lifebearer and feminist icon. And whereas Stowe sustained her Marian interest within a modified Protestant version of Christian orthodoxy, Fuller venerated the Virgin as transcendental image of the awakened soul. In *Woman in the Nineteenth Century,* Mary becomes Fuller's prototype of the empowered female whose self-reliant autonomy derives from a pneumatic inspiration that displaces conventionalized marital authority. "Would she [Woman] but assume her inheritance," the author insists, "Mary would not be the only virgin mother."[2]

By the close of the century, Harold Frederic is able to exploit the Madonna theme for purposes of artistic irony and social satire. In his underrated masterwork, *The Damnation of Theron Ware* (1896), an artless Methodist minister confronts a new American Catholic subculture in which the Marian image of "holy womanhood" merges confusedly with the pagan cultus of liberated licentiousness. Or so at least things appear to the Reverend Theron Ware as he gazes longingly toward the un-attainable Celia Madden. But while Theron's overheated male imagination sees in Celia an alluring amalgam of Madonna and presumptive harlot, what she embodies in actual social terms is the new independent woman of the 1890s. In a brilliant stroke of social commentary, the author shows how Celia at once scandalizes and entrances Ware when she brings him into her inner sanctum decorated with nude statues *and* paintings of the Virgin. For Frederic, then, as realist observer, the Madonna theme matters less in its theological aspect of universal myth than in its sociological reflection of cultural myth, psychosexual conflict, and changing models of womanhood at a given historical moment.

Carrying my rather broad survey beyond Frederic and Henry Adams a little further into the current century, I have decided to close with a discussion of T. S. Eliot, who may not seem to belong here on at least three counts. Not only does the poet's modern context introduce issues distinct from some of those pertinent to the nineteenth-century mainstream of this inquiry, but also his own national identity weighs in as only ambiguously American. What is more, Eliot's chosen Anglo-Catholic (albeit non-Roman Catholic) religious affiliation sets him slightly apart from the solidly Protestant background of self-identification characteristic of all the other writers I examine.

Nonetheless, it seems to me that Eliot's anomalous position makes his work in some ways all the more revealing of oxymoronic tension in the cultural development and transformation of an American Madonna. It is probably no accident that "Dry Salvages," the section of *Four Quartets* where Eliot interposes his most explicitly Marian poetry, also contains the work's most American setting of reminiscence. It is also notable that "Ash-Wednesday," a work that marks a turning point in the poet's own spiritual passage, abounds in Marian imagery integrally related to the speaker's perception of interior reality. Hence the Virgin became for Eliot a touchstone of traditional yet deeply felt personal faith as well as a symbolic vehicle for cultural criticism. Cognizant of the mythic roots of Marian piety beneath Christian orthodoxy, Eliot emblematized the Madonna as a garden oasis of solace and spiritual sustenance amid the mythopoeic impoverishment of the wasteland era.

WHAT FURTHER CONCLUSIONS might be drawn overall about the origins and implications of this theme? At one level, the American Madonna appears to be yet one more reflection of that nostalgic medievalism that characterized the Romantic era internationally and that survived in some quarters into this century. At another level, it betrays a persistent American urge toward the archaic, toward the recovery of natural roots in the deep psyche, that recalls Emerson's atavism in seeking "an original relation to the universe." Alternatively, in its more socially conservative aspect, homage to the Madonna could translate into conformity with an ideal of sacred womanhood enforced by the Victorian cult of sentimental domesticity. In his Introduction to a devotional book published in 1889, a Protestant clergyman identifies Mary as the queen of "home influences" and "the model of all womanly, wifely, motherly excellence."[3] The Divine Woman has realized her presence in America through both sociohistorical and archetypal versions of myth. Accordingly, a broad assortment of interpretive methods—including cultural criticism, myth and psychological criticism, iconographic study, feminist revaluation, and theological analysis—is needed to appreciate her significance as most vividly revealed through literary imagination.

Inevitably, too, such an inquiry must touch on issues of marriage, sex relations, and domesticity that involved the actual experience of Americans. Particularly from the standpoint of present-day women's concerns, the Madonna motif raises intriguing questions about how myth impinged on the social circumstance of real-life women. Thus, the man's recovery of psychic femininity in connection with Marian piety is not *bound* to enhance the social possibilities and autonomy of women in the empirical world. Indeed, the reverse might occur. So the Madonna, which Goethe linked to the *Ewig-Weibliche* or "eternal feminine," remains liable to feminist suspicion. Contemporary critiques by Mary Daly and Marina Warner, for example, disparage the cult of the Virgin as socially regressive insofar as this Woman is presumed to represent a unique ideal and miraculous achievement that actual women cannot hope to replicate. Others, particularly those combining Christian commitment with more moderate feminist values, have lately argued for Mary's continuing spiritual and social relevance to modern aspirations.[4] But while questions about the effect of Marian beliefs on women's social status certainly warrant empirical investigation, I do not presume to settle that issue here. Within the literary and imaginative terms of this study, my intent is rather to elucidate mythopoeic perceptions of these matters in selected texts and to suggest, in turn, how attending to the Madonna theme as broadly conceived can deepen appreciation of the artistry and import of those texts.

If the origins of the Marian cultus can be related to first-century mystery religions or to pre-Christian and even prehistorical beliefs, it is also clear that the mother of Jesus took on a distinctive and integral significance within the development of Christian doctrine. This emphasis drew especially on the Gospel nativity narratives in Matthew and Luke, above all on the Lukan account of God's Annunciation to Mary and the ecstatic poetry of her response in the Magnificat. Yet from the standpoint of strict exegesis, there is, of course, little New Testament justification for elevating Mary to anything like the privileged status of a demigod or coredeemer.

There is even some scriptural basis for wondering how explicitly she affirmed the beliefs taught by apostolic Christian followers of the Way.[5] Orthodox church teaching has always defined Mary of Nazareth as decidedly human, as ancillary to Christ in the work of redemption, and as by no means equivalent to a fourth person of the Divine Trinity.

Yet beyond these technical reservations, it remains an awesome fact for orthodoxy that God became flesh in and through her flesh. Hence her ancient—and perennially controversial—title of Theotokos (mother of God), confirmed by the Ecumenical Council of Ephesus in 431, carries momentous implications. That this title was ratified in Ephesus (figure I.1), where the cult of virginal yet sexually charged Artemis had ruled, is telling. Just as the Christ of faith came to signify considerably more than was carnally visible in the historical Jesus of Nazareth, so also by the fourth century the typological significance of Maria Theotokos—as new mother of the church and of the human race—had developed well beyond the originative locus of Miriam the Galilean. This is not the place to rehearse the story of Mary's elevation to cultus figure through the course of patristic and medieval history in both Byzantine and Western Christianity.[6] Suffice it to say that from the designation as Theotokos, expansion of Mary's transhistorical or mystical identity followed quite logically. Eventually, then, the mother of Jesus would be mystically linked to the antecedent tradition of Hebrew Wisdom, to the affective imagery of the Song of Songs, and to the apocalyptic "woman clothed with the sun" from chapter 12 of the Book of Revelation.

Insofar as Mary dramatized God's impregnation of all creation in her bringing to birth the New Creation, her symbolic expansion assimilated as well the precedents of the archaic Earth Mother and the fertility goddesses of ancient Canaanite, Egyptian, and Greek religious notoriety. Hildegard of Bingen's Christian verse-hymns from the twelfth century celebrate Mary as the fructifying vessel of incarnate Love, the human womb of divine creation in all its theophanic glory.[7] In Christian iconography and devotional writing, one can even discern mythic remnants of the divine consort or *hieros gamos* motif, so that Mary appears as in some sense both the lover and mother of the bridegroom Jesus.[8] As exalted Queen of Heaven, Christianity's royal bride shows an evident symbolic kinship with figures like Ishtar, Ashera, Astarte, and Isis. She is wedded not to Joseph but to the overshadowing and impenetrating Spirit-Christ. And within biblical tradition this bridal conceit is supported, once again, by erotic language from the Song of Songs and by poetic accounts of Lady Sophia presented in the books of Proverbs, Ecclesiasticus, and Wisdom.

Such observations suggest that, even within Christian orthodoxy, Mary Theotokos reflects the feminine face of a God who ultimately transcends all categories of sexual identity. *Almost* deified, then, as *virgo genitrix* and palpable bearer of the divine Word, the mythical Madonna must be accounted at least "more honorable than the Cherubim, and more glorious beyond compare than the seraphim."[9] Despite excesses of devotion lamentable under the brand of "Mariolatry," emotive involvement in the Marian mystery has long exercised a kind of poetic attraction transcending functional definition. In his own unorthodox terms, C. G.

Jung applauded the Roman church's 1950 doctrinal declaration of the Virgin's bodily Assumption into heaven because he took this development to signify acceptance of the feminine principle as complementary to the Divine Trinity. A psychic quaternary had been recovered, a proper archetype of wholeness had been recognized, with "the entry of the Mother of God into the heavenly bridal-chamber."[10]

By contrast with the "maternal character" thus displayed in Catholicism, Jung found Protestantism tied inextricably to a "paternal spirit" of rationalism that forbad iconic access to divine womanhood. Yet this dismissal of Protestant possibilities may have been premature. Just as Marian devotion has persisted quite vividly in Anglican writings from the seventeenth century through the nineteenth-century Oxford movement and beyond,[11] so also it has maintained a recessive position in the spirituality and hymnody of mainstream Protestantism. In the nineteenth century, Americans encountered highly sympathetic readings of Marian aesthetics in Anna Jameson's *Legends of the Madonna* (1852), a well-known study by an Anglo-Irish Protestant. Both Hawthorne and Fuller were well acquainted with Jameson. At around the same time, works such as Johann Jakob Bachofen's *The Mothers: Myth, Religion, and Mother Right* (1861) signaled a revival of modern interest in the Goddess.

Accordingly, the Madonna symbology I discern in selected U.S. writers of Protestant background is *not* to be construed as a covert allegiance to Roman Catholicism. The Virgin Mother has never "belonged" exclusively to that church. As we have already observed, her mythopoeic ancestry goes back at least as far as the Great Goddess cultus that held sway before 3,000 B.C., and nowhere in Christendom has she been known with greater depth and iconographic force than in the non-Roman spirituality of Eastern Orthodoxy. None of the American writers I discuss came close to becoming a Roman Catholic.

On the contrary, Hawthorne and Stowe envisioned a reconstituted Protestantism that might accept more fully the religious value of divine femininity without, in their view, succumbing to the authoritarian rigidity and institutional corruption of Roman Catholicism. From a dissenting point of view, questionable doctrines such as the 1854 papal pronouncement on Mary's Immaculate Conception might actually violate the poetic mystery of the Madonna by objectifying it in rationalistic terms.[12] Neither were the writers under discussion oblivious to the sentimental excesses and aesthetic offenses sometimes engendered by Roman Catholic Mariolatry. Though they might be drawn toward certain aspects of Roman Catholicism including its Marian cultus, they were apt to seek within that cultus a more archetypal expression of psychic femininity than the institution's hierarchy was prone to acknowledge.

Yet, curiously, these Protestant writers invoked Marian or Magna Mater themes in a way that their Roman Catholic counterparts in this country generally have not. In the modern United States, for example, the Madonna fascination seems comparatively rare in works by such notable and religiously committed Roman Catholic fictionalists as Flannery O'Connor, Walker Percy, and J. F. Powers. In the Catholic France of Paul Claudel and Charles Péguy, that is hardly so. It is as though the American Catholic writer needed to frustrate stereotypical expectations of Mariolatry, whereas the American Protestant needed to recover the Virgin's archetypal femininity with an opposite rhetoric of response.

Thus, beyond the individual cases of Protestant authorship considered here, their common investment in the Madonna suggests an intertextual pattern of symbolic compensation and reaction. While tracing notable variations on the Madonna theme, I also try to delineate a persistent cultural pattern of yearning or nostalgia for religious myth combined with resistance to post-Enlightenment rationalism and native American pragmatism. Eventually, it seems, something more than an accident of nomenclature draws together in Marian sisterhood figures like Hawthorne's Miriam, Stowe's Mara or Mary Scudder or Little Eva, and Adams's real-life Marian Hooper. That the Madonna Ciccone of current mass media fame draws appeal from debased representations of the sacred testifies, however ironically, to the persistence in American culture of a spiritual force whose trajectory I have tried to trace forward from early in the previous century.

FIGURE I.I. *Ephesian Artemis.* From the Ephesus Archaeological Museum, Ephesus, Turkey (Erich Lessing/Art Resource, New York). The Marian cultus soon assimilated the precedents of goddesses from throughout the ancient Mediterranean and Near Eastern world. At Ephesus, in the Church of St. Mary, the Ecumenical Council of 431 confirmed attribution of the title Theotokos (God-bearer, or Mother of God) to Mary.

THE SACRED WOMAN

The Problem of Hawthorne's Madonnas

Of Holy Mothers and Dark Ladies

When Nathaniel Hawthorne took up residence with his new bride at the Old Manse in Concord, Massachusetts, in 1842, he was acutely aware of the house's churchly legacy. Built by Emerson's ministerial grandfather in 1765, it had been inhabited thereafter by a long succession of clergymen, and Hawthorne found its garret full of dusty theological tomes that he felt "none the less a Christian" for ignoring. The author of the prefatory essay on "The Old Manse" retains a religious confidence in divine beneficence, in the "infinite spiritual capacity" of the human soul, and in some version of "saving grace." He aspires to write a novel "that should evolve some deep lesson" suitable to the Manse's sacred space. And yet he feels so oppressed by the house's "grim prints of Puritan ministers," who frown on his new-found Eden from the walls of his study, that he and Sophia replace these "bad angels" with "the sweet and lovely head of one of Raphael's Madonnas."[1]

The gesture of displacement is telling. It says a good deal about what one recent commentator has called "the feminization of masculine poetics" in nineteenth-century America.[2] It also enlarges our sense of Hawthorne's religious sensibility as centered in a belief system which, because of the author's well-known reticence and reluctance to define himself doctrinally, has eluded close description. Of course, there is no lack of commentary on Hawthorne's imaginative involvement with, and presumed ambivalence toward, New England Puritanism. By now, it seems fairly apparent that this moral analyst of the Colonial past was, indeed, as Lawrence Buell describes him, a "post-Puritan" product of liberal, Unitarian influences in his nurturing environment.

Still, whether one identifies Hawthorne's personal religious stance as closer to agnostic secularism or to Christian neo-orthodoxy, it seems to encompass a broader span of psychic and emotional coloration than that typically associated with liberal Protestantism. As Buell wisely observes, "Hawthorne's neo-orthodoxy, if that is the right label, can thus be seen as a sort of rebuke not just to Arminian-Transcendentalist optimism but to the whole drift of mainline Protestant thought."[3] Implicated in this rebuke are those peculiar propensities toward Roman Catholicism, mixed though they are with countervailing antipathies, that Hawthorne betrayed, especially toward the close of his career. Though it hardly seems credible that, as one contemporary rumor had it, Hawthorne thought to become a Catholic during his Italian sojourn, he was plainly attracted in ways that anticipate the later Anglican and Roman Catholic affiliations of his two daughters.

Instead of trying to deal here with the entire question of Hawthorne's attraction toward Catholicism, which an earlier generation of scholars—particularly Leonard J. Fick—has already addressed in general terms,[4] I want to highlight one neglected aspect pertinent to my larger study: his fictive portrayal of Mary, the Mother of Jesus and figurative Christian relative of the primeval Mother Goddess. Though Henry Adams declared in 1900 that the energy of the Marian Virgin was "unknown to the American mind," Hawthorne's creative mind was clearly engaged by her concept and iconography.

In the traditional Catholic and European mythology surrounding the biblical Mary, this fictionalist from Protestant New England discovered several things. First, the Madonna offered him a symbolic analogue for his enduring faith in the sacred, saving force mediated through womanhood. Biographically, the prospect of mediated access to the Father God through a feminine face of divinity might be particularly welcome to someone who had, like Hawthorne, suffered an early deprivation of access to his human father and who was apt to regard his biological mother in curiously virginal terms.[5] The Marian mythology implied a critique not only of liberal Christianity, with its presumed excess of demythologizing rationalism, but also of the aggressive, anti-imaginative, mercantile temper that ruled in the nineteenth-century culture of a Judge Pyncheon. In a word, imaginative interest in the Marian mythology and its goddess affiliations stimulated Hawthorne—as it did other writers we shall consider—to recover for his readership an anima dimension of feminine spirituality otherwise underrepresented in Victorian America.

Within the fictional canon, Hawthorne's exploitation of Marian symbolism is most significant in *The Marble Faun,* though it also appears in *The Scarlet Letter,* in *The Blithedale Romance* with variant stress on the pre-Christian Goddess, and less overtly in some of the tales. At least two different faces of the sacred woman figure in Hawthorne's imaginative response. The first is St. Mary the Virgin, with her mystique of surpassing purity and latent sexuality. The second and ultimately more significant is the Mother Mary, physical bearer of the divine Word and compassionate intercessor for humankind. Both perspectives combine to create the overall picture of a Christian Magna Mater in Hawthorne's fiction, though we shall also see them clashing at times to image personal and cultural tensions in the author.

Hawthorne's portrayal of sacred womanhood under the dual aspect of Virgin and Mother shows some correlation with the pattern of opposition between his "fair" and "dark" heroines as analyzed in the criticism of previous decades. The fair-haired lady, a virginal innocent, is typically represented by dovelike New England maidens such as Phoebe in *The House of the Seven Gables,* Priscilla in *The Blithedale Romance,* or Hilda in *The Marble Faun.* In theological terms, the fair lady has been associated with grace, spirituality, and the prospect of salvation; the dark lady, with sin, bodily temptation, and the threat of damnation.

That Hawthorne's fiction so persistently dramatizes the redemptive love mediated through godly women would seem, at one level, to confirm the author's appreciation of women and of feminized religion. Like the mythologized Marian Madonna, interceding women such as Phoebe in *Gables* (a "Religion in herself," 2:168) and Elizabeth in "The Minister's Black Veil" offer fallen men a divine communion devoid of wrath or blame. Some of these sanctifying heroines even bear the right name. In "The Man of Adamant," for example, the specter of Mary Goffe typifies that "pure Religion" whose "faith and love united" invites Richard Digby to save his soul. Hawthorne likewise stresses the emphatic "purity" of Mary Inglefield or the invaluable filial love of Marygold, the name he confers on King Medea's daughter in "The Golden Touch." Manifesting in his own authorial self traits of "feminine" sensibility,[6] Hawthorne also testified repeatedly and with religious fervor that his beloved wife, Sophia, had saved him from a life of damning isolation.

At another level, to be sure, the Hawthorne who recorded his famous complaints about "scribbling women" and uppity feminists lies open today to charges of rank misogyny. When he fictively identifies his dark lady with erotic iniquity, does he not betray a conventional male-Victorian suspicion of actualized womanhood as well as, perhaps, his own fear of sex? And when he rhapsodizes on the spirituality and household wonderworking of fair heroines like Phoebe, is he not guilty of obscuring women's authentic experience and aspirations behind a romantic-patriarchal image of the disembodied angel? In short, if Hawthorne "really believed that women were ethereal angelic substances," as charged by Louise DeSalvo,[7] then his figure of the chaste Madonna-Savior amounts to nothing more than a superimposition of social myth onto male fantasy.

There is enough conservative idealization of the angelic woman in Hawthorne's fiction to give some credence to this hostile assessment. But the image of women and gender relations emerging from his larger canon is finally more variegated than the binary contrast between fair heroine and dark temptress can convey. As James D. Wallace observes, the author's antifeminist prose statements about women writers betray "profoundly conflicted feelings."[8] And, as Nina Baym points out, even some prefeminist criticism recognized the impressive, virtuous traits of his "dark" characters like Hester Prynne and the cloying deficiencies of his fair maidens.[9] Neither can Hawthorne's women—including his wife as well as his characters—always be assigned to a single side of the traditional dualism or categorized reliably by complexion.[10] In fact, a case can be made that in the post-1842 "Old Manse" tales, especially, Hawthorne *points up* the murderous consequences of pursuing a disembodying ideal of female purity. Nina Baym contends quite plausibly that in stories like "The Birthmark" Hawthorne shows us how "the woman's saving grace and her body" are inseparably linked, despite the male protagonist's rejection of her erotic physicality.[11]

Thus, even Hawthorne's disreputable or exotically ambiguous female characters can embody a potentially redemptive but nonvirginal aspect of the archetypal Madonna. That is, the Hawthorne Madonna is not always or wholly a disembodied angel. Aside from the long romances, Beatrice of "Rappaccini's Daughter" offers a memorable if problematic instance. Inwardly innocent in moral terms, she nonetheless bears the unmaidenly "pollution" imposed on her by her father's experimentation.[12] She also displays a sexual potency threatening to Giovanni's superficial character and "a queen-like haughtiness" indicating womanly rather than girlish self-possession (10:112).

Like her Dantesque namesake, Beatrice Rappaccini offers to lead a male protagonist toward the holy beatitude of love. Admittedly, the "Eden of the present world" (96) in which she offers this grace is always already fallen, perverted by designing men like her father and Baglioni. So Giovanni suspects the inner woman of corruption. Yet the tale assures us that her heart has remained pure, despite her thoroughgoing corruption before eyes of carnal skepticism. Had Giovanni sustained faith in "better evidence" (120) than that supplied by rationalistic empiricism, had he been able to gaze truly on this Beatrice with the inner eye of love, he might have discovered something of God's new paradise even in the midst of Rappaccini's artificial hell.[13] He could even have believed her through what his eyes beheld, as Beatrice first assures him, had his vision ripened from the heart, as does the pilgrim-narrator's view of Beatrice Portinari and of her soul-sister Mary by the close of the *Paradiso*.

As figurative divine woman, then, Beatrice plays the role not mainly of Eve but of second Eve in Hawthorne's peculiar allegory. Standing apart "from ordinary women" (127), she impresses Giovanni early on with the "benign power of her feminine nature, which had so often enveloped him in a religious calm" and shown her worthy "to be worshipped" (122, 114). Like the new and future Eve typologized in Genesis 3.15, she readily destroys the garden's resident reptile—in this case, "a small orange-colored" thing (102). But she retains in her body the venom of this world's corruption as well as the dark flower of its hope. She is in one aspect a blessed Virgin, recalling with her floral similitude that rose of Dante's paradise in which the divine Word took flesh, that celestial queen and enclosed garden who discloses her salvific power only to those who, like St. Bernard, see with the ardor of genuine love.[14]

Giovanni, however, comes to fear her as demonic temptress. In this capacity, with her ominous connection to the purple shrub and perhaps also to a patricidal Beatrice Cenci, she expresses an aspect of the archetypal Magna Mater—the terrible anima—that he cannot assimilate into his most "most rational view" of the happenings in Padua. This aspect of the dark lady finds some precedent in traditions of the Black Madonna. Failing to acknowledge the deficiencies of his own psyche, to confront his shadow side, Giovanni can only dichotomize the image of Beatrice as "angel or demon" (109), as supernal beauty or femme fatale.

In the end, it seems she is neither, or in some qualified psychosexual sense both. From a feminist viewpoint, socialized habits of male misperception are clearly to blame for the story's catastrophe. A perennial victim of unresolved projections, the woman becomes at once—or alternately—idealized and demonized. In Giovanni's case, the error is arguably not just that he idealizes Beatrice—since the narrator, too, portrays her as a singular and sanctified being—but that the ideal he conceives is defective. Richard Brenzo (158) observes that Giovanni wants to shape Beatrice into his own image of the divine woman, disjunct from the earth she inhabits. Accordingly, Giovanni's sense of her as Madonna is more ethereal than spiritually incarnational.

By contrast, it is worth recalling that Christianity's historical Madonna was no "angel." Though St. Luke tells us that Mary's soul magnifies the Lord, it was in and through her body that she became blessed—or condemned, because her bodily state as pregnant maiden looked as suspect to other skeptical eyes as the physicality of Beatrice does to Giovanni. That grace can coexist incarnationally with corruption is one of Hawthorne's central themes, one to which "Rappaccini's Daughter" bears forceful though problematic witness. For even the poisoned body of Beatrice is not unambiguously "corrupt" within the altered biosphere she is forced to inhabit.

All the same, nobody can doubt that the usual Hawthornian fable of encounter with womanhood is told from a decidedly male point of view. Either as radiant goddess or as terrible anima, as mother or as virgin, the woman typically offers Hawthorne's protagonist a chance to recover some essential element of health missing from his own soul.[15] Only in a rare instance such as Hester Prynne's does a female character emerge with a fully realized life of her own. In an allegorical piece like "Egotism, or the Bosom Serpent," for instance, the estranged wife, Rosina, is given so little visualized autonomy that she presents herself finally as little more than a voice or shadow of Roderick Elliston's better self. Bending over a husband afflicted with "diseased self-contemplation," she presents "the shadow of his anguish reflected in her countenance, yet so mingled with hope and unselfish love, that all anguish seemed but an earthly shadow and a dream" (10:283). Here is another unvirginal figure of the second Eve, a rosewoman who once again destroys the invading serpent. Her redemptive word and touch presumably awaken Roderick from the peril of loving his sin above all else, and the abruptness of Roderick's restoration "to his right mind" and rescue "from the fiend" suggests the operation of grace that we are supposed to regard as a genuinely inexplicable gift. Roderick's acceptance of his proffered salvation is, of course, a rarity in Hawthorne's fiction. Yet this success is qualified for us as readers by the story's failure to dramatize any palpable recognition of otherness beyond the image making of a solitary self.

The notion of a divine Madonna as some sort of literalized reflection or projection of the soul is pervasive in Hawthorne's writing. Often she appears in the mythological shape of a pre-Christian water goddess or earth mother. Thus, in "The Vision of the Fountain," Hawthorne's fantasizing narrator takes the reflection of a village schoolgirl in a spring-filled basin for a "dewy goddess" and naiad. He tells us that the face of this fair divinity appears "deeper in the fountain" than his own, that she bewitches with eyes that mirror his. Elsewhere, as in "Rappaccini's Daughter," "The Village Uncle," and The Marble Faun, other specters of fountain goddess, mermaid, or nymph are evoked. In "Drowne's Wooden Image," an artist pours his soul into the creation of a ship's figurehead, which, as another sort of seagoing goddess, contains a life akin to "the hamadryad of the oak."

Hawthorne's literary imagination does, therefore, recognize the archetypal connection of the divine woman to a seminal ocean—as well as to the gracious mother earth evoked in pieces like "The Old Manse," "Earth's Holocaust," and "The Hall of Fantasy." The marine references must owe something to Hawthorne's knowledge of pagan mythology, especially as focused in the oceanic birth of Venus. Hawthorne could scarcely forget this scene, inasmuch as Sophia had decorated his bedroom washstand at the Old Manse with a pictorial rendering. Meanwhile, an image of Ceres, Magna Mater of the Eleusinian mysteries, adorned his study in company with the Raphael Madonna.[16] It is doubtful that the author knew explicitly of Mary's traditional link to the sea, as inscribed linguistically through a Latinate pun on her title as *maris stella*. But a reading of *The Divine Comedy*, in which Dante portrays the Virgin as surrounded by a river of light, could evoke some of the relevant water mythology.

In any case, the watery abode of the Goddess suggests that larger mystery whereby Hawthorne's dark lady represents a psychological dimension of the terrible anima, a domain mapped by Jung and Erich Neumann.[17] In starkest form, this devouring woman haunts both early and late fictions appareled as a witch ("Young Goodman Brown"), an old crone ("The Hollow of the Three Hills"), or a seductive enchantress ("Circe's Palace," "The Golden Fleece," "The Gorgon's Head"). Yet, as Philip Rahv's classic commentary underscores, even Hawthorne's more complex characterizations of the dark lady retain part of this mythic aura of danger, enchantment, and female demonism.[18] Thus, Hester's links with Mistress Hibbins's witchcraft and the forest add unmistakable shadings of the dark or terrible anima to her portrayal. In combination with the horrific glimpse of Medusa inserted into "Zenobia's Legend," equivalent hints of female sorcery and a questionable past help to darken the image of Zenobia in *The Blithedale Romance*. Even more sinister pieces of slander are attached to Miriam in *The Marble Faun*.

Hester's Divine Maternity

Of all the major characters, though, Hester endures as Hawthorne's most powerfully and sympathetically drawn version of dark womanhood. It may not be coincidental that she is also the only mother involved in this competition, and a single mother at that. As such, she combines some of the archetypally erotic, menacing traits of the lady with the nurturing tenderness of the Virgin Mother. Hester's maternity has lately begun to absorb new critical attention, marking a shift from previous concentration on her roles as lover, self-reliant iconoclast, or sinner. It is not only a common mood of social rebellion but also a shared vocation of beset motherhood that brands her a follower of "the sainted Ann Hutchinson" (1:48).[19] Accordingly, a closer look at Hawthorne's apparently offhand reference to Mary in "The Market-Place" scene that opens *The Scarlet Letter* reveals this passage to be loaded with prophetic statements about Hester's maternity and womanhood.

That the author dares to analogize Hester Prynne with a Madonna figure is scandalous, I would suggest, on account of his audience as well as her condition. Even if the latter-day human model were unimpeachable, Marian iconography was not quite the proper subject on which to rhapsodize in front of Protestant New Englanders, to say nothing of their Puritan ancestors. And so despite a "strange earnestness" in the narrator's voice, we are not surprised to find his word portrait framed in subjunctive disclaimers:

> Had there been a Papist among the crowd of Puritans, he might have seen in this beautiful woman, so picturesque in her attire and mien, and with the infant at her bosom, an object to remind him of the image of Divine Maternity, which so many illustrious painters have vied with one another to represent; something which should remind him, indeed, but only by contrast, of that sacred image of sinless motherhood, whose infant was to redeem the world. Here, there was the taint of deepest sin in the most sacred quality of human life, working such effect, that the world was only the darker for this woman's beauty, and the more lost for the infant that she had borne. (1:56)

The Hester-Mary analogy nonetheless proves itself apt at several levels. Though the beautiful Hester is no virgin, her child lacks a visible father, and the rose emblem with which she is initially linked is likewise a traditional Marian emblem. But it is the mother rather than the virgin aspect of Mary that Hawthorne invokes most pointedly in his image of "Divine Maternity." Hester's role as spiritual mother extends beyond the tender protection she affords her own Pearl of great price. In time it expands to encompass as well her nurturing of lost souls and, iconographically, her pietà gestures of comfort in the final scaffold scene.[20] And it is partly through her mediating power that Dimmesdale, who proves himself more helpless child than lover in the forest scene, reaches the liberating moment of his confession.

From the teasing ambiguity of Hawthorne's reference to "Divine Maternity" emerges the further suggestion that the woman is herself divine, enclosing and shaping divinity within her fecund body. Such a notion, though anticipated by the controversial "Mother of God" epithet from the patristic church, is audacious even as applied to Mary, to say nothing of its relevance to the presumably sin-stained Hester. Sharing in the scandal of Hester's presence before *her* audience by almost daring to scandalize his own, Hawthorne thereby establishes that sacred love can indeed coexist with sin; that redemption can and must work through the infirmity of human flesh. The strictly antithetical categories of perception enforced alike by moral Puritanism and by pre-Romantic rationalism dissolve before the intuitional mystery of a "Divine Maternity" that is rooted in the Magna Mater archetype.[21]

Hester, then, is painted less as the Hebrew maid of Nazareth than as an icon of that divine motherhood the Christian church envisions within the person of its own blessed mother. In prophetic terms, the image of Hester in travail suggests further comparison to the persecuted yet secretly glorified woman with child of Revelation 12. Again in the opening scene, Hawthorne stresses Hester's "sacred" affiliations by imaging a "halo" of beauty surrounding her against the backdrop of ignominious affliction. In this portrait, she is also consecrated, or set apart as singular, by virtue of the embroidered letter she bears. The letter, "fantastically embroidered and illuminated upon her bosom," had "transfigured the wearer," whom it encloses in a mandala-like "sphere by herself" (53–54). Likewise, in considering the later

forest scene, one need not insist on a purely Romantic or antinomian reading of
Hester's story to grant that, in *some* qualified religious sense, her regenerating encounter with Dimmesdale must have indeed "had a consecration of its own" (195).[22]

Admittedly, there is something decidedly posed or artificial about the image of
Hester as "picturesque" Madonna, as an "object" of the sort "so many illustrious
painters have vied with one another to represent." Standing initially in silence before a gazing and critically assessing multitude, she risks becoming a mere artistic
object. A Madonna in this sense is only a picture, an abstract image of femininity
devoid of a woman's own life or subjective response.[23] She is somebody else's work
of art. With a thousand eyes "concentred at her bosom" (57), Hester faces the
simultaneous if paradoxical indignity of becoming a voyeuristic sex object as well.

Yet Hester soon manages to step out of the picture frame, taking possession of
her own portraiture and shaping her own re-creation as a vitalized icon of divine
maternity. Refusing to be sketched permanently in the passive stance of victim, she
has repelled the town beadle "by an action marked with natural dignity and force
of character, and stepped into the open air, as if by her own free-will" (52). In so
doing, she presents a vivid contrast to the "darkly engraved portraits" seen in faces
of the town's ruling elite. Transcending the image of solitary shame, she becomes,
instead, the very picture of dignity, elegance, beauty, and motherhood. For she bears
"in her arms" the child who is both her sorrow and joy. Standing to confront her
grief, she images not only the young mother but also the mature *stabat mater*.[24] Even
as she remains the object of scrutiny and comment from the crowd, she also looks
out toward her spectators, imaginatively projecting upon that scene other scenes
from "memory's picture-gallery" (58). And Hester's portrait truly comes to life
the first time she speaks—partly to outline herself as a defiant sort of Miriam-like
Madonna who will speak no further, partly to insist that her child can claim no
earthly father.

This last suggestion of a mother's parthenogenetic creativity finds its symbolic
corollary in the scarlet letter. Like Pearl, the aboriginal "A" is at once something
Hester has been given and something she has made her own. Whereas the Puritan
community endeavors to make Hester an art object in the figure of Jezebel, she
produces a counterimage of herself as mother-artist by illuminating with "much
fertility . . . of fancy" the token she brandishes on her breast. So even townsfolk
come eventually to view the letter with awe and reverence, as lending the "self-
ordained" Sister of Mercy who wears it "a kind of sacredness" comparable to that
associated with a nun's cross (53, 161,163). Denied residence in the central settlement, Hester must also create her own version of community—her own holy family, as it were—with Pearl. In fact, the notion of a holy family recalls specific phrasing, from Mary Peabody's novel *Juanita,* that is said to have influenced Hawthorne's
Madonna passage in *The Scarlet Letter*.[25]

Iconographically, the opening tableau of Hester and Pearl as Madonna and Child
fits into a symbolic triptych that is completed by the other two scaffold scenes. In
the final scene, Hester remains the mother of Pearl; more curiously, she also adopts
the posture of both lover and grieving mother toward Dimmesdale. The pietà pose
has been commonly mirrored in the book's pictorial illustrations (figure 1.1), while

FIGURE 1.1. "It was revealed." The pietà pose is reflected here in Eric Pape's illustration for the 1900 Riverside edition of *The Scarlet Letter*. Courtesy of the Homer Babbidge Library, University of Connecticut.

the mother-lover conflation finds precedent in myths of the Goddess as well as in Marian devotional tradition.[26] Yet the capstone rendering of Hester's divine womanhood comes in the final chapter, "Conclusion." This last image is figured not as visual artistry but as verbal prophecy.

By now, Hester has returned from Europe to her seacoast cottage in America, choosing voluntarily to resume the burden of wearing the letter. She also dedicates herself to counselling troubled souls, especially women. Strangely, though, she insists that the world must await a prophetic woman other than she to reveal "a new truth" concerning "sacred love" and "the whole relation between man and woman." She muses that this agent of future revelation must be someone purer and less afflicted than she.

The curious prediction is apt to dismay readers who read in it Hawthorne's definitive capitulation, his retreat from the radical force of his main character.[27] Yet this final articulation is laced with irony, starting with its claim to prophetic knowledge despite Hester's presumed incapacity to prophesy. It is not even clear that Hester expects her prediction to be fulfilled within historical time, particularly if the relevant passage is keyed to the apocalyptic mood already established in the book's penultimate chapter on "The Revelation of the Scarlet Letter."[28] In fact, Hester's denial that she herself could serve any office of public revelation need be accepted no more absolutely at face value than the antinomian claims of private revelation (in the mode of "sainted" Anne Hutchinson) with which she had previously been associated:

> Earlier in life, Hester had vainly imagined that she herself might be the destined prophetess, but had long since recognized the impossibility that any mission of divine and mysterious truth should be confided to a woman stained with sin, bowed down with shame, or even burdened with a life-long sorrow. The angel and apostle of the coming revelation must be a woman, indeed, but lofty, pure, and beautiful; and wise, moreover, not through dusky grief, but the ethereal medium of joy; and showing how sacred love should make us happy, by the truest test of a life successful to such an end! (263)

But *could* a "mission of divine and mysterious truth" rest upon a woman "burdened with a life-long sorrow" if not sin? One would certainly suppose so, judging from the case of Christianity's Mother of Sorrows. At least Sophia Hawthorne was once moved to remark on how the deep eyes of Mary, in Perugino's visual rendering (figure 1.2), were "nearly quenched with tears" as testimony to a grief that "communicates itself to all who see her, for it is a real and not a painted grief."[29] And might not Nathaniel Hawthorne's own tale of "guilt, passion, and anguish" afford plentiful illustration that whatever revelation mortals receive of "sacred love" comes enveloped in affliction?

So it would seem. Hester's disclaimer of her own prophetic role evidently springs from her encounters with ruined ambitions and death, from chastened recognition that she can scarcely embody *the* Divine Woman in any literal, transcendent sense. She is only the town counselor-in-residence, that familiar recluse in a gray robe. Nonetheless, the book's final image of Hester incorporates part of her own prophecy concerning divine womanhood, thereby completing her earlier portrait as spirit-filled Madonna. Especially through the enduring artistic medium of Hawthorne's tale, Hester does fulfill a prophetic office as agent of revelation and mediation between humanity and godly love. If not permeated with joy, she retains much in her character that strikes us as lofty, pure, beautiful, and wise. In this last apocalyptic pose, she appears not mainly as repentant sinner or iconoclast, not even as weary compromiser, but as spiritual mother-prophet. Typologically, she appears here not as the scarlet whore from Revelation 17 alluded to earlier in the narrative but as the afflicted female embodiment of God's covenanted people from Revelation 12.2 who "cried, travailing in birth, and pained to be delivered" (King James, or Authorized Version).

Queen Zenobia of Blithedale

In his third full-length fiction, especially in the "Eliot's Pulpit" chapter of *The Blithedale Romance,* Hawthorne muses still more explicitly on the role of the Divine

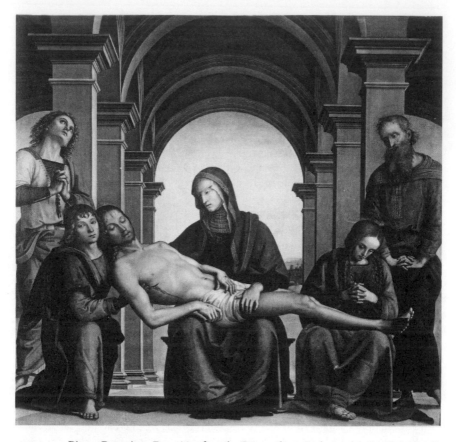

FIGURE 1.2. Pietro Perugino, *Deposition from the Cross,* otherwise known as *La Pietà* (detail). From the Uffizi, Florence (Alinari/Art Resource, New York).

Woman as minister and mediator toward sinful man. Yet in this work, as in *The Marble Faun,* Hawthorne polarizes his representation of mythic womanhood between the story's two female protagonists. For all their contrasts, Priscilla and Zenobia remain soul sisters in that both evoke impressions of the woman as sacralized other, as figurative goddess. Such, at least, are the figures they trace through Coverdale's fevered male imagination as narrator. Yet in this case the mostly pre-Christian Madonna recalled from archetypal memory bears the dual identity not so much of virgin and mother as of virgin and queen.

In this bifurcated scheme, Priscilla, of course, fills the role of virgin. She is the shrinking maiden, the innocent who pales by comparison with her vibrant and voluptuous half-sister, Zenobia. Not only Priscilla's "virgin reserve and sanctity of soul" (3:203) but also her "Sibylline attributes" (2) seem to set her beyond the normal limits of space, time, and corporal solidity. Marketed by Westervelt as a white goddess of marvels who enjoys "communion with the spiritual world" (201), Priscilla appears pristine, disembodied, insulated from the earth behind her diaphanous veil.

To be sure, this numinous aspect of Priscilla is only a staged apparition. Whatever her psychic gifts, her aura of mystery ultimately derives not from any transcendent mediation of "the Absolute" (201) but from Westervelt's manipulative projections of an all too human stamp. Apart from the daydream of romance, then, Priscilla looks more the part of undernourished victim than she does goddess of the new age. If her apparel as the veiled lady betokens her inaccessibility, it links her ambiguously not only with a sacred sisterhood, with the spiritual realm of the Marian Madonna, but also with the Eastern harem,[30] as reinforced through hints of latent sexuality such as those surrounding her silk purse. These several connotations of the veil envelop Zenobia as well, culminating in her macabre deathshroud reference in the farewell prophecy that "her face will be behind the black-veil" (227–28).

Yet insofar as Priscilla does typologize the simple younger and virginal aspect of goddess mythology, she remains a disembodied woman. Her character lacks fictive presence because she has been reduced to a signifying absence, to a kind of decadent Madonna invoked to mediate illusions of spiritual transcendence in a new age of pseudoscientific faith.

By contrast with this dispirited maiden, the vital and "high spirited" (2) Zenobia fully embodies female eroticism. Irving Howe aptly calls her "a kind of New England earth goddess"; she is accordingly, for Nina Baym, a woman in whom "all kinds of passionate and creative energies have united in a fundamental Eros,"[31] to which Coverdale—both as male associate and as narrator—responds with fearful ineptitude. Even more distinctively, Hawthorne associates Zenobia—within her role as erotic goddess and typological earth mother—with the divinizing title of "queen."

Zenobia's cognomen, connecting her to the queen of ancient Palmyra, is the most obvious token of this identification, which is supported by numerous hints of her queenly bearing. But what does "the queenliness of her presence" (44) signify in the context of Hawthorne's narrative? Most plainly, it betokens the royal autonomy and pride endemic to her character. It likewise expresses Zenobia's singularity, her naturally aristocratic stature as "the freshest and rosiest woman of a thousand" (46). More than that, Hawthorne's insistence on the potency and rare magnificence of this woman points toward the supernatural sovereignty long attributed to the Goddess.

Paralleling the natural tendency to conflate earthly monarchy with divinity, the impulse to associate female avatars with the title "Queen of Heaven" originated with primordial Near Eastern rituals that incorporated throne and coronation imagery and that persisted in ancient venerations of Isis, Astarte, Ceres, and Venus. Although the Hebrew prophet Jeremiah denounced cultic worship of "the Queen of Heaven" (Jeremiah 7.18), during the early centuries of Christianity this title also became attached to the historical Mary of Jesus as her cultus developed through apocryphal writings, hymnody, and iconography. By the sixth century, Maria Regina had been firmly enthroned in Rome. Through his familiarity with works like George William Curtis's *Nile Notes of a Howadji* (1851), Hawthorne would certainly have encountered suggestions that the Mary of Jesus bore kinship to Isis, as did Cleopatra and Zenobia to Venus. The historical assessments he met in Edward Gibbons's *History of the Decline and Fall of the Roman Empire* and Anna Jameson's *Memoirs of Celebrated*

Female Sovereigns (1831) could likewise remind him of the persistent tendency to worship and deify earthly queens such as Semiramis of Assyria, Cleopatra of Egypt, and the tragically magnificent Zenobia of Palmyra. Gibbons, for example, writes that third-century Zenobia "exacted from her subjects the same adoration that was paid to the successors of Cyrus."[32]

Within this tradition of divinized female sovereignty, the fictive Zenobia's role as would-be queen of Blithedale is laden with symbolic irony. For aside from the worshipful homage rendered her by Priscilla, Zenobia aspires to rule at Blithedale as a queen without a kingdom—that is, without subjects who will acknowledge her sway in this new, ostensibly egalitarian order of society. Yet when Coverdale casually mentions Blithedale's constitution, we might recall how the real-life documents describing association at Brook Farm in West Roxbury exploited Christian rhetoric by envisioning ideal community as the millennial fulfillment of what George Ripley termed "a divine order of human society" or of what Elizabeth Peabody identified as the "kingdom" of God set forth by Jesus.[33]

In fact, a good deal of inherited Christian rhetoric about churchly fellowship echoes through Coverdale's narrative. Blithedalers half-seriously imagine themselves to be a "little army of saints and martyrs," pilgrims in the tradition of New England's founders. Or they are an "apostolic society" engaged in the mission of blessing mankind, of ushering in a "millennium of love" (24), of completing the "reformation of the world" begun by their Protestant forebears. We soon realize, however, that no such dreams of divine society can be realized at this post-Christian plantation where individuals worship only the sovereignty of the imperial self.

Thus alienated from the living spirit of historical Christianity, Blithedalers come closer to achieving social and spiritual regeneration when they try to recover the pre-Christian, pastoral roots of natural religion in their "modern Arcadia." But they never come very close. As adopted experimentally by New England's leisured elite, pastoral life becomes here a false anachronism; and as he composed his romance in 1851–52, the author who once wrote "The Maypole of Merry Mount" retained his old scruples about any wholesale modern abandonment to a pagan faith of eroticism and fertility worship. Nonetheless, Zenobia emerges as the most compelling presence in this book—not only by virtue of her emotional intensity and tragic grandeur, but also because she radiates symbolically much of the archaic potency associated with the queenly goddess.

In this archetypal configuration, Zenobia bids to rule in two complementary guises: as the Venusian queen of Eros and as the May Day queen of fecundity. As latter-day embodiment of Venus, Zenobia shows herself plainly enough to be a divine woman who exudes erotic energy. Granted, Coverdale's prurient rhapsodizing on Zenobia's "fine, perfectly developed figure" (17), her "singular abundance" of "dark, glossy" hair (15), and her "full bust" (44) may slight the "fine intellect" encased in this body. So one must make allowances for Coverdale's distorted vision. Even so, Zenobia's physicality generates undeniable impressions of amplitude, of singularity, of superabundant "bloom, health, and vigor" (16).[34]

Emblematic of her almost transcendent singularity is the "single flower" she dons freshly each day in her hair. If this hothouse exotic bears a repellent sense of artifice, it may also be read as a token of exuberant sensuality and creativity in ways that Nina Baym has argued. The meaning of this flower must also be unfolded in conjunction with the story's overall pattern of floral imagery, in which Zenobia's flesh and beauty of person are persistently identified with roses. Right down to her "rosy finger-tips," she *is* a "perfectly-developed rose"—indeed, "the freshest and rosiest woman of a thousand" (34, 46–47). And what the rose woman inevitably signifies is love. Love in the form of eroticism? Yes, certainly as regards Zenobia, the core of whose personality Coverdale for once rightly identifies as "passionate love" (102).

Yet the rose symbol can traditionally encompass a variety of loves, both sacred and profane, in addition to sexual passion. We recall, for example, that Hawthorne's Endicott crowns Edgar and Edith with a wreath of roses in "The Maypole of Merrymount," thereby recognizing a devout nexus between their marital union and the Christian God of love. The rose is Dante's culminating image of all-embracing sacred love in the *Paradiso*; it is also a traditional flower of Mary, signifying the divine tenderness of maternal love. Some such tenderness Coverdale briefly locates not in Zenobia but in Hollingsworth, whose priestly ministry toward afflicted humanity strikes him as "the reflection of God's own love" (43). In fact, Zenobia's ultimate failure to love her sister, Priscilla, epitomizes the larger failure of Blithedale. Here the world was supposed to see how exemplary ties of fraternal and communal charity could be reknit more broadly across the whole fabric of society following the pattern of familial love. Where human relations end up instead is in a "perfectly inextricable knot of polygamy" (98), with pathologically disordered eroticism restricting all other loves. Even so, Zenobia makes important attempts to love Priscilla, as indicated by the anguished warning she presents in "Zenobia's Legend." She even makes charitable albeit ineffectual overtures toward Coverdale.

Thus, the creative potential of love, as mediated through Zenobia's quasi-mythic womanhood, never comes to bloom at Blithedale. Despite Hawthorne's suspicions of feminist ideology, this blight results largely from male deficiencies: from fears of involvement and eroticism on the part of Coverdale, from controlling ambitions on the part of Hollingsworth and Westervelt. Coverdale will ultimately profess to desire, if that is the right word, a fireside goddess like Priscilla rather than Zenobia, who confronts him with the life force of eternal womanhood. So threatening is the creative autonomy of this force that it eventually condemns Zenobia to personal isolation and death. By contrast, it is intriguing to notice that "Queen"[35] Margaret Fuller, one prototype of Zenobia, was willing to invoke the Marian Madonna to affirm the generative capacity of spirited, self-reliant womanhood. "Would she [modern woman] but assume her inheritance," wrote Fuller toward the close of *Woman in the Nineteenth Century,* "Mary would not be the only Virgin Mother." Zenobia's autonomy leaves her indeed "alone of all her sex," but in a solipsistic pit of despair, without fruitful issue in the world.

As queen of fecundity, then, Zenobia comes no closer to achieving regenerative rule at Blithedale than she does as queen of eros. From the first, despite the community's search for agrarian harmony, a note of discord from seasonal order is struck when the story opens in an April snowstorm. Yet if the community were ever to experience a spring renewal of nature and society, that occasion would presumably have been marked by its celebration of May Day. And significantly, at this reminiscence of Europe's cultic vegetative festival, Zenobia holds sway as a kind of presiding spirit or fecundity goddess. She assumes natural prominence as the Maylady, or queen of the May. Coverdale speculates that it is she who may have, by her "sole decree," declared May Day "a moveable festival" (58) to be celebrated later than ordered by the calendar. It is subsequently she "whose part among the maskers" in the darker autumnal rite of masquerade and crisis encounter with Hollingsworth and Priscilla "as may be supposed, was no inferior one" (213). It is likewise she who, while Maying with Priscilla, "showed no conscience" (58) when it came to taking by imperial will whatever it suited her to gather from nature's vegetative bloom.

Though the version of May Day celebrated at Blithedale looks like child's play, Hawthorne must have remembered Thomas Morton's notorious frolics at Mount Wollaston well enough to retain cognizance of the festival's orgiastic antecedents. Some hint of that old-time pagan religion survives in Zenobia's coy remark that she would not be assuming "the garb of Eden" until "after May-day" (17). For Morton, in fact, May Day at Merry Mount was undeniably a fecundity festival of the Goddess—variously compounded of Venus-Cytherea, Maia, Athena, and, by Bradford's accusation, licentious Flora—though an occasion legitimized by its overlay onto the Anglican liturgical feast of St. Philip and St. James. May is also the traditional month of Mary. *The New English Canaan* even suggests that Morton envisioned a link between his community's place-name of "ma-re mount" (with its latinate pun indicating proximity to the sea) and the oceanic Venus or Aphrodite who presumably inspired his poetic effusions and May Day rites.[36]

So in the reminiscence she inspires of the Earth Mother's fecundity, Zenobia at agrarian West Roxbury resembles Mother Ceres, the earth-mothering grain goddess Hawthorne would soon be describing in *Tanglewood Tales*. Similarly, in her relation to Priscilla, Zenobia enacts something of the classic pairing of mater and maid, of Demeter-Ceres and Kore-Persephone. And when Coverdale expounds in the same breath on the beauty of womanhood and on the parental bearing of nature as "loving mother" (62), he evidently has Zenobia on his mind. Repeatedly toward the story's outset, Zenobia is described more or less playfully as a new Eve— literally, the mother of all living. Nonetheless, she ends up as mother of no one and nothing. She engenders no progeny, just as Blithedale's field of dreams yields no enduring harvest.

A turning point in Zenobia's half-conscious ambition to reestablish rule of the matriarchal goddess at Blithedale comes midway through the narrative, with the critical chapter titled "Eliot's Pulpit." Gathered at the rock where a saintly Puritan patriarch had once addressed Native American pagans, Hawthorne's four principals enthrone Hollingsworth—not Zenobia—at the ruling center of their Sabbath day discourse. With this reinvestment of patriarchal power in a "godlike" man (124), Zenobia's "living voice" is drowned out by elevated claims of male pulpit authority. (So also is her voice, like the oral eloquence of Margaret Fuller, overwritten by texts such as Coverdale's or Hawthorne's.) Within the ensuing mock debate about

women's place and prerogatives, Hollingsworth at least exposes his masculine condescension toward women—if not his betrayal of Zenobia's love—quite openly.
Coverdale, by contrast, shrinks from any actualized embodiment of feminine force
while styling himself verbally as a champion of women's social and spiritual
empowerment.

THUS PROTESTING THAT HE has "never found it possible to suffer a bearded priest so
near my heart and conscience, as to do me any spiritual good," Coverdale seems
for the moment to echo the author's personal sentiment and experience. Yet he
goes on to make an extraordinary recommendation:

> Oh, in the better order of things, Heaven grant that the ministry of souls may be left
> in charge of women! The gates of the Blessed City will be thronged with the mul-
> titude that enter in, when that day comes! The task belongs to woman. God meant
> it for her. He has endowed her with the religious sentiment in its utmost depth
> and purity, refined from that gross, intellectual alloy, with which every masculine
> theologist—save only One, who merely veiled himself in mortal and masculine shape,
> but was, in truth, divine—has been prone to mingle it. I have always envied the
> Catholics their faith in that, sweet, sacred Virgin Mother, who stands between them
> and the Deity, intercepting somewhat of His awful splendor, but permitting His love
> to stream upon the worshipper, more intelligibly to human comprehension, through
> the medium of a woman's tenderness. (121–22)

Clearly a passage like this says a good deal about the strong hold the Madonna
image maintained in Hawthorne's imagination. Nowhere does he express more
passionately the desire for a divine woman to serve as spiritual minister and mediator toward sinful man. Stressing here the Madonna's role as compassionate intercessor, the author may also betray his own psychic need to sacralize female sentiment and domesticity—in the person of someone like Sophia—as solace from the
world's dark brutality. Yet interpreting this speech, insofar as it issues from
Coverdale's self-deceived narration rather than from direct authorial testimony,
becomes trickier within the dramatic context of "Eliot's Pulpit." Even Zenobia
hesitates to endorse it in so many words. Perhaps she senses, in Coverdale's extravagant paean to womanhood, a certain disingenuousness on his part, a declaration of radical chic to which he will scarcely commit himself in practice. Coverdale,
after all, resents the fact that a man with politically incorrect views on gender relations manages to monopolize the affections of two women whom *he* might have
desired. Perhaps, too, Zenobia detects a veiled reproach in the way Coverdale extolls
Madonna-like "tenderness," a trait he implicitly favors over that divine autonomy
of high-spirited womanhood more clearly represented in herself.

Hollingsworth, then, is not the only male character in the romance who threatens to deprive "woman of her very soul" (123). True, this blacksmith reformer
completes the tale's fire imagery by making of Zenobia something of a vestal sac-
rifice who must be slain on the altar of his pride as Vulcanic "high-priest" (70). But
Coverdale, too, bids to deprive Zenobia of her soul. As readers have observed, his
storytelling tends to reduce her flamboyant humanity and creative divinity to a "work
of art" (164), a "full-length picture" (155), and ultimately a "marble image" of death

(235). By the time Zenobia's lifeless body is recovered from the river at midnight, little is left in her of that holy splendor and tenderness Coverdale attributes to the Mary of Jesus. In her defiance, she seems to bear more the scandalous spirit of another Mary: Mary Gove Nichols, a feminist free-love advocate, lecturer, and associationist contemporary with Hawthorne.[37]

Still, it remains uncertain whether Coverdale reads rightly when he finds impious hostility in the final body language of Zenobia's arms and hands. In fact, she dies wordlessly absent from her interpreting community, preserving to the last her royal autonomy in a world unreceptive to the chthonian, erotic force of her self-determined womanhood. Such an ending may suit a book dedicated to showing at once the imperative to establish genuine community in America and the futility of trying to do so, at least through ideological design. Yet following this particular demise of the Goddess in *The Blithedale Romance,* Hawthorne's fascination with divine womanhood resurfaces all the more expansively eight years later in his final completed romance. Here, in fact, he would give fullest play to the mythic topos of the Madonna, lending her a more Christian and European coloration than he had envisioned in the pagan queen of West Roxbury.

The New England Maiden and the Fallen Goddess of *The Marble Faun*

Given the European setting and mythic texture of *The Marble Faun,* one is perhaps not so surprised to find this work permeated by Marian allusions and iconography. Statues, paintings, shrines, and tales of the Virgin lay everywhere open for exploitation in Italy as Hawthorne knew it during his stay in 1858–59. If anything, popular attention to Mary had been heightened at this time because of Pope Pius IX's recent declaration of the Immaculate Conception doctrine in 1854, an event to which Hawthorne testifies cognizance in his Italian Notebooks (14:387).

Inevitably, Hawthorne's encounter with Italy confronted him with the nexus between Mary and the goddesses venerated before her in the ancient world. "The Catholics have taken a peculiar pleasure in planting themselves in the very citadels of paganism," he noted, "whether temples or palaces" (14:116). Within the first two pages of *The Marble Faun,* he underscores the same point: Rome's Christian churches are "built on the old pavements of heathen temples, and supported by the very pillars that once upheld them" (4:6). In sacred spaces like the Temple of Vesta, then, one could observe at first hand the architectural shift by which "the Virgin took the place of Vesta" (14:135).

In Hawthorne's view, images of Venus as well as of Mary could stir artists to capture the beauty, wholeness, and eternal youth of divine womanhood in a manner equivalent to religious revelation. "The sculptor must have wrought religiously," he asserted in his notebook, to produce "so tender and chaste" an image of transcendent femininity as he observed in the *Venus de Medici* exhibited in Florence's Uffizi gallery (figure 1.3). This "miracle" of beauty not only warranted lifelong contemplation but also might endure "as one of the treasures of spiritual existence hereafter" (14:307–9).

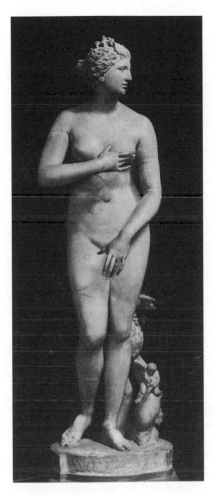

FIGURE 1.3. *Venus de Medici*. From the Uffizi, Florence (Alinari/Art Resource, New York).

Just as Venus, in at least some of her artistically formed "revelations," appeared to be "nothing short of divine," so also the best portrayals of Christianity's Madonna sometimes offered the viewer "a sort of revelation" (14:403, 318). However unscrupulous Hawthorne thought artists could be in their portrayals of nudity, they had certainly grasped the Venus-Mary interaction so far as "They seem to take up one task or the other—the disrobed woman whom they call Venus, or the type of highest and tenderest womanhood in the mother of their Savior—with equal readiness, but to achieve the former with far more satisfactory success" (4:337). Hawthorne found even a poor rendering of Venus and Cupid memorable because the painting imaged "maternal care" in a way that might well remind us of the classic Madonna and child pose (14:318).

This is not to say that Hawthorne was uniformly impressed by the countless paintings, statues, and frescoes of Mary he met in Italy. He had tried to respond to representations by Cimabue, Correggio, Fra Angelico, Guido, Michelangelo, Murillo, Overbeck, Perugino, Raphael, Vandyke, and many other known or anonymous artists. Still, he was bored by the repetitive treatment and lack of divinity he found in the Virgins collected at Borghese. He was likewise repelled by early Madonnas of the Sienese school and recorded his particular distaste for the famous Cimabue Virgin housed in Florence. Yet he admired the holiness and tenderness of Raphael's treatments, not to mention those of Perugino, to whom "the Virgin often revealed herself . . . in a loftier and sweeter face of divine womanhood than all the genius of Raphael could produce" (14:377, 324). In a flush of enthusiasm, though, he declared Raphael's *Madonna della Seggiola* in Florence "the most beautiful picture in the world" (14:305). On the more popular plane, Hawthorne could also appreciate some of the folk expressions of Marian piety that flourished in nineteenth-century Italy. Thus, *The Marble Faun* introduces us as early as chapter 5 to a streetcorner shrine of the Virgin, which stands as a landmark in the book's moral geography to match against the popular wayside shrines that Hawthorne's wayfarers later meet in the countryside in chapter 32.

TURNING DIRECTLY TO this text, the reader discovers immediately that among major characters the uncontaminated Hilda is most overtly identified with the Virgin Mary. As stressed in chapter 6, "The Virgin's Shrine," Hilda is a self-appointed votary of the heavenly queen, tending her lamp and even praying at times to this blessed personage who was indeed, as she puts it, "a woman once" (69) but above all a tender mother. Bereft of her own earthly mother and removed from her natal home, Hilda yearns to embrace a celestial surrogate: "If she knelt—if she prayed—if her oppressed heart besought the sympathy of Divine Womanhood, afar in bliss, but not remote, because forever humanized by the memory of mortal griefs—was Hilda to be blamed? It was not a Catholic, kneeling at an idolatrous shrine, but a child, lifting its tear-stained face to seek comfort from a Mother" (4:332).

Besides paying homage to images of Mary, Hilda is clearly supposed to image the Virgin in her own person. She is therefore surrounded by doves, praised for her "patient faith" and "generous self-surrender," and venerated by Kenyon (60). To Kenyon's mind, at least, this New England maiden is surely an Immaculate Conception. That she dwells in a tower high above the mortal fray, preserving the "ethereal" and "white shining purity" of her nature as "a thing apart" from the "perplexed and troubled world" gives him vast satisfaction (128, 287, 112). He can rest assured that somewhere, at least, simple feminine virtue stands protected from iniquity and ambiguity. When the shrine's lamp finally burns out, we are to believe that Hilda has, in effect, absorbed its light and subsumed the Divine Woman into herself as an American household goddess.

For all that, Hilda has scarcely proved an attractive character to the book's original or subsequent readers. While Kenyon renders her sanctimonious homage, her priggish innocence is apt to draw more contempt than veneration from present-day readers. Indeed, one needs only a little feminist perception to see Hilda reflecting the worst sort of "madonna" image of womanhood. As such, she projects a male fantasy of domestic tranquility, a disembodied ideal remote from flesh and blood humanity. More lamentably still, one cannot help sensing from the narration that a good deal of Hawthorne, in consort with Kenyon, embraces this view of Hilda as sanctified Madonna.

Yet within the cross-purposes of Hawthorne's imperfectly unified fiction, the matter is complicated by other shadings—perhaps subconscious—of authorial intention. Another part of Hawthorne, it seems, ironically undercuts Hilda's figurative identification with Mary by allowing her connection with only one of the Madonna's two central aspects. Thus, while *The Marble Faun* accents to the point of excess Hilda's attribute of virginal purity, it portrays her as the very antithesis of maternal compassion. She may serve as a latter-day type of Vesta but hardly as Our Lady of Mercy. In the severity of her cloistered virtue, Hilda lacks altogether the fecund mystery and compassion associated with the Mother Mary. Though she softens a little toward the end, her unyielding righteousness offers no refuge for sinners or mediation for troubled souls. So Hilda is *not* the holy woman whose soul, in the words of Simeon's prophecy (Luke 2.35), would be pierced by the sword of her son's affliction, but one whose innocence pierces others "like a sharp steel sword" (66).

What is more, in aesthetic terms this pale, derivative copyist of the old masters lacks the truly generative vitality associated with the Mother of God and with the feminine poet of the Magnificat. In this regard, as in several others, the vibrantly original Miriam of this tale comes closer than Hilda to fulfilling a Marian model of womanhood.

Admittedly, Miriam's complex function as a character cannot be reduced to a single figurative abstraction. Indeed, as the sexually tainted and sometimes irreligious woman of passion, she strikes us as more nearly femme fatale than Madonna. In biblical terms, her moody, spirited character may recall for us the rebellious Miriam of the Old Testament, or else, in view of the book's plentiful Edenic imagery, we may see Hawthorne casting her into the role of a seductive Eve, the terrible anima who tempts Donatello to commit mortal sin.

Yet as patristic exegesis would have it, the first Eve leads by direct line of typological progeny to the second Eve of Nazareth, whose Hebrew name matches precisely that adopted by Hawthorne's Miriam. And Miriam's dark beauty, emotive depth, and Jewish affiliations all render her a more plausible image of Mary than her opposite, the "fair-haired Saxon girl" in the tower. Unlike Hilda, who tries to insulate herself from transgressors, Miriam remains fully engaged with sinful, afflicted humanity. Her worldly experience of grief finds a parallel sympathy in that "celestial sorrow" (58) which the biblical Mary shares in her son. And whereas Hilda shrinks from the very mention of a fortunate fall, involving the paradoxical drama of redemption in which Christ's mother plays a leading role, Miriam bears crucial responsibility in Donatello's marvelous but tragically incomplete moral education.

We might say, then, that within Hawthorne's complex typology the Judaic Miriam fulfills at once the roles of a first and second Eve in relation to Donatello. Like Hester, Miriam also adopts something of a psychological mothering role toward her lover, whom she calls a "boy" and "child." But ultimately her spirit of self-abnegation, which surpasses that of Hilda, renders Miriam more Marian than

Eve-like. If she does not succeed in mediating any final salvation for Donatello, neither does she retain any final office in the story as siren or temptress.

In pagan archetypal terms, too, it is Miriam rather than Hilda who embodies the primal, creative, and regenerative force of womanhood. As such, Miriam appears as a newly re-embodied water nymph or lady of the fountain—both in the "Faun and Nymph" engagement at the Villa Borghese and later in association with Count Donatello's ancestral estate at Monte Beni. She also assumes mythic stature as lady of the dance, both in the golden age frolics of Borghese forest and in the melancholic saturnalia of the Roman carnival.

Moreover, it is Miriam who figures as the living counterpart of the *Venus of the Compagna* statue that is unearthed outside Rome toward the close of the tale. This pivotal episode becomes paradigmatic, in turn, of the projected "recovery" and moral ascent of Donatello. Based on an actual find observed by the author in 1859, the incident may even be taken more broadly to dramatize the symbolic recovery of the Goddess in Western culture. It is precisely from archaeological evidence, including digs yielding figurines of divine womanhood, that new theories of Great Goddess culture began to develop in conjunction with research undertaken by nineteenth-century scholars such as Johann Jakob Bachofen.[38]

In chapter 46, Hawthorne at first lets us suppose that Kenyon deserves credit for discovering this Greek marble "image of immortal Womanhood." Shortly thereafter, we learn that Donatello and Miriam had come upon it two days earlier, in the midst of an excavation, and left it exposed for Kenyon to rediscover. Significantly, Donatello was the one who had first "detected the fallen goddess," with his "keen eyes," while discoursing with Miriam. Miriam reflects that now, as though privileged to receive an apparition of divinity, "the eyes of us three are the only ones to which she has yet revealed herself" (427).

Kenyon feels less enthusiasm about recovering this Venusian goddess than he does about the prospect of finding his own missing goddess in the person of Hilda. No wonder. Hilda, after all, remains much the safest goddess around. Her mythic identity as a pale descendant of the Hebraic Lady Wisdom/Sophia and Christian dove/Holy Spirit has lifted her far above the chthonic turbulence that marks Miriam's paintings of Jael, Judith, and Miriam herself.[39] Only briefly does Kenyon celebrate the return of divine womanhood represented in the Venusian goddess. Similarly, Kenyon had earlier shown himself capable of letting the queenly, divinely passionate womanhood of Cleopatra burn into marble through his own artistry, though almost despite himself. But he fails to respond sympathetically to Miriam when this real-life, full-bodied version of queenly womanhood visits his studio.

Like Miriam herself, then, the emblematic figurine of Venus remains "Donatello's prize" (427). He apparently does not get to keep the marble figure or to stay with the woman. But a story that began in subterranean terror, and that marched us toward the existential abyss through a literalized depiction of "the fall of man," now takes something of an upward turn. As if previewing his own moral elevation, Donatello sees "the fallen goddess" raised up from soil of "the wild Campagna." Like Miriam, this goddess is decidedly "earth-stained" (423), but she presents an image of newly restored wholeness and beauty that signifies salvation. In Christian terms as well as in Thorvaldsen's idiom of three-stage process, the episode is plainly resurrectional, reversing the momentum that led toward the fall: "a goddess had risen from her long slumber, and was a goddess still" (424).

Miriam had already received a token of her potential rejuvenation several chapters earlier, at her reunion with Donatello in the Perugian marketplace. Here Donatello calls her back into existence by intoning one word: her name. "'You have called me!' said she" (320). Through this annunciation, "Miriam" effectively becomes the woman's real name, just as she becomes from that moment a kind of new Eve, devoid of danger to Donatello. Yet within the tale, we never see either Miriam or Donatello attaining the final fruits of redemption. In fact, Miriam's final vocation of divine womanhood draws her closer to the Mary of Sorrows than to Venus. Like Sodoma's sublime fresco of Christ bound to a pillar, her life ends up illustrating the challenge of "reconciling the incongruity of Divine Omnipotence and outraged, suffering Humanity" (340).

Once Donatello has also been initiated to sin and grief, it is telling that he seeks a mediating refuge from his crime in the Mary of roadside shrines. Here, in way stations of pilgrimage where ancient rural grottos of the Goddess once stood, the "mild face of the Madonna promised him to intercede, as a tender mother, betwixt the poor culprit and the awfulness of judgment. It was beautiful to observe, indeed, how tender was the soul of man and woman towards the Virgin mother, in recognition of the tenderness which, as their faith taught them, she immortally cherishes towards all human souls" (297).

Hawthorne's Search for Sacred Love: From Puritan Fathers to Divine Mothers

In his overall response to Marian piety, Hawthorne evidently understood that the Madonna cultus of the Roman church, like many of the Christian edifices he saw in Rome, was built upon a pagan substructure. But apparently this discovery, together with the Roman church's aura of ritualism and aestheticism, provoked no sensation of scandal or repugnance in him. He was *not* so Puritan as that. He objected rather to what he saw as that church's moral corruption, self-serving parochialism, unnatural requirement of priestly celibacy, and authoritarian governance. For these reasons, conversion was out of the question. Or, as Hilda replies to Miriam when questioned about her devotion to the Virgin: "You must not call me a Catholic." Yet, she goes on to insist, "A Christian girl—even a daughter of the Puritans—may surely pay honor to the idea of Divine Womanhood, without giving up the faith of her forefathers" (54).

The remark is equally appropriate for a distant son of the Puritans. Though divine *womanhood* stands in some tension of gender relation to the faith of Puritan fore*fathers,* Hawthorne was also inclined to offer some form of homage to the Virgin Mother. He speculated on occasion that a revived, reconstituted Protestantism might incorporate some of these Roman "advantages" while avoiding its faults. "Protestantism," he confided to his notebook while in Rome, "needs a new Apostle to convert it into something positive" (14:195).

Short of finding this new apostle, and unable to embrace Europe's culture and religion as his own, Hawthorne saw no choice but to return to America, where he was left with his Hilda-like Sophia and a religion of womanly domesticity to support what faith remained to him toward the close of his career. The prospect was scarcely encouraging. Hilda had looked everywhere for "a face of celestial beauty, but human as well as heavenly, and with the shadow of past grief upon it; bright with immortal youth, yet matronly and motherly; and endowed with a queenly dignity, but infinitely tender, as the highest and deepest attribute of her divinity" (4:348). And just as Hilda canvassed churches and galleries without locating precisely the Virgin Mother she sought, a face that combined in feminine form Christ's human tenderness and numinous splendor, so also Hawthorne failed to discover the integrating faith he sought in the American cult of domesticity.

The signs of this failure are written all over *The Marble Faun*. The bifurcation evidenced here, whereby the image of Mary as pure virgin and as compassionate mother is split irreconcilably between Hilda and Miriam, reflects that larger division of sensibility that plagued Hawthorne's later career. We are left in *The Marble Faun* with a richly evocative and provocative work, perhaps even a major work of literature, but one desperately at odds with itself.

What Hawthorne ended up making of the Madonna theme in larger terms shows a comparable ambivalence of intent. Both countercultural and culturally conservative forces figured into his fictive portraits of divine maternity. On the more prophetic side, the Marian Magna Mater provided a vehicle for combining appreciative reminiscence of pagan myth with the iconography and emotion of Christian belief. As such, the Divine Woman satisfied a nineteenth-century Romantic ideal, expressing spiritual and intuitional longings suppressed by the mercantile rationalism of Hawthorne's age. This woman also challenged the predominantly masculine symbol system Hawthorne inherited from the theology of his Puritan-Unitarian forebears. She embodied a creative generativity subversive of machine productivity, a contemplative alternative to the strenuously competitive model of Victorian manhood. Yet in its contrary, more conservative aspect, Hawthorne's ideal of sacred womanhood supported and reflected the sentimental values of his marketplace culture.[40] *This* version of "the feminization of American culture" ends with Hilda enshrined in fireside veneration, Miriam and Zenobia lost, and Hester displaced by prophecy of a new female apostle better able to embody the divine truths of "sacred love."

THE VIRGINAL SOUL OF
MARGARET FULLER'S
Woman in the Nineteenth Century

Queen Margaret's Mythmaking

Both in her own estimation and as tagged by detractors who mocked her claims to intellectual superiority, Margaret Fuller held sway as New England's queen. The regal title might censure her for betraying an uncommon arrogance antagonistic to American democracy. More favorably, it might typify the sovereignty achieved through Transcendental self-reliance or a singular vocation to lead others—especially women—toward artistic and cultural ambitions loftier than those supported by common standards of taste in the United States. Sophia Peabody Hawthorne, rejecting the central argument of *Woman in the Nineteenth Century* for female emancipation, labeled this work with its regal opening citation ("The Earth waits for her Queen") in a letter to her mother as "the speech which Queen Margaret Fuller has made from the throne," and Fuller herself imaged her "natural position" as that of a monarch ordained to govern "without throne, sceptre, or guards."[1]

But something more is signified by Fuller's persistent image of a queen who gains and exercises power without benefit of kingly cohort or male consort. At once personally and culturally emblematic, the monarchical woman embodies Fuller's lifelong ambition to achieve an imaginative re-creation of self capable of yielding permanent self-rule. Inspired to conceive and to carry to term her own second birth of soul, of affections, and of aesthetic intellect, Fuller as virginal yet maternal queen emanates powers of parthenogenetic creativity.

For Fuller, this aspiration to regenerate herself—and, by extension, her nineteenth-century sisters stillborn into that fixed domain of cultural identity defined as "true womanhood"[2]—often expressed itself symbolically through mythology. Fuller's eclectic mythologizing drew mainly from ancient Greek, Roman, Egyptian, Hebrew, and Christian paradigms. She enriched it further through her extensive reading in German romanticism. But the archetypal Goddess, bearing her sundry names from this vast span of cultures, remains a pervasive presence throughout Fuller's prose and poetic writings. In meditating on the Goddess, Fuller accented her queenly capacities for dominion as well as her recurring representation as maternal virgin. Although several mythological women figure notably in Fuller's symbolic equation, the mother of Jesus plays a crucial and varied thematic role that warrants special investigation. It is striking that Fuller invokes Mary, whom she understood as indeed a historical figure with mythic import, at several critical junctures in *Woman in the Nineteenth Century*. This strong identification with Mary is all the more unexpected in view of the author's youthful exposure to Unitarian rationalism and adult rejection of orthodox Christianity.[3]

Only toward the conclusion of her life, when she gave birth to Angelo Ossoli in Italy, could Fuller know the satisfactions of biological maternity. In an earlier journal fragment, she confessed that "the woman in me has so craved this experience" of childbirth "that it has seemed the want of it must paralyze me."[4] Yet through the mythological medium of her written and spoken discourse, she had intended all along to dramatize not merely the procreative but also the creative spiritual force of awakened womanhood. Her own "children of the muse" (p. 7) were vitalized through fruitful utterance. Years before her actual pregnancy, Fuller showed fascination with the maternal metaphor in her quest for cultural, intellectual, and spiritual fecundity. Though maternity and marriage remain problematic concerns in her writing through the 1845 publication of *Woman in the Nineteenth Century,* as indeed they continue to be for feminist thinkers such as Kristeva, Dinnerstein, and Chodorow,[5] Fuller encompasses both within her prophecy of woman's future potential. Her pointed affirmation of nineteenth-century womanhood gains further authority within her presentation of a universal vision supported by mythology.

Study of how and why Fuller exploited mythological materials, particularly those involving goddess or Marian elements, is therefore essential for appreciating the artistry and argument of her writing. Aside from Jeffrey Steele's highly revealing treatments of goddess imagery in Fuller's shorter writings and Marie Mitchell Olesen Urbanski's brief but apt analysis of *Woman in the Nineteenth Century,*[6] critical interpretations of the written corpus remain scarce—perhaps because modern readers persist in lamenting its faults as compared with the brilliance of her unpreserved speech. Instead of attending to the author's literary expression, most commentators have confined their interest to biography or ideology. By probing Fuller's literary uses of mythology, however, one discovers new reasons for appreciating not only the innovative force of her best writing but also the intuitional and religious grounds of her case for emancipation.

"Her Own Creator": Images of Self-fashioning in Minerva, Leila, and Mary through 1844

To follow the course of Fuller's mythmaking is to trace an uneven progress from images of the passionate seeker, haunted by self-doubt and powerless isolation, toward icons of the enspirited woman celebrating her self-reliant yet associative identity. In this regard, the biographical context of Margaret Fuller's personal struggle for autonomy clearly does inform her testimony concerning the general character and destiny of womankind. Rarely indeed does a literary career better illustrate the present-day cliché that the personal is political. Biographers have already established that Fuller labored to regenerate her identity at once through and against the authority of three paternal figures: Timothy Fuller, Emerson, and Goethe. At least the first two male precursors exercised a peculiar anxiety of influence, allowing Margaret Fuller access to spiritual and intellectual power even as they imposed restrictions or betrayed personal weaknesses that drew her resistance. Hence, it is instructive to consider first the personal preoccupations revealed in Fuller's partly uncirculated poems and essays from 1839 to 1844 before examining how she attempts to fuse personal with public values and mythological with political concerns in *Woman in the Nineteenth Century*.

Congressman Timothy Fuller, Margaret's obsessively organized father, surely exercised a decisive influence on his firstborn child through the ambitious program of intellectual training he applied during her childhood in Cambridge, Massachusetts. As Charles Capper's excellent biography confirms, Margaret developed a complex response to the challenge posed by Timothy's intrusive and competitive yet ultimately stimulating example.[7] Exalting him as a kind of father god, she naturally passed through phases of worship and rebellion, followed by painful loss after his death from cholera in 1835. Her losses became all the more grievous as she faced repeated disappointment in her friendships and overtures toward erotic intimacy, a path of abandonment that reached its nadir when not one but two cherished soul mates, Samuel Ward and Anna Barker, married each other rather than her in 1840.

Yet these upheavals, in conjunction with episodes of mystical or religious awakening and the stimulus afforded by Transcendental pronouncements, led Fuller to conceive the rebirth of her own spiritual identity.[8] As outward loss drove her to exploit every interior resource, she searched to express her emerging self-renewal through mythological delineations of the Goddess. The resulting process of conversion combined heterodox religious impulses with psychic yearnings validated by her nascent feminism. By 1839, she had begun to shape a new professional identity focused toward women through her presentation of the Boston Conversations; she had also assumed editorship of the *Dial*. Thus, Jeffrey Steele observes that Fuller's "1844 poetry articulated a mythologized realm in which she transformed the self into a powerful goddess." Furthermore, Steele points out that as "her poetry developed, real people tended to be replaced by mythological figures"; she had corresponded with Anna Barker in 1835, but by 1844 "she addresses the moon, Diana, Apollo, and the Virgin Mary."[9] This mythical self-fashioning involved rejecting Timothy Fuller's legacy of Enlightenment rationalism, as well as softening the call to Emersonian discipleship, especially by 1840, when the Master and putative friend received with suspicion her testimonies of mystical engagement.[10] Nathaniel Hawthorne's notoriously nasty assessment of Fuller following her death holds at least a glimmer of metaphoric truth in its suggestion that she credited herself with "having been her own Redeemer, if not her own Creator."[11]

Three mythic women dominate the Fuller writings in question: Minerva, Leila (in conjunction with Isis), and Mary. A fitting emblem of regenerate and self-reliant womanhood, the mythological Minerva had, as Fuller reportedly remarked during one of her Boston Conversations for Women in 1841, skipped infancy and "sprang full-armed into being."[12] Minerva also exemplified highly cerebral and "masculine" traits because she had issued motherless from the head of Jupiter.

As an exceptional woman forging a vocation as artist and intellectual, Fuller identified readily with this goddess of wisdom who nourished craft, beauty, and civilization. After citing Fuller's account of Minerva-Athena in unpublished notes for the Conversations as "a child of counsel, birth of the brain, a virgin & warrior," Capper discerns that the sketch amounts to "a rather good, if unintended, history of her life."[13] Although Minerva does not gain clear literary prominence in Fuller's writing until "The Great Lawsuit" and *Woman in the Nineteenth Century,* where she becomes psychic complement to the Muse aspect of womanhood, she also figures briefly in various letters, essays, and poems. Thus, while praising Goethe's portrayal of redemptive female characters in a critical essay written for the the 1841 *Dial,* Fuller declares that "Woman is the Minerva, man the Mars." Writing to Emerson, she associates Minerva with her own search for creative inspiration. And emblems she finds expressive of Minerva, particularly "the Sphinx, the owl, the serpent," supply imagery for her 1844 poems and other writings. In her 1844 poem on the "Winged Sphynx," Fuller evidently represented her quest for regenerative potency in the voice of a mythical demiwoman who struggled against brutishness toward realization of her "Soul divine." Not only the maternity but also in some sense the virginity of goddesses like Minerva must be understood metaphorically. Accordingly, when the Sphinx grows beyond her phase of dark striving to present an "aspect Chaste, Serene," she earns the threefold title that encodes this childless poet's ideal of womanly identity: "virgin mother queen."[14]

Never named in classical mythology, the mysterious goddess identified as Leila is more nearly Fuller's own creation. She becomes, therefore, a fitting emblem of woman's capacity for fecundity and transcendent self-renewal. In her 1844 poem "To Sarah," Fuller writes that she first chose Leila as a name for herself "by the sound, not knowing why" but subsequently relished knowing "that Leila stands for night," for the darkness that brings forth stars "As sorrow truths."[15] Three years earlier, in a mystical essay titled "Leila," Fuller had published an evocative prose account of this figure, portraying her as at once an unsettling presence within the writer's own being and a transcendent goddess. This multivalent goddess is personal yet an abstracted spirit linked to "the elemental powers of nature" (53), elusive yet alluring.

In its venture toward a feminist re-vision of theology, the essay starts off sounding a note of regret that "most men," who "shrink from the overflow of the infinite" (53), fail to encounter Leila's divine mystery. But the narrator responds to her as a mystical presence surging from boundless depths, as a darker version of Minerva's "Saint of Knowledge." Leila's eye reflects the soul's "sense of eternity" as well as the soul of nature—particularly of elemental ocean, night, star, moon, fire, and wind. Indeed, one naturalistic-cum-Christian identity Leila recalls is that of *maris stella* (star of the sea), for the narrator addresses her as Star while invoking her presence in the watery deep. "At night I look into the lake for Leila," she writes. "If I gaze steadily and in the singleness of prayer, she rises and walks on its depths" (56, 54–55).

Leila, the vibrant woman of night, hardly enforces cultural ideals of sunny domesticity. Instead she witnesses to the power of the subliminal self, of dreams, of id instincts linked to demonism and invocations of female potency. Fuller identifies her with occult ritual, with the blood red carbuncle sought by alchemists and fictionalized by Novalis. Leila thus fulfills Fuller's own vocational dream to become "the poetic priestess, sybilline."[16] Leila also functions as a composite icon of the vestal virgin, bacchante, earth mother, Venus, Diana, Phoebe, Io, Hecate, and Isis. Accordingly, Fuller's 1844 poem devoted to "Leila in the Arabian zone" insists that such goddess figures "Only Leila's children are" (233).

Two emblems of the archetypal fertility goddess express Leila's profound access to chthonic powers. One is the "magic Sistrum," a rattle Isis uses to bridle the reptilian Typhon.[17] The other is the serpent. Adopting the sistrum as her personal emblem, Fuller suggests in various writings that this talisman channels the life force or "ceaseless motion" that inspires all organic being and art. For the goddess to release and regulate this force, which resembles the Holy Spirit, is for her to command that "God-ordained, self-fed Energy" of "Nature in Eternity" by which "Brutes are raised to thinking men" and living souls ("Sistrum," 235; "Leila in the Arabian Zone," 233).

The sistrum of Leila-Isis represents, therefore, the feminization of powers equivalent to those Emerson had already attributed to the poet-Transcendentalist. In 1836, Emerson had rhapsodized in the final chapter of *Nature* that the Spirit's influx would render nature fluid and dispel "disagreeable appearances," including snakes and prisons.[18] Five years later, Fuller celebrates Leila's magical charism to effect a comparable transformation: "At her touch all became fluid, and the prison walls grew into Edens. . . . The redemption of matter was interwoven into the coronal of thought, and each serpent form soared into a Phenix" (57).

Leila's links to elemental wildness nonetheless conjure also a more positive association with serpents. In the ancient Middle East and Neolithic Europe, snakes imaged the regenerative fecundity and oracular or ecstatic wisdom engendered by the Great Goddess.[19] Beyond her brief allusion to snake potency in "My Seal Ring," where the power of the "serpent rod" recalls Exodus 4.1–5, Fuller enlarges on this theme in her "Double Triangle, Serpent and Rays":

> Patient serpent, circle round,
> Till in death thy life is found;
>   Double form of godly prime
> Holding the whole thought of time,
>   When the perfect two embrace,
> Male & female, black & white,
>   Soul is justified in space,
> Dark made fruitful by the light;
>   And, centred in the diamond Sun,
>   Time & Eternity are one. (233)

In the visionary symbol of the uroboros, or snake biting its own tail,[20] Fuller
located a figure of ideal self-integration that she would pictorialize encircling a triangle for the frontispiece of *Woman in the Nineteenth Century*. Self-reliant and all-
encompassing, the uroboros combines "godly" and erotic energies. Within the
mystical circle of the serpentine body, a unifying embrace connects death and life,
time and eternity, male and female. In effect, Fuller invokes the snake goddess to
sanctify the personal and exemplary quest for female autonomy set forth in *Woman
in the Nineteenth Century*. The oroboros is kin to the "wondrous circle" (57) of Leila.
Yet her vision of psychic and spiritual integration ultimately transcends the gender
split between "male & female," just as the internalized meaning of Leila "ever transcends sex, age, state, and all the barriers behind which man entrenches himself from
the assaults of Spirit" (54).

What kinship, though, might possibly exist between Fuller's wild-haired Leila,
a kind of snake goddess of night, and Christianity's serene and wholesome Mary?
For one thing, Leila qualifies as another virgin mother, one who retains her virginal autonomy while producing "immortal births of her unshrinking love" (57).
Then too, Leila fills a decidedly religious role as mediator and vessel of the Holy
Spirit. Fuller's narrator considers her "a bridge between me and the infinite" (54),
and she manifests the Spirit under traditional signs of "mysterious wind" and fire,
a fire concretized in the "heart-blood-red of the carbuncle" (54, 55). She also in-
fuses transcendence into human time and space through an acceptance of incarnation, thereby recalling not only Mary but also Christ as divine savior:

> But floating, hovering, brooding, strong-winged bliss shall fill eternity, roots shall
> not be clogged with earth, but God blossom into himself for evermore. Straight at
> the wish the arrow divine of my Leila ceased to pierce. Love retired back into the
> bosom of chaos, and the Holy Ghost descended on the globes of matter. Leila, with
> wild hair scattered to the wind, bare and often bleeding feet, opiates and divining
> rods in each over-full hand, walked amid the habitations of mortals as a Genius, visited
> their consciences as a Demon. . . . Of late Leila kneels in the dust, yea, with her
> brow in the dust. I know the thought that is working in her being. To be a child,
> yea, a human child, perhaps man, perhaps woman, to bear the full weight of acci-
> dent and time, to descend as low as ever the divine did, she is preparing. I also kneel.
> (56–57)

Nowhere does Fuller expose more clearly the startling kinship between untamed
Leila and "Mary Mild" than in her 1844 poem on "Raphael's Deposition from the
Cross" (see Appendix). This moving piece, which Jeffrey Steele deems her finest
poem,[21] also suggests why Fuller so esteemed and identified with the Marian
Madonna.

The poem's opening address to Mary as "Virgin Mother" (238), though conventional, corresponds metaphorically to the twofold ideal of autonomy and fecundity with which Fuller was personally preoccupied during her spiritual search
in 1844. Declining to analyze the biology of Jesus' birth, she affirmed elsewhere
that "whatever the actual circumstances were, he was born of a Virgin, and the tale
expresses a truth of the soul."[22] She had written to Caroline Sturgis in 1840 that if
she sensed within herself "any apparition of the Divine," she could bless herself

"like the holy Mother" but that, also like Mary, she longed "to be virgin."[23] In the poem, she represents the integrity and attentiveness of her interior discipline in Gospel imagery of the wise virgin who keeps her lamp "constant trimmed" and her "fond resolve undimmed." And she would repeatedly seize on maternal imagery to express her yearning to become the fertile vessel from which a vital soul and muse might emerge.

Yet the dominant mood she sustains through the first two-thirds of her poem is one of horrific loss, epitomized by Raphael's depiction of the Mother of Sorrows:

> Virgin Mother, Mary Mild!
> It was thine to see the child,
> Gift of the Messiah dove,
> Pure blossom of ideal love,
> Break, upon the "guilty cross"
>
> The seeming promise of his life;
> Of faith, of hope, of love a loss
> Deepened all thy bosom's strife,
> Brow, down-bent, and heart-strings torn,
> Fainting by frail arms upborne.
>
> But 'tis mine, oh Mary mild,
> To tremble lest the heavenly child
> Crucified within my heart
> Ere of earth he take his part,
> Leave my life that horror wild
> The mother who has slain her child. (238)

Beneath the poet's effusion of grief—mixed with remorse—over the imagined death of a child lie several layers of actual personal loss. Fuller had suffered the broken "promise" of ambitious vocational hopes, the decease of loved ones,[24] and the keen erotic and emotional privations of "love . . . unreturned." Having earlier pictured herself as a mourning version of Mary, she would later reclaim this identification while tending men wounded during the siege of Rome. "I was the Mater Dolorosa," she wrote her sister, "and I remembered that the midwife who helped Angelino into the world came from the sign of the Mater Dolorosa."[25] And when Fuller describes herself in *Summer on the Lakes* as bearing an excess of affliction at boarding school though chosen among women to rule "like a queen, in the midst of her companions" (121), she does so under the name of "Mariana." Evidently, she was captivated by the image of Mary as archetypal woman of sorrows.

Yet by the close of "Raphael's Deposition," her Marian figure assumes a greater, more active role than that of piteous victim. Rising above passive endurance, Mary becomes a potent Dark Madonna[26] conjoined with Leila, enchanting woman of night: "Leila, take thy wand again." This Dark Madonna eventually brings to life "a muse-like form," her "new-born" child of inspiration, not only through Christ's resurrection but also through her own resolve to bear pain beyond death so as to make of night and the tomb another womb. With Emily Dickinson, then, the poem affirms that "Power is only pain—/ Stranded, thro' discipline"[27]—or, in Fuller's pointedly Marian imagery, through a "rosary" of "beaded years" and "pearly tears." For herself, too, Fuller desperately wishes to affirm that the seemingly passive enterprise of mourning could offer stimulus for renewal.

Fuller's Mary also summons power from the hidden, contemplative recesses of her soul, unlike the "startled figures" of eight other mourners in Raphael's tableau without the deeper wisdom to "apprehend / the thought of him who there lies low" or the saving vitality in "this deepest of distress" (239). Mary enjoys privileged access to the Holy Spirit, a point dramatized in traditional iconography by her swooning posture during the deposition (figure 2.1). Fuller likewise describes her as "fainting by frail arms upborne." She faints not only in shock but also in a kind of mystical transport. Raphael portrays Mary's swoon on the right of his canvas as symmetrically equivalent to the death trance of Christ on the left, thereby supporting the notion of her coredemptive rather than diminutive status.[28]

In her poem, Fuller represents the triumphant rebirth and apotheosis of self through several figures, including plant and gem imagery conjoined with name-

FIGURE 2.1. Raphael, *Entombment,* commonly known in the nineteenth century as *The Deposition*. From the Galleria Borghese, Rome (Alinari/Art Resource, New York).

based punning. The poem's second section draws into conjunction three women's names, each of which initiates a line of address: Rosemary, Margaret, and Leila (58, 61, 65). For the speaker to expand and renew a potent female identity is to amalgamate her own personal name, "Margaret," with the mythic name of her muse, "Leila," as well as with the "Mary" or "Rosemary" who embodies historically the Christian archetype of divine womanhood.

In its first meaning, of course, the poem's "Rosemary" functions as an herbal symbol of remembrance and consolation:

> Angels weeping, dirges singing,
> Rosemary with hearts-ease bringing,
>   Softly spread the fair green sod,
> Thou escape and bathe in God. (239)

Yet the punning nexus of this plant name with Mary of Nazareth is undeniable. The traditional and Dantesque figure of Mary as God's rose unites her to Christ, a "pure blossom of ideal love" (4). It also recollects the floral imagery with which Fuller surrounds her goddess descriptions in earlier mystical essays like "The Magnolia of Lake Pontchartrain" and "Yuca Filamentosa." Biographically, too, Fuller's acute memory of her mother's domestic garden seems to have strengthened her belief in the maternal character of all "secret powers."[29]

In the culminating lines of "Raphael's Deposition," floral imagery signals a shared influx of regenerative life into the dead Christ, the mourning Mary, and the poem's speaking self:

> "Maiden wrap thy mantle round thee"
> Night is coming, starlit night,
>   Fate that in the cradle bound thee,
> In the coffin hides thy blight;
>   All transfused the orb now glowing,
>   Full-voiced and free the music growing
>   Planted in a senseless sod
>   The life is risen to flower a God. (240)

Another imagistic scheme, involving gems and alchemical allusions, reinforces the poem's theme of transformation and mystical marriage. Most intriguing in this regard is the etymological wordplay on "Margaret" as pearl. Margaret's "pearly tears" become at last precious, linked as they are with "a ruby heart" and with that Virgin Mother who once bore the pearl of great price.[30]

The Mary Victoria of *Woman in the Nineteenth Century*

Those unfamiliar with the shorter writings Fuller produced through 1844 may be all the more baffled to encounter mythological and Marian material interlayered throughout *Woman in the Nineteenth Century* (1845). Here, after all, we should not expect to ponder the timeless universals of mythology but to confront the urgent pain of nineteenth-century women. And we should not expect to see the mild mother Mary honored beside iconoclasts and occupational pioneers in a feminist polemic aimed at enlarging the scope of liberty and action currently available to women.

Fuller intends, however, to base her argument for social and political change on deep foundations. Mythology and religion supply these footings because they extend beneath immediate instances to express what human beings—and particularly women—need "as soul to live freely and unimpeded" (261). Instead of surveying the full range of women's particular grievances, Fuller proposes to "go to the root of the whole" and to articulate "the true destiny of woman" (258).

Thus, the religious substructure of Fuller's argument is essential to understanding *Woman in the Nineteenth Century*. For despite her heterodox leanings, Fuller brought to this work a spiritual intensity that should not be discounted. Already by 1840, she had written William Channing that she aspired to "preach the Holy Ghost as zealously" as "the old religionists" had dispensed less compelling doctrines (14). Though she once admitted that she had "no confidence in God as a Father," she nonetheless urged her students in Providence to seek "that religion which can alone support us in this sorrowing world."[31] *Woman in the Nineteenth Century* favors self-dependence for women based largely on the author's personal testimony, in Miranda's voice, that "religion was early awakened in my soul" (262). Fuller had even confided to her journal that, whatever her moral faults, there were "none more religious" than she.[32]

Accordingly, the opening pages of Fuller's prophetic discourse set forth the promise of actualized selfhood-womanhood and renovated male-female relations in religious terms. The author describes this promise as a "holy work that is to make the earth a part of heaven," as "the open secret of love passing into life" under the leading of "a divine instinct" linked to "the Word" (245, 248). To discover the living God, she urges, is to welcome that millennial era of "a truly human life" that is also truly divine. Moreover, this promise of "a love that made all things new," already expressed in a "holy child," *can* be realized by readers of her prophecy: "Whatever the soul knows how to seek it cannot fail to obtain. This is the law and the prophets. Knock and it shall be opened, seek and ye shall find" (250, 249). Indeed, *Woman in the Nineteenth Century* ends in self-fulfilling prophecy to the extent that it embodies one woman's achievement in declaring a vocation as writer and in claiming an identity as womanly soul.

Unlike the esteemed Mary Wollstonecraft, then, Fuller does not develop her case for emancipation mainly through an appeal to secular rationalism. If the French Revolution brought natural rights philosophy some distance toward practical fulfillment, its egalitarian principles yet fell short of the "promise of heaven" Fuller envisions for womankind. So if the author must invoke a male exemplar of emancipation, she will name Moses before Locke, Paine, or Jefferson.[33] Her mention of the Hebrew liberator, which complements her provocative analogizing of women with black slaves, reinforces the point that women must obtain more than new political rights and social liberties to reach "the promised land" of divinization (252–53). Even as they petition for legal property rights within marriage, they must strive to elevate the frequently degraded idea of marital union to its highest form—"the religious, which may be expressed as pilgrimage towards a common shrine" (289). Beyond equality, nineteenth-century woman should aspire to divinity, to that full flowering of her soul and intellect consistent with her "especial genius" (309). She should live "*first* for God's sake" (346).

It follows for Fuller that before young girls inquire after a path of vocation in public life, they must ask the root question of "What shall I do to enter upon the eternal life?"(306) Yet her discourse shows considerable optimism about the prospect that obstacles now impeding the flow of "divine energy" can be the eliminated through feminist reform:

> . . . without attaching importance, in themselves, to the changes demanded by the champions of woman, we hail them as signs of the times. We would have every arbitary barrier thrown down. We would have every path laid open to woman as freely as to man. Were this done and a slight temporary fermentation allowed to subside, we should see crystallizations more pure and of more various beauty. We believe the divine energy would pervade nature to a degree unknown in the history of former ages, and that no discordant collision, but a ravishing harmony of the spheres would ensue. (260)

The literary form in which Fuller expresses her vision of nineteenth-century womanhood and gender relations is, of course, problematic. As we have already heard, tones of religious prophecy and exhortative homily resound through *Woman in the Nineteenth Century*—but without benefit of fully coherent rhetorical structures.[34] Within the sprawling miscellany comprising this prose poem, one finds a curious mélange of voices, frequent gaps in narrative sequence, and a superabundance of allusions and examples.

From the standpoint of cohesive economy, the book version published in 1845 looks even worse than the essay Fuller originally published in *The Dial* under the title of "The Great Lawsuit: Man *versus* Men. Woman *versus* Women." The original version, whose title Fuller said she preferred, lacks the seemingly digressive elaborations and appendices added in 1845. It is usual to suspect that Fuller attached an eightfold appendix to *Woman in the Nineteenth Century* for reasons of insecurity, indifference to literary form, and haste to turn her essay into a full-length book.[35]

I would argue that many of the later additions, including the appendices, actually strengthen Fuller's work—not only because they introduce comment on practical issues such as prostitution, but also because they expand a critical network of mythological reference. It is harder to argue for the uniform cohesiveness of *Woman in the Nineteenth Century* because the book clearly suffers from repetition and imperfect integration of the materials it exploits. A Transcendental principle of organically adaptable form may justify in part the baggy shape of a work that illustrates multiple versions of woman's vocation, or the unsettled state of the woman question in nineteenth-century America. Alternatively, Elaine Showalter, drawing in turn on Barbara Walters, has proposed that the gaps in a text like Fuller's are "sites of contradiction" that reveal "the writer's conflict between her internalization of patriarchal rhetorical forms and her need to articulate a feminine subjectivity." As feminist polemic, *Woman in the Nineteenth Century* would therefore show a characteristic oscillation between the "rhetorical, legalistic, logical, and objective" idiom of "women's rights" and the "literary, personal, discursive, and emotional" idiom of "women's wrongs."[36]

In any case, at least one disjunction in Fuller's discourse seems serious enough to threaten the consistency of her overall argument. On the one hand, she emphasizes that woman, notwithstanding culture and biology, is fundamentally a living soul capable of self-reliance and that the equality of men and women, of black and white Americans, is based on the Transcendental principle that "there is but one law for souls" (261). So far she advocates an egalitarian culture beyond privilege or distinction of gender. On the other hand, she also supports an essentialist view of gender difference centered on the "especial genius of woman." Distinctive attributes of "femality" set women apart as "electrical in movement, intuitive in function, spiritual in tendency" (309).

This ideological tension, which has yet to be resolved definitively in present-day gender studies, dramatizes Fuller's insistence on writing an idea of woman that was still undergoing creative evolution. Though conscious that she needs to qualify the sexual dichotomizing encouraged by her Romantic feminism,[37] she also wants to reconceive Transcendental categories so as to find in "representative woman" the normative but not exclusive locus of human spirituality: "In so far as soul is in her completely developed, all soul is the same; but as far as it is modified in her as woman, it flows, it breathes, it sings, rather than deposits soil, or finishes work, and that which is especially feminine flushes, in blossom, the face of earth, and pervades, like air and water, all this seeming solid globe, daily renewing and purifying its life. Such may be the especially feminine element, spoken of as Femality" (309–10).

Fuller does not understand "Femality" to be an exclusively female trait. Neither does she accept an exclusively biological or sociological definition of womanhood. Sensitive to the sexual contradictions of her own nature, she offers instead a picture of psychic androgyny in which "male" and "female" both contend and interfuse: "Male and female represent the two sides of the great radical dualism. But, in fact, they are perpetually passing into one another. Fluid hardens to solid, solid rushes to fluid. There is no wholly masculine man, no purely feminine woman. . . . Man partakes of the feminine in the Apollo, woman of the masculine as Minerva" (310).

The meta-structure of *Woman in the Nineteenth Century* can be simply described, in fact, as a teleological progression from specters of radical dualism at the outset to a vision of unific harmony and mystical marriage at the end. The preliminary state of war that Fuller portrays involves not only contention between men and women but also discord within the self, epitomized by figurative Minerva and the Muse as contending aspects of womanhood.[38] What is more, Fuller launches her discourse by pointing up the disparity between womankind's lofty promise and currently degraded state in society. *This* radical dualism confronts us immediately when she starts off juxtaposing two provocative citations:

> "Frailty, thy name is Woman."
> "The Earth waits for her Queen." (247)

Teasing out the dialectical possibilities of this opener through the remainder of her work, Fuller draws the main text to a joyful conclusion directed toward the final word, "Queen," from a poem of her own composition: "So shalt thou see what few have seen, / the palace home of King and Queen" (349). Following several extracts from other writers, a coda section then culminates in another self-composed poem, "The Sacred Marriage," which celebrates imminent revelation of "the future Deity" and realization of "the Union in the Soul" (378). If, as one has reason to suspect, Fuller at the start is mischievously citing a self-created aphorism in "The Earth waits for her Queen,"[39] the formal symmetry with which the work enacts her self-fulfilling prophecy of creative autonomy becomes all the more affecting.

Within the terms of this polarity, much of *Woman in the Nineteenth Century* is devoted either to elaborating women's wrongs or to acclaiming the right if not transcendent accomplishments of representative women, despite society's constraints. These women of promise include named contemporaries such as George Sand, Catherine Sedgwick, Angelina Grimké, and Queen Victoria. But Fuller also draws heavily on literary, historical, and mythical figures for her idea of woman. Inspiring instances of the idea are variously discovered in Isis, Mother Anne Lee, Goethe's Macaria, Abby Kelly, and Native American Ratchewaine (Flying Pigeon). In Fuller's vision, contemporary women join spirits with a full pantheon of goddesses: Ceres and Proserpine of the Eleusinian cultus ("significantly termed the 'great goddesses,'" 269), Isis, Rhea, the Sphinx, Diana, Minerva, Vesta, Iduna, Wisdom-Sophia, and Frigga.

Admittedly, a culture's social practices, including its marriage provisions and the status it accords actual women, rarely live up to the idea of woman it enshrines in myth. But instead of discounting these mythologies as irrelevant or baneful fantasy, Fuller presses the challenge to fulfill more of their prophetic import in practical life.

Mythologically, for example, woman's power to rule the seas is manifest in fables of Venus, in the Marian *maris stella*, and, as we have already seen, in Fuller's own composite Leila. The first extract in Fuller's appendix to *Woman in the Nineteenth Century* recounts the story of Isis's glorious appearance to Lucius as "a divine form emerging from the middle of the sea" (350); and in 1844, while Fuller was revising "The Great Lawsuit," Hawthorne published in *Godey's Magazine and Lady's Book* a tale recollecting the zeal of American shipowners to set a "female figure" with "the grace and loveliness of a divinity" at the head of sailing vessels.[40] The *idea* of woman, as figurehead, had already led American ships. Why, then, shouldn't a bodily woman with nautical expertise become captain? Yet when Fuller expostulated toward the close of *Woman in the Nineteenth Century* that women might aspire to any office, some readers thought it laughable she should propose to "let them be sea-captains, if you will" (345).

Still, the book finds copious illustration of realized womanhood in its sweeping survey of contemporary life, history, literature, and religious mythology. Within this cloud of witnesses, Mary of Nazareth occupies a prominent position. Although some of the references to Mary serve only to amplify themes sounded through other examples as well, the biblical Virgin Mother also fills a distinctive rhetorical purpose in Fuller's exposition.

The most obvious reason to invoke Mary in Fuller's scheme is the lofty position she claims for enspirited womanhood in a culture still nominally Christian. In the finer fruit, at least, of Jewish–Christian tradition, "we find woman in as high a position as she has ever occupied": "No figure that has ever arisen to greet our eyes has been received with more fervent reverence than that of the Madonna." The Marian image "exercised an immediate influence on the destiny of the sex," albeit one whose salutary potential has yet to be fully realized. Applauding the renovation of Adamic myth that elevated womankind from helpmate to Mother of God, Fuller sees in Mary the promise of new dignity and autonomy for women:

> . . . is it in vain that the truth has been recognized, that woman is not only a part of man, bone of his bone, and flesh of his flesh, born that men might not be lonely, but that women are in themselves possesssors of and possessed by immortal souls. This truth undoubtedly received a greater outward stability from the belief of the church that the earthly parent of the Saviour of souls was a woman.
>
> The assumption of the Virgin, as painted by sublime artists, Petrarch's Hymn to the Madonna, cannot have spoken to the world wholly without result, yet, oftentimes those who had ears heard not. (272–73)

Yet the sovereign dignity of Mary, particularly in her pose as *regina caeli* (queen of heaven), defines only part of her exemplary identity for woman in the nineteenth century. For beyond the circle of her own apotheosis, Mary acted as female coredeemer, as one who accepted a vocation directed outwardly toward others. Thus, Fuller points out that when Dante portrayed Beatrice as guide and savior who led him "to wisdom through love," he "sought, in her, not so much the Eve, as the Madonna" (280). The distinction is telling. Likewise in Goethe, she sees a "redeeming power" generously invoked by the soul of Faust's former lover Margaret through intercession with the *mater dolorosa* and *mater gloriosa* (316), feminine powers that effect the ultimate salvation both of Faust and of Margaret-Gretchen whom he had ruined. Indeed, Goethe's appeal to the saving power of eternal womanhood at the close of *Faust,* part II, offered the latter-day Margaret important stimulus for developing her own feminist vision. So did Goethe's evocation of mystical maternity (which Fuller recalls in reference to "The mother of all things," 301)—and, most likely, other precedents in German Romantic literature, such as the strong appeal to Marian mythology and piety evident in mystical writings by Novalis.[41]

Fuller even mentions approvingly those legends of medieval chivalry, illustrated by a Rhine ballad (273–74, 335), in which Marian piety inspires the protection and moral redemption of errant males. Read in gender-specific terms, the Marian maxim that "as through woman man was lost, so through woman must man be redeemed" sounds indeed like a sentimental commonplace of nineteenth-century thought promoting the cult of True Woman. But Fuller also extends belief in woman's redemptive power to sanction the capacity and obligation of women to assist other women. However much men may "share and need the feminine principle," they will not voluntarily transform the existing social order or lead a woman to self-dependence. Currently, women remain "the best helpers of one another" (344). Hence, Fuller urges women readers to "consecrate" themselves toward the betterment of imprisoned women by offering "tender sympathy, counsel, employment" so as to "Take the place of mothers, such as might have saved them originally" (329).

Paradigmatic Mary qualifies the standard of self-centered autonomy because she can be regarded as at once secure in her own integrated identity and dedicated to fostering new life in others. As mother, she not only affords Jesus biological sustenance but also extends the Spirit's vitalizing influence to subsequent generations of humanity. Fuller associates her spiritual fecundity as mother of all with her presumed experience as archetypal mystic, as one conjoined in rapture to the Most High. Before Mary, other spirit women had already been "greeted, with solemn rapture . . . as heroines, prophetesses, judges in Israel"; but having "made Eve listen to the serpent," the ancient Hebrews "gave Mary as a bride to the Holy Spirit" (266). Woman's superior endowment of electrical, magnetic, intuitive elements qualifies her peculiarly for this mystical vocation, one in which she derives strength of soul paradoxically from her "willing submission"—not to men, but to a pneumatic presence answered from within:

> Mysticism, which may be defined as the brooding soul of the world, cannot fail of its oracular promise as to woman. "The mothers"—"The mother of all things," are expressions of thought which lead the mind towards this side of universal growth. Whenever a mystical whisper was heard, from Behmen down to St. Simon, sprang up the thought, that, if it be true, as the legend says, that humanity withers through a fault committed by and a curse laid upon woman, through her pure child, or influence, shall the new Adam, the redemption, arise. Innocence is to be replaced by virtue, dependence by a willing submission, in the heart of the Virgin Mother of the new race. (301)

Among the many goddesses and versions of virgin motherhood explored throughout *Woman in the Nineteenth Century,* Mary fills a pivotal role by virtue of her engagement with human history as an actual woman of Galilee. It is precisely because Mary, unlike Isis or Ceres, once rose "to greet our eyes" (272) in the flesh that her *theosis* and the mythology of her queenly glory afford such an uplifting example for nineteenth-century women. To be sure, Fuller's book dwells much more on the apotheosized Madonna and on the *idea* of Mary's life than on what might be gleaned concretely about that life from Gospel narratives. But as we have seen, Fuller brought to the work prior meditation on Mary's altogether human experience as the *stabat mater*—as one who had stood and wept for grief, yet endured.

Fuller was also much taken with the human drama implicit in St. Luke's Gospel tale of the Visitation (figure 2.2). When Mary, pregnant with Jesus, runs into the hill country to greet her pregnant cousin, Elizabeth, unborn John the Baptist responds by leaping in Elizabeth's womb. After Elizabeth is "filled with the Holy Ghost" (Luke 1.39–41), Mary answers her cousin's joy with the sublime Magnificat. This poignant episode of woman-to-woman encounter (with further hint of cross-gender conjoining as John greets Jesus in utero) dramatized what sisterly self-dependence in the Spirit might look like. For Fuller, it imaged a deep intimacy—with other women, particularly—that she craved but rarely found. She demonstrates as much, balancing the joyous Lukan episode with a self-pitying adaptation of the Ceres-Persephone myth, in an 1844 letter to Caroline Sturgis:

FIGURE 2.2. Mariotto Albertenelli, *Visitation*. From the Uffizi, Florence (Alinari/Art Resource, New York). Anna Jameson, in her influential *Legends of the Madonna,* praises the artist's "simple majestic composition" in this painting.

If it should suit us both in September and we could be together in harmony, in a beautiful place, and some new plant grow up under my hand, and perhaps under yours, to redeem the hours, so that we might remember the time and place as a portion of *home* it would be joyful and like the hour of Elizabeth and Mary.

But if not so, Ceres is well accustomed to wander, seeking the other Magna Dea, and to be refused the cup of milk by the peasant, and to have snatched from her the princely nursling that she would baptize with fire.[42]

For the most part, then, Fuller portrays Mary as retaining a core humanity that renders her a godly woman but not wholly a goddess. She therefore declines to follow the lead of Goethe's Doctor Marianus, who does invoke the *mater gloriosa* as "goddess" toward the close of *Faust,* part II. Though affiliated with goddesses and gifted with a transcendent destiny, Mary represents for Fuller the highest position historically attained by one of her sex.

In this regard, the author's Mariology shows a curious consonance with Christian orthodoxy. Despite her liberal approach to biblical hermeneutics and heterodox denial of God's *unique* incarnation in Christ, Fuller did seem to accept the historical base of Gospel narratives concerning Jesus and his mother. "Few believe more in his history than myself," she once claimed, "and it is very dear to me."[43] Replying to an inquiry during one of her Conversations, she distinguished Mary from Venus in that "the Madonna represented more than passing womanly beauty"; Mary "was prophetic, and lived again in her child." Insofar as Fuller defines mythology as "the history of the development of the Infinite in the Finite,"[44] her view of glorified Mary could be described as mythical—but as rooted also in historical finitude in a way that Venus, Isis, and Ceres clearly were not.

It is relevant to mention here that Fuller, like Hawthorne, developed an affection for Raphael's *Madonna del Pesce* (figure 2.3), a disarmingly earthy painting in which child Tobias presents Mary with a fish. The fish may signify divine healing and regeneration—Anna Jameson's visual commentary called it "an early type of baptism"[45]—but the human tenderness of Raphael's scene is most striking. William Henry Channing reports that Fuller liked the copy hanging in her home at Jamaica Plains because she saw its rendering of Mary as "not divine, like the Foligno" and "not too bright and good for human nature's daily food."[46]

It is precisely because the author views Mary more as representative woman than as ghostly aberration of her sex that she summons up her example for the peroration of *Woman in the Nineteenth Century:*

> It is a vulgar error that love, a love to woman is her whole existence; she also is born for Truth and Love in their universal energy. Would she but assume her inheritance, Mary would not be the only virgin mother. Not Manzoni alone would celebrate in his wife the virgin mind with the maternal wisdom and conjugal affections. The soul is ever young, ever virgin.
>
> And will not she soon appear? The woman who shall vindicate their birthright for all women; who shall teach them what to claim, and how to use what they obtain. Shall not her name be for her era Victoria, for her country and life Virginia? (347)

A prototype of the "ever young" virgin soul,[47] Mary supplies one name for "self-sufficing" (269) woman, regardless of her age, marital status, or station in society. Such women, mystically assured of their participation in divine life, are emboldened to claim fitting vocations in the life of society. Even or especially in democratic America, the spirited woman claims regal sovereignty over her destiny. She must rule her own domain, and may also intervene to advance the forgotten interests of others.

Aptly, three queens stand behind this proclamation of a new age of female sovereignty in which "Mary is not the only virgin mother." Two of the three are earthly monarchs. Victoria, a potent exemplar of nineteenth-century womanhood, is "the

FIGURE 2.3. Raphael, *Madonna del Pesce*. From the Prado, Madrid (Alinari/Art Resource, New York). A favorite of Margaret Fuller, this image is also likely to have adorned Hawthorne's residence at the Old Manse and at subsequent locations.

name of the queen of our mother-land" (305). This Victoria gives birth to an entire era of sensibility, as well as to Edward VII; yet she retains the virgin's "self-sufficing" confidence and freedom from male control. Within Fuller's larger composition, Victoria also names "noble" Victoria Colonna, an Italian widow who triumphed over loss to compose sonnets and whose integrity showed her worthy to wear "a coronet of pearls" (300). The second queen is likewise British. "Virginia" names a geographic space of English claims once imagined to span the entire continent; but Sir Walter Raleigh had named this territory after the Virgin Queen, Elizabeth, whose reign conceived explorations that eventually issued in the United States.

The patriotic mythology surrounding England's Virgin Queen drew heavily, in turn, on images previously formed of the Virgin Mary. And the Queen of Heaven ("del ciel Regina," 351), as she is characterized in the Petrarch poem Fuller cites in the appendix, represents yet another "Victoria." Fuller's fascination with visual art, and particularly with "the assumption of the Virgin, as painted by sublime artists," no doubt reinforced her awareness that the traditional sequence of Marian images ends with some version of Our Lady of Victory. Indeed, the extrabiblical doctrine of Mary's Assumption celebrates her victory over bodily death, and the iconography of her crowning marks a triumph shared with Christ over all powers and principalities of evil. Thus, Fuller's allusion to Mary as model of awakened womanhood develops here a rich literary signification from patterns of association formed among three common names: Mary, Victoria, and Virginia.

Nonetheless, from the standpoint of present-day assumptions, one may still find it odd that Fuller should enlist Mary in the struggle of contemporary, active women to claim new roles in society. How might Miranda or the psychically "masculine" Minerva locate her patron saint in a figure presumed to model virtues of obedience or passive acquiescence? What, after all, did the biblical-historical Mary ever *do* beyond satisfying traditional domestic roles of wife and mother in an uncultured village? And what could Fuller's adventurous *improvisatrice*,[48] in search of novel experiences and cultured sophistication, learn from a settled and devout virgin like Miriam of Nazareth?

For Fuller, though, the figure of Mary represented potency of spirit rather than passivity before the will of men. Like her rebellious namesake, Miriam, Mary had a mind—and soul—of her own.[49] "It was not the opinion of woman current among Jewish men," Fuller argues, "that formed the character of the mother of Jesus" (335). Although motherhood was Mary's chief vocation, she fulfilled this office not only biologically but also mystically—and through decidedly unconventional means. Thus, she transcended traditional female roles from inside the roles; she also assumed offices of apostle, prophet, and oral poet more typically occupied by males.

Fuller did not, in any case, believe that women would realize the ideal of emancipated womanhood simply by producing or achieving as much as their male counterparts in society's competitive marketplace. Such a masculinist ambition could scarcely feed the world's underlying hunger for "Truth and Love in their universal energy." So that members of both sexes might satisfy their vocations and need for psychic complementarity, Fuller urged that every sphere of public employment be opened to women. But, like Stowe, Fuller conceived the central challenge of the day in spiritual rather than sociological terms and as therefore requiring not merely a redistribution but a redefinition of power.

The associative self-dependence represented by Mary's virginity also helped to validate Fuller's own status as an unmarried woman at the time she composed *Woman in the Nineteenth Century*. Her work sounds least modern, perhaps, when it identifies celibacy "as the great fact of the time" (312). Fuller, though, had personal reason to invest credence in the spiritual fecundity of sublimated sexuality. She also had reason to suspect that, given the social norms of her day, unmarried women were usually better situated than wives to become self-reliant souls. The transcendent force of woman's "electrical" and "magnetic" energy might flow more readily through a soul prepared to "meditate in virgin loneliness" (313).

Accordingly, the Chippewa woman Fuller extols for living out her youthful dream that "she was betrothed to the Sun" (301), rather than to any mortal male, preserves a consecrated independence. Far from barren, she had managed to "blossom sweetly" in the sun's rays. So also Fuller cites Petrarch's address to Mary, a "perfect woman" (351) clothed with the sun, as "a consecrated living temple of the true God in your fruitful virginity."[50] Both the main text and the coda section of *Woman in the Nineteenth Century* conclude with invocations of transcendent power and images of a fruitful *hieros gamos*. Earlier, in an 1841 journal entry centered on affliction, Fuller had identified Mary more explicitly as the object of invocation: "Return Madonna, for none since thee has been the mother of a perfectly holy child" (19).

By the close of her 1845 prophecy, however, Fuller shows less inclination to venerate Mary as a discrete figure than she does to assimilate the example and idea of the Madonna into her own idea of woman in the nineteenth century. For Fuller, Mary as Virgin Mother exemplified a twofold personal ideal: the realization of spirited autonomy, as well as creative fecundity. No less than Miranda "a child of the spirit" (261), the Madonna mediated transcendence even as she retained her engagement with wounded humanity. She also joined history to myth, as Fuller aspired to do within the whole of *Woman in the Nineteenth Century*. Above all, Mary exemplified the divine potency of womanhood. If Raphael's Sibyl embodies "female Genius" that "alone understands the God,"[51] all the more might his Madonnas be said to do so.

In calling for the advent of a woman "who shall vindicate their birthright for all women," Fuller extends the orthodox typological equation beyond Eve and Mary toward prediction of a new Mary Victoria for her age. As one might have supposed, this collective personification of womanhood moves further from commitment to historical Christianity than the responses to Mariology developed by Harriet Beecher Stowe. It is even more "post-Christian" than the subsequent response of Henry Adams, whose Marian piety ran not so much toward a prophetic antitype as to a mythical but highly personal, interlocutory Madonna fixed in an imagined past. Strange to say, Fuller identified Mary with a revolutionary shift in sensibility that led, after deeper secularization than she had sponsored, toward appearance of the "New Woman" who would announce her emancipation in the public arena and fictions of America before the close of the nineteenth century. The New Woman gains clear ascendancy in works by writers like Kate Chopin, Charlotte Perkins Gilman, Harold Frederic, Henry James, and Theodore Dreiser—but not before Harriet Beecher Stowe would rediscover religious icons of a divine mother with saving power to regenerate the sinful society of antebellum America.

THREE

CALVINISM FEMINIZED

Divine Matriarchy in Harriet Beecher Stowe

Godly Maternity and Motherly Jesus

Confronting her New England religious heritage with more personal credulity than Hawthorne ever did his, the seventh child of Lyman and Roxana Beecher found herself engaged in a lifelong struggle to assimilate—and to remake—her ancestral Calvinism. The fruit of this engagement is evident in the subject matter of later novels, such as *The Minister's Wooing, Oldtown Folks,* and *Pogunuc People,* as well as in the apocalyptic urgency and evangelical fervor of *Uncle Tom's Cabin.* Deficient in several crafts of the belletristic novelist, Stowe yet knew how to infuse her writing with the powerful rhetoric of conversion preaching. In fact, her best fiction often shows a temper closer to symbolic romance than to novelistic realism, with the author drawing on mythic and personal energies to sustain her heightened rhetoric. Thus, episodes in *Uncle Tom's Cabin* such as Eliza's perilous crossing of the Ohio River or the deaths of Eva and Tom amount to rituals of passage laden with mythological import.

Inspired with regenerative confidence that the last will be first in God's kingdom, Stowe exalted society's powerless people—children, blacks, and women—in her tales of the lowly. And as critics like Elizabeth Ammons and Dorothy Berkson have demonstrated for *Uncle Tom's Cabin,*[1] her recognition of women and endorsement of feminine piety centered especially on the saving force of maternity. Stowe's agonistic involvement with Edwards and the original faith of New England's fathers issued at length in a reconceived Christianity of American mothers.

At one level, of course, this paean to motherly love betrays the influences of a postrevivalist and sentimental Christianity, of emerging bourgeois values, and of feeling loosed from all strictures of logic. As Berkson suggests, it also shows Stowe's

53

theological impulse to displace the monarchical God of Edwardsean Calvinism with a divine principle of maternal compassion. At the same time, one can see the author's matrifocal spirituality flowing directly from evangelical tradition insofar as her motherhood theme grounds more incarnationally that classic Reformation-Pauline metaphor of conversion as a "new birth."

For Stowe, the resulting focus on divine womanhood, which is central to her vision of this life and the next, drew particular inspiration from the biblical Mary. That Stowe reflected deeply on the Marian Madonna is a little-known fact one might not have predicted in a woman of her era, place, and religious background. She shared this interest with her brothers Charles and Henry Ward Beecher.[2] One indication of it can be seen in her zeal for visual art, particularly as stimulated by her three visits to Europe. In her Hartford residence on Forest Street, tour guides today point to a copy of Raphael's *Madonna of the Goldfinch* (figure 3.1) hanging conspicuously in the front parlor to illustrate her pioneering display of Madonna artifacts among the households of local Protestant gentility. What is more, Stowe owned copies of at least three other sacred Madonnas—including the *Holy Family del Divino Amore* and Raphael's *Madonna del Gran Duca*—in addition to secular renderings of the mother and child motif. After her first European tour in 1853, she reported to her sister-in-law that she had just installed a "picture of Madonna and child from Dresden" (Raphael's *Sistine Madonna*, figure 3.2) in her home at Andover, Massachusetts. She remarked elsewhere that this picture "formed a deeper part of my consciousness than any I have yet seen."[3]

So her iconographic fascination with the theme is plain. And in conjunction with her fiction, Stowe's written discourses on Mary in her verse and nonfictional prose—especially as delineated in *Woman in Sacred History*—offer us valuable understanding of the personal, cultural, and theological significance of her interest. Her Marian attitudes help to clarify, in turn, the distinctive sort of domestic, matrifocal feminism that informs fictions such as *Uncle Tom's Cabin* and *The Minister's Wooing*. It is scarcely accidental that several of Stowe's redemptive heroines—Mary Scudder in *The Minister's Wooing,* Mara in *The Pearl of Orr's Island,* and Mary Higgins in *Pogunuc People*—even bear Marian names. But why was this Protestant writer so entranced by the ostensibly Catholic image of the Madonna?[4]

Stowe's revalorization of the Madonna presented Mary not as virgin so much as paradigmatic mother, focusing especially on her conjunctive relation to a maternal Jesus. Thus accommodating Marian piety to Protestant orthodoxy, Stowe sought to refashion her inherited Calvinism into what she conceived to be a more encompassing Christianity. In biographical terms, Stowe's interest in the Marian Madonna may have been stirred not only by her European travel experiences but also by highly sanctified memories of her own mother, Roxana Beecher, who died when Harriet was only five. Brother Henry Ward Beecher even testified, "My mother is to me what the Virgin Mary is to a devout Catholic."[5]

Two revealing expressions of Stowe's responses to the biblical Mary can be located in her devotional account of "The Blessed Woman"—included in her *Footsteps of the Master* (1877)—and in her volume of character portraits celebrating *Woman in Sacred History*.[6] Devoting separate chapters of *Woman in Sacred History* to "Mary the Mythical Madonna" and "Mary the Mother of Jesus," Stowe seems at first to

FIGURE 3.1. Raphael, *Madonna of the Goldfinch.* From the Uffizi, Florence (Alinari/Art Resource, New York).

reject the mythical Mary altogether on the usual Protestant grounds of scant biblical evidence. To allow unscriptural legends, iconography, and pagan associations to image a Mary who overshadows Jesus is, she charges, a grave mistake.

Yet the resistance here to deifying Jesus's mother may derive less from biblical hermeneutics than from Mrs. Stowe's urge to identify with Mary's palpable experience of womanhood. For Stowe, the woman highly favored is no timeless goddess but a figure of history. Though "the crowned queen of women," Mary manifests her blessedness not through supernal powers but in her exemplary bearing among those "that have lived woman's life."[7] Not surprisingly, Stowe identifies this womanhood chiefly with maternity.

Indeed, Stowe's domestic sense of Mary as mother is so strong that it all but effaces the title of virgin from her nonfictional commentary. Rejecting in usual Protestant fashion the theory of Mary's *perpetual* virginity, Stowe reflects instead with knowing

FIGURE 3.2. Raphael, *The Sistine Madonna*. From the Gemäldegalerie, Staatliche Kunstsammlungen, Dresden (Foto Marburg/Art Resource, New York).

sympathy on the trials Mary faced by virtue of "the unbelief of her other children."[8] Moreover, Mary's maternity extends beyond the momentous act of birthing Christ to include her teaching of Jesus and domestic familiarity with him.

This sense of an integral association between Mary and Jesus is central to Stowe's theology. It helps to explain not only her Protestant reluctance to view Mary as an autonomous goddess but also her arresting insistence on the feminine character of Jesus: If Jesus lacked a biological father, "all that was human in him" derived from Mary's nature. Accordingly, "there was in Jesus more of the pure feminine element than in any other man. It was the feminine element exalted and taken in union with divinity." So intimate is this association that to express it, Stowe combines imagery of marriage and parthenogenesis: "He was bone of her bone and flesh of her flesh—his life grew out of her immortal nature."[9]

To Mary alone—not to Joseph—Stowe assigns the peculiar advantages of domestic intimacy with Jesus.[10] While granting Mary exalted status, Stowe denies Joseph even his traditional singularity as Jesus' only genealogical link to the messianic kingship of David; she endorsed a curious exegesis of Luke 3.23–38 whereby Mary, too, stands by birth within the house of David. Yet Stowe rejects medieval inclinations to discover the godliness of maternal compassion by transferring adoration from Christ to Mary. Precisely because Jesus took flesh as consubstantial with Mary in utero, partaking of her human nature alone, he is uniquely qualified to satisfy those yearnings "of the human heart to which it has been said the worship of the Virgin Mother was adapted."

Yet Mary herself retains for Stowe a crucial role as exemplar. It is evident that Stowe identified personally not only with Mary's motherhood but also with Mary's ironic attainment of public significance through values and activities centered in the private, domestic sphere.[11] Stowe does praise Mary's self-abnegating acceptance of the divine will, to the point of echoing the blessed woman's "Behold the handmaid of the Lord" in the course of describing the newfound faith and vocation beyond perplexity she found in her own religious experience.[12] But Stowe also attributes to Mary the divine fire of poet and prophet. Sharing the name of Miriam, "the first great prophetess," Mary likewise "inherited, in the line of descent, the poetic and prophetic temperament" befitting her noble Davidic ancestry. The mind of Jesus' mother was "capable of the highest ecstasy of inspiration,"[13] as shown in her one great effusion, the Magnificat.

Plainly, Stowe identifies, too, with Mary's perseverance in facing keen personal loss. She dedicates her 1867 verses on "The Sorrows of Mary" quite explicitly "to mothers who have lost sons in the late war,"[14] and surely the "anguish of disappointed hopes"[15] that pierced the stabat mater was comprehensible to a mother who in 1849 lost one son to plague and in 1857 another, nineteen years old, to death by drowning in the Connecticut River. In fact, Stowe's ability to draw mythic power from her own maternal mourning over baby Charley became crucial to her conception of Uncle Tom's Cabin, just as her affliction over Henry's state of soul at the time of his death helped to precipitate The Minister's Wooing.[16]

In the final analysis, Stowe's nonfictional writings testify that she could not fully resist the imaginative attraction of "Mary the Mythical Madonna." Even as she laments displacement of "the real Mary" by poeticized imagery, she writes appreciatively of iconographic representations by Raphael, Titian, and Fra Angelico, as well as of legends passed down through apocryphal writings. She cannot help embracing the tale, related by Anna Jameson in Legends of the Madonna, that Jesus appeared first to his mother after his resurrection. "This legend has something in it so grateful to human sympathies," she confesses, "that the heart involuntarily believes it." "Though the sacred record is silent, we may believe that He, who loved his own unto the end, did not forget his mother in her hour of deepest anguish." Stowe likewise finds appealing the mythic tradition of the Greek church that "Mary alone of all her sex was allowed to enter the Holy of Holies, and pray before the ark of the covenant."

By envisioning Mary as a "second Eve" and quintessential mother worthy of "love and veneration," Stowe comes close to recognizing her—if not invoking her—as the mother of us all. In a later novel, she would voice hope that eventually the influence of Mary, "the great archetype of the christian motherhood, shall be felt through all of the laws and institutions of society." But she is careful to distance herself from Catholic allegiances, observing that the Mariological excesses of the Roman church "have tended to deprive the rest of the world of a great source of comfort and edification by reason of the opposite extreme to which Protestant reaction has naturally gone."[17]

Birthpangs of the New Order in *Uncle Tom's Cabin*

Against the backdrop of such concerns, the prophetic purpose of *Uncle Tom's Cabin* can be seen all the more clearly. Just as the Marian Magnificat looks toward that era when God shall put down the mighty but exalt the humble and meek, so also Stowe's best-seller represents a womanly triumph of evangelical rhetoric on behalf of "the lowly." And, despite the book's technical deficiencies as novel, it is indeed a masterwork of rhetoric. Addressed above all to the maternal soul and conscience of the nation, *Uncle Tom's Cabin* is also a book full of motherly characters—to the point where even its black hero, Tom, has been aptly described as figuring a feminized and maternal Christ.[18]

Already in the book's second chapter, "The Mother," Stowe invokes a heroic image of motherhood in the flight of Eliza Harris. Warned as Mary had been that on account of her male child "a sword will pierce through your soul,"[19] Eliza nonetheless enjoys almost miraculous protection as she flees from bondage across the Ohio River, her figurative Jordan and Red Sea, on dancing ice floes. What drives this thrilling exodus, Stowe suggests, is Eliza's powerful assent to faith and hope, combined with "maternal love, wrought into a paroxysm of frenzy by the near approach of a fearful danger" (104). And just as Stowe perceived something stronger in Mary's assent to Gabriel's annunciation than shrinking submissiveness, so also she highlights the fierceness of Eliza's parental commitment.

Another case of compelling maternity is presented by Senator Bird's wife, named Mary, who intercedes successfully with her husband on behalf of the fugitives. In view of the familiar charge that Stowe's sentimental portrayal of womanhood reduces all argument to mere feeling, it is worth observing that Mary applies a fairly rigorous logic of consistency and biblical authority in making her case against the fugitive slave law. By contrast, Senator Bird, who lacks Mary's concrete, integral sense of moral reality, succumbs initially to a fallacy of uprooted abstraction in which "his idea of a fugitive was only an idea of the letters that spell the word" (155). Yet ironically, he patronizes his wife as having more heart than head, just as Haley dismisses Mrs. Shelby's concern for her slaves as irrational because women "ha'nt no sort of calculation" (46).

Even more than Mrs. Shelby or Mary Bird, Rachel Halliday, whose comfort Eliza enjoys in the Quaker settlement, presents an image of archetypal maternity. It is surely no accident that in the epigraph appearing one chapter before Halliday's introduction, Stowe cites Jeremiah's prophetic account of Rachel weeping for her children (192). Rachel Halliday supplies potential nurture to the whole of afflicted humankind because "hers was just the face and form that made 'mother' seem the most natural word in the world" (216). As Jane Tompkins observes, Halliday personifies for Stowe something of divine presence because as she is "seated in her kitchen at the head of her table, passing out coffee and cake for breakfast, Rachel Halliday, the millennarian counterpart of little Eva, enacts the redeemed form of the last supper."[20]

Yet Stowe portrays only one virgin mother within her gallery of memorable women. Or at least one could argue that the child-saint Eva, who is evidently a holy virgin, qualifies metaphorically as a mother by virtue of her role in mediating the new birth to characters such as Topsy, Miss Ophelia, and her father, Augustine. Hers is thus a true, spiritual motherhood in opposition to the false, fleshly mother-hood of Marie. Consistent with the book's ironic reversals in which the last be-come first, Stowe develops here a curious sort of reverse typology in which Eva replaces Mary (or second Eve) and in which the child emerges as more effectively maternal than her own mother.

Beyond the ironic nomenclature by which Eva supplants Marie, Stowe exploits other dimensions of Eva's name. As Evangeline, she serves, of course, as the book's strongest evangelical instrument of conversion. For the author of *Uncle Tom's Cabin*, conversion to the cause of immediate emancipation, with its conviction of slavery as sin, must be founded at base on the heart's conversion to Christ. But Stowe portrays Eva as stimulating this twofold conversion not through her speech so much as through a quality of presence that bears the Word into the world. As an antitype of Eve, Eva epitomizes—within the sentimental terms of Stowe's narrative—the saving power of natural womanhood. Recreating her namesake's title as "the mother of all living" (Genesis 3.20), Eva also epitomizes a more universal maternity than that presented by Marie.

At the same time, Eva reveals herself to be a new Eve in that she bears the Word into a world enslaved by sin and offers herself as agent of the new birth. She also absorbs the pain of others; like the *mater dolorosa* of Luke 2.48–51, she knows what it is for such sorrow to "sink into" her heart (326). Through her devotional exer-cises, this "fair star" (383) consents to act as feminine intercessor before God for her sinful father. When St. Clare sees her off to church, where he will not follow, he nonetheless bids her "pray for me" (278). This intercessory role parallels and sup-ports that of St. Clare's own mother.

However embarrassing by present-day standards of critical taste, Eva's death scene plainly occupies a pivotal place in the book—and in this character's brief career as mother of conversions. Of course, Stowe does not hesitate to milk the episode for all the Victorian sentiment that a pious maiden's early demise could supply. Pre-cisely the sort of nineteenth-century conventions regarding death that Dickinson mocks so brilliantly in "I heard a fly buzz when I died" come in for solemn treat-ment here: the circle of chastened mourners, the sacramentalized curls of hair Eva confers as "a last mark of her love," an edifying farewell discourse reminiscent of that given by Jesus in St. John's Gospel, and the mourners' urge to glimpse some-thing of the saint's dying vision of joy, peace, and love.

Yet beyond its individual demonstration of holy dying, Eva's translation is in-tended to signal the larger birth pangs of a new order opening from the womb of eternity. As such, the scene incorporates birthing similitudes in its mention of Eva's spasmodic agony leading toward exhaustion, its passage through the tension of midnight vigil when eternity's veil "grows thin" (426), to that blessed change which Tom describes as an opening wide of heaven's door. Still presented as beautiful despite her crimson coloring, Eva dies nobly of consumption. In Stowe's idealized fable, she is indeed consumed—immediately and integrally, without apparent corruption of body or conflict of spirit—into the dawn of God's kingdom. No wonder a favorite hymn of Stowe's was the comforting song of death beginning, "O mother dear, Jerusalem."[21] This untraumatic form of Eva's rebirth parallels the translation of Mary, otherwise termed her Assumption or (in Eastern Orthodox usage) Dormition, as set forth in apocryphal and iconographic traditions later described by Stowe in detail. Such traditions regard Mary's assumption as an instance of realized eschatology in which Jesus returns to escort Mary not merely in his role as son but also as bridegroom of his beloved.[22] So also Tom counsels watchfulness for the bridegroom's rendezvous with Eva at midnight.

In tandem with this scene, Stowe later depicts a more traumatic version of passage toward the new birth in Tom's martyrdom at the hand of Simon Legree. Already a reconceived *alter Christus,* Tom is delivered to the kingdom's larger life as "He began to draw his breath with long, deep inspirations; and his broad chest rose and fell, heavily" (591). Moreover, Stowe associates his death mystically with the birth pangs of the apocalyptic endtime. And plainly the archetype of Tom's triumphant passion is found in Jesus' life-giving labor on the cross: "In his patient, generous bosom he bears the anguish of a world. Bear thou, like him, in patience, and labor in love; for sure as he is God, 'the year of his redeemed *shall* come.'"[23] In the closing pages of her book, the author underscores the natal trauma of this coming age of cataclysm or millennialistic renewal, "an age of the world when nations are trembling and convulsed," when "a mighty influence is abroad, surging and heaving the world" (629). As George Harris interprets the signs of these times, "the throes that now convulse the nations are . . . but the birth-pangs of an hour of universal peace and brotherhood" (611).

Predictably, readers unsympathetic to Stowe's religious values have scorned Tom's nonviolent resistance, his self-sacrificing resignation, as a form of passive docility demeaning to African Americans—no matter that in his defiant love Tom refuses to flog a fellow slave, that he will die rather than betray Cassy and Emmeline, and that his response makes possible both their escape and the liberation of slaves on the Shelby estate in Kentucky. Admittedly, certain aspects of Tom's characterization warrant the modern epithet of an "Uncle Tom," even if his singularity renders him not so much a direct model for behavior as a motivating inspiration for readers or for witnesses like Sambo and Quimbo.

At base, however, Tom's bearing continues to scandalize our own culture of self-assertion and self-development because it embodies Stowe's conviction that kenotic or self-emptying love is ultimately more powerful than what Ann Douglas has described as "the masculine hubris endemic to Western capitalism and imperialism" (Introduction 27). In dramatizing that spiritual conviction, Stowe draws on conventional pieties surrounding motherhood and childhood; at the same time, she subverts normative values insofar as she argues not simply for a redistribution but for a redefinition of power. That the "powerfully made"(68) and indubitably masculine Tom nonetheless functions as a kind of heroine, incorporating values traditionally branded as feminine or maternal, is a notable finding of recent feminist criticism. And when Tom assures Legree that he (Tom) "can die," the affirmation carries for Stowe an active import understandable only within the visionary terms of his role—shared with Eva—as divine mother of the nascent kingdom of God.

Because Tom carries maternal compassion so fully in the body of his own person, *his* biological mother need not play a role in this narrative. Yet two other mothers in *Uncle Tom's Cabin,* both deceased, continue to influence their sons despite or through their absence. These are the absent mothers of Simon Legree and of Augustine St. Clare. Even Simon Legree, it seems, might have claimed salvation had he not rejected definitively the humanizing and divinizing influence of his mother. From beyond the grave, she haunts this would-be reprobate with the specter of an unresolved identity and almost irresistible grace. Linked to Eva by association with a golden hair thread, Legree's mother signifies not only the shadow of potential regeneracy, but also the supressed anima of this "grotesquely masculine tyrant."[24] Despite her son's perdition, her intercessory power bears fruit—even at a heavenly distance—by making possible the escape of Emmeline and Cassy.

As a choice version of what Puritans would recognize as the "natural man," an unconverted but sympathetic man of the world, the ironically named Augustine St. Clare does achieve full conviction of his personal depravity. He might therefore be considered ripe for regeneration. Yet before his deathbed change, he is incapable of passing beyond this stage toward the assurance of grace and forgiveness needed for "effectual calling." He also abandons hope when he fails in his romantic ideal of love. Briefly, *this* Augustine believes more deeply in his capacity for sin than in his ability to embrace the saving goodness of God. He can appreciate, intellectually, the evil of slavery though he is helpless to affirm, existentially, the imperative of emancipation. Accordingly, his predicament reflects Stowe's moral critique of Calvinism. Without the intervention of heaven-sent intermediaries, "Saint Clare" can be neither saintly nor clear of vision.

Yet he is peculiarly susceptible to the influence of feminine grace by virtue of his "marked sensitiveness of character, more akin to the softness of woman than the ordinary hardness of his own sex" (239). And we know that his Bible-loving mother had been, literally, another Evangeline. In St. Clare's estimation, she "was divine," or at least immaculately conceived in the sense that she betrayed "no trace of any human weakness or error about her" (333). We are told that St. Clare's father once overruled her, despite his supreme reverence for her, as brazenly as he would have "the virgin Mary herself" (336). Yet as a woman of Protestant (French Huguenot) stock who plays Catholic organ music, she transcends sectarian categories. That St. Clare's maternal piety leads toward a virtual identification of motherhood with divinity seems apparent when, on his deathbed, he declares he is returning "HOME, at last" and invokes "Mother!" as his final word. Thus St. Clare's absent mother ultimately regains a kind of divine presence.

In her closing exhortation to the congregation of all America, Stowe warns of wrath from above unless the nation reverses its course toward a dis-union of states effected by slavery and sin. If "this Union" of states is "to be saved," to regain health and wholeness, her readers must seize the "day of grace" and assist the birth of God's kingdom in a convulsive era (629). By the close of *Uncle Tom's Cabin*, Stowe establishes that within her hopeful vision of the mother-savior lies the mother-healer who could restore integrity to dis-membered families, souls, and sections of the United States.

The Ministry of Mary in *The Minister's Wooing*

Seven years after releasing *Uncle Tom's Cabin* in book form, Stowe confronted more directly her own religious and familial heritage in a New England novel featuring an overtly Marian protagonist. Despite its title, *The Minister's Wooing* focuses less on the historically based character of Samuel Hopkins than it does on the saintly figure of Mary Scudder. If Hopkins fictionally encompasses Lyman Beecher so as to epitomize for Stowe New England's Calvinist patriarchy,[25] it is telling that Mary ends up displacing Hopkins as the novel's theological center. Similarly, Stowe had already advanced her own claim, within a family of noted clergymen, to exercising a ministry of the Word through her authorship of works like *Uncle Tom's Cabin*.

In *The Minister's Wooing*, the rhetorical urgency and drama of *Uncle Tom's Cabin* give way to a novel of ideas and of reflections developed from visualized tableaux. Significantly, the book's opening still life of Mary Scudder shows her enshrined as the New England maiden, an image superimposed on her iconographic portrayal as the original Virgin Mary. The picture of this girl, who at first means never to marry, comes complete with a descending dove, forming an overall impression of "simplicity and purity" reminiscent "of some old pictures of the girlhood of the Virgin."[26] Indeed, the Roman Catholic Virginie de Frontignac later confides to Mary that "I always think of you when I think of our dear Lady" (394). In her grief, Stowe's American heroine is also likened to the Sistine Madonna and associated with one of da Vinci's Madonnas. Linked repeatedly to the ocean beside Newport, she is even decked out playfully for her nuptials by Madame de Frontignac to resemble a "sea-born Venus" (432).

This image of Mary's divine womanhood—reinforced by further comparisons to Catherine of Siena, to Dante's Beatrice, and to the saintly wife of Jonathan Edwards—is qualified only slightly by recognition that the dove painted into the mise-en-scène actually belongs to her heathenish cousin James. Stowe quickly establishes that at another level Mary is herself the dove, one in whom the Holy Spirit ultimately bears vitalizing power as "priestess, wife, and mother" (567).

Like Eva, Mary Scudder fulfills a crucial vocation as the mother of new birth for others. She is a regenerative agent not only for James Marvyn but also—if with less certain results—for the notorious Aaron Burr, grandson of Jonathan Edwards. She even succeeds in "wooing" the learned Doctor Hopkins some distance from his overcerebral, self-tormenting Calvinism toward a Christianity allowing greater scope for beauty and divine compassion.

While preserving Mary's image of unspotted virtue, Stowe attributes to her the same initiated understanding of affliction that James remembers seeing pictorialized in "the youthful Mother of Sorrows" (36). Even before she finally achieves bio-logical motherhood at the story's conclusion, then, and particularly after gaining precocious wisdom in her grief over James's supposed death at sea, Mary appears less the virginal innocent than her friend, the nearly ruined "Virginie." Stowe's New England maiden qualifies as a mother-nurturer to others because of her initiation "as a sanctified priestess of the great worship of sorrow" (380).

Yet the way in which Mary Scudder quickens conversion differs in at least one crucial respect from that displayed by Eva St. Clare. Mary, unlike Eva, draws on sexual energies directed initially toward herself on the way to stirring male desires for the love of God.

Thus, in *The Minister's Wooing,* Stowe ventures to affirm that agape need not efface eros in the divine economy of grace. To be sure, disordered eros gives rise to the rapaciousness of Burr or the psychic bondage of Virginie. Rightly directed, however, natural impulses might elevate the soul toward higher loves, as in the instance of Dante's love for Beatrice. Stowe demonstrates this theological hypoth-esis by indicating how much of the regenerative inspiration Mary supplies to James Marvyn, Hopkins, and Burr is fueled by eroticism. So *this* Mary is clearly lover as well as spiritual mother—and, without conscious design, she fulfills much of her latter role through the former.

In *The Minister's Wooing,* Stowe underscores her conviction that a progressive scale of affections connects the theological orders of nature and grace, that natural love is indeed sacramental. In contrast to the all-or-nothing ideality of austere Cal-vinism, she insists, "There is a ladder to heaven, whose base God has placed in human affections, tender instincts, symbolic feelings, sacraments of love, through which the soul rises higher and higher, refining as she goes, till she outgrows the human, and changes, as she rises, into the image of the divine" (87).

Within this scheme, Mary Scudder clearly qualifies as high priestess of the natu-ral sacrament by which God leads us to good through "the love we have to each other" (82). Thus, James testifies that Mary's image, standing "between me and low, gross vice" (70), has drawn him upward toward God. Yet in her office as mediator and intercessor, Mary stands by no means "alone of all her sex." Instead, she typi-fies for Stowe that charism of spiritual maternity shared by many women and some men. Mary Scudder belongs to "the great company scattered through earth who are priests unto God,—ministering between the Divine One, who has unveiled himself unto them, and those who as yet stand in the outer courts of the great sanc-tuary of truth and holiness" (74). And even a woman such as Virginie can serve eventually as the "pure priestess of a domestic temple" (230).

In contrast to this sacramental theology, the hyper-Calvinistic theology of the rungless ladder demands a heroic, unmediated leap of virtue to the point of accept-ing one's own damnation for the greater glory of God. Stowe suggests that Hopkins's sublime theory of benevolence betrays a masculinized privileging of heroic achieve-ment and individual force of will. At its worst, the damned theology of Hopkins ends up exalting the nobility of man's self-abnegating exertions over the gracious benevolence of a God who presumably wills to save all repentant sinners. Ironi-cally, this New Divinity comes close to supplanting Calvinism's favored covenant of grace with a new covenant of works centered in human volition, to replacing the charitable bonds of communitarian Christianity with a virtue borne of heroic individualism.

Depicted novelistically as a sound-hearted eccentric, Doctor Hopkins embodies true virtue both in his personal charity toward African slaves and in his willingness to free Mary from her promise to marry him. But the novel portrays him as a good man largely despite, rather than because of, the theological system he espouses. For Stowe, the rationalistic, disjunctive logic supporting his theology is far less sound than the spirit-wisdom that sustains the faith of characters like Mary and Candace. In underscoring this point, the author elaborates a gender division in which the epistemology and semiotic expression of male clerics are superceded by those of holy women.

The male-sponsored, rationalistic approach emphasizes verbal knowledge and expression as epitomized by the doctor's monumental treatise. It is essentially analytic, cerebral, abstracted. By contrast, Stowe's pneumatological way accents iconic or wordless communication, intuitive and poetic knowledge, and matrifocal values.

It is fair to question the gender-specific validity of this theoretical opposition. One may likewise question what appears to be the antiintellectual tenor of Stowe's sentimental focus on a religion of feeling. Yet the spirit-based epistemology favored in *The Minister's Wooing* carries a logic of its own.

Thus, the Puritan logic of "evidences" for election is shown to be ultimately illogical insofar as it purports to find rationalistic criteria for judging motions of the Spirit. During James's fearful absence at sea, there is no external, empirical evidence to prove that this natural man ever found personal evidence of his conversion and salvation. Hence Hopkins offers no hope for him. Yet Candace, eschewing the "white folks' way of tinkin" and following another "mode of testing evidence," rightly affirms that "Mass'r James is one o' de 'lect' and I'm clar dar's considerable more o' de 'lect than people tink" (447–88, 349).

It is indeed reasonable for Candace to conclude that "Jesus didn't die for nothin', —all dat love a'n't going to be wasted" (349). It is likewise reasonable for Mary to protest, in a key exchange with Hopkins, that we may never know we have achieved disinterested love of God because "our love of happiness and our love of God are so inseparably connected" (293), just as our inclination toward self-love bears some connection to God's preceding and unlimited love for us. It is scarcely antiintellectual of Mary to observe that Hopkins sometimes mistakes "the elaboration of theology" for "preaching the gospel" (90) or that, by trying to deconstruct virtue, he risks analyzing it out of existence—or, at least, out of practice.

Perhaps nothing in the book illustrates more graphically the unreasonableness of rationalism, when abstracted from the incarnate context of human feelings, than the response of Simeon Brown to the challenge of renouncing his interest in the lucrative slave trade. Reflecting a sensibility that calculates all virtue in relation to the summum bonum of personal wealth, Brown reaches a predictable conclusion. Yet his cerebral rationalism, if not his heart or his inner faith, accords with the epistemological assumptions of Hopkins more closely than the good doctor can admit.

By contrast, Candace and Mary demonstrate other, more womanly ways of knowing. Stowe regards those with such "instinctive and poetic" capacities as "winged" spirits who fly ahead of the walking logicians (294). As Stowe's African reembodiment of the archaic Earth Mother, Candace not only displays special powers of intuitive prophecy but also exercises the universal motherhood typified by the Christian Madonna. Thus, Candace rocks the grieving Mrs. Marvyn "as if she had been a babe" (347), reminding her of how tenderly Jesus of Nazareth "looked on His mother" and assuring her that such a Savior "knows all about mothers' hearts" and "won't break yours" (348).

This black mother's aboriginal power as intercessor likewise emboldens her to invoke the authority of the Spirit when she assures Ellen Marvyn, contrary to one version of Calvinist evidence, that James *has* been "called an' took" (349) among God's elect. Candace bustles about the house, half comically, as a latter-day goddess of abundance and the hearth, an "African Genius of Plenty" (445) resembling one of those rotund fertility figurines from the Neolithic era. But she also performs Christian intercession as a Black Madonna (figure 3.3) who spreads her "ample skirts" over the transgressions of her white and black children and who has "secret bowels of mercy" (112) for James when he is convicted of youthful misbehavior. Hers is indeed a queenly motherhood, as underscored by Doctor Hopkins's joking reference to her name as that of an ancient Ethiopian queen (138); and for nineteenth-century scholars like J. J. Bachofen, "Candace" became a generic term associated with the matriarchal phase of woman's spiritual rule in society.[27]

In *her* office as evangelizing intercessor, Mary Scudder likewise mediates the Spirit—as when she quickens Hopkins's soul, passions, and instinct for beauty through "the silent breathing of her creative presence" (93). And though James finds her "a living gospel" (37) who shelters the Word, she achieves this end not mainly through verbalized discourse but through an iconic force issuing from silence. Particularly in her pain, she is framed descriptively as an image of reflective and attentive meditation, like her namesake who ponders words in her heart. Stowe underscores the inspirative power mediated through her face, gestures, and listening presence. As Kristeva says of the Virginal Maternal, Mary Scudder's semiotic import extends "to the extralinguistic regions of the unnamable."[28] Because the language of the Virginal Maternal issues from the Spirit's silence, it is fitting that James progresses toward his shipboard conversion not through any direct verbal initiative but through possession of *Mary's* bible, that physical relic whose extralinguistic power extends the presence of her physical body.

Yet the author's feminized theology reflects more an adaptation and transformation than a wholesale rejection of masculine precedents in her Christian tradition. It is scarcely surprising that, within the sacred bower of Mary Scudder's bedchamber, the library that feeds her imagination includes not only the Bible and a few secular writings but also the works of Jonathan Edwards. Holy New England women could find much to sustain them in the contemplative Edwards—the Edwards who recognized the beauty of divine virtue and the virtue of beauty, or who appreciated the emotive power of affections in drawing souls toward conversion.

Only the ultra-Calvinist Edwards, the rigorist who highlighted divine sovereignty and human depravity, needed to be shelved. For Stowe, this less congenial exponent of the rungless ladder and a monarchical God had, like his follower Hopkins, lost contact with that homelier life sanctified by Mother and Child: "These hard old New England divines were the poets of metaphysical philosophy, who built systems in an artistic fervor, and felt self exhale from beneath them as they rose into the higher re-

THE SOUL-DRIVER EXPERIENCES A MERCANTILE DRAWBACK.

Marks.—" If we could get a breed of gals that did'nt care, now, for their young uns, I tell ye, I think t'would be 'bout the greatest mod'rn improvement I knows on."

FIGURE 3.3. The figure of the Black Madonna—and particularly the image enshrined at Jasna Gora, Poland—has long been revered in Europe. This illustration from the 1852 London edition of *Uncle Tom's Cabin* points up another form of Black Madonna that Stowe envisions in her fiction. The author's description of Candace in *The Minister's Wooing* is perhaps the most vivid single instance of the case. Courtesy of Dodd Research Center, University of Connecticut.

gions of thought. But where theorists and philosphers tread with sublime assurance, woman often follows with bleeding footsteps;—women are always turning from the the abstract to the individual, and feeling where the philosopher only thinks" (25).

In a subsequent letter, Virginie de Frontignac enlarges the meaning of these "bleeding footsteps" when she exclaims with reference to Mrs. Marvyn's loss that "the bleeding heart of the Mother of God can alone understand such sorrows" (382) as the book's grieving women—and, presumably, its author—have known. No wonder Mrs. Marvyn, after James's return, sits "looking into her son's eyes, like a picture of the Virgin Mary" (565–66). Stowe's narrative returns often to this notion that the heart of the *mater dolorosa* lies close to the mystery of a suffering God and that "Sorrow is divine" (360). For "the All-Father treats us as the mother does her 'infant crying in the dark;' he does not reason with our fears, or demonstrate their fallacy, but draws us silently to His bosom, and we are at peace" (425–26).

Despite her resistance to a masculinized tradition of semiotics and epistemology, Stowe draws heavily on orthodox biblicism in framing the millennial-apocalyptic imagery that dominates the conclusion of *The Minister's Wooing*. The novelistic Hopkins had earlier sublimated his erotic attraction to Mary Scudder within his devotional zeal for the Book of Revelation, an apt transposition of the fascination with millennialistic prophecy shown by the historical Hopkins.[29] Emotionally absorbed by the biblical prospect of apocalyptic marriage, he might well take his white-garbed Mary as a figure of the "mystical bride," "the Lamb's wife," a "celestial bride" (94) whom he is gifted to embrace in earthly marriage. Yet though the book ends in the eschatological mood of a wedding and miraculous return, Mary is never to be *his* bride.

Instead, in a curious twist on biblical figures, it is the natural man James who finally emerges as the resurrected bridegroom. In the chapter "Old Love and New Duty," Mary's reencounter with James is described in a manner that recalls Gospel accounts of Jesus's postresurrection appearances to Mary Magdalene and others. At the same time, this episode, which comes upon Mary Scudder "like life from the dead" (513), is described as another Annunciation, with further allusion to the mystical transport of St. Paul in 2 Corinthians 12. Summoned from daydream as if beyond the waking world, Mary suddenly hears "footsteps behind her, and some one said, 'Mary!' It was spoken in a choked voice, as one speaks in the crisis of a great emotion; and she turned and saw those very eyes, that very hair . . . and, whether in the body or out of the body God knoweth, she felt herself borne in those arms, and words that spoke themselves in her inner heart, words profaned by being repeated, were on her ear" (506).

The figurative ambiguities whereby Mary Scudder becomes at once spiritual and erotic bride, both mother and lover, correspond to traditional symbolizations of the Madonna as both mother and spouse of God. This pattern reflects as well Stowe's faith that youthful womanhood might embody the power of eros coextensively with that of agape and communal *caritas*. Finally, *The Minister's Wooing* is less a romantic love story than a narrative of community. Mary's love for James becomes incarnate within the beloved body of her *koinonia*, with the wedding room aptly resembling "the Episcopal church at Christmas" (560). So also Virginie, purged of grosser affections, continues to intercede with God for love of Burr even after his death.

Other Appearances of the Madonna-intercessor in *Agnes of Sorrento*, *Poganuc People*, and *The Pearl of Orr's Island*

The figurative richness and complication revealed in *Uncle Tom's Cabin* and *The Minister's Wooing* give way to less nuanced evocations of Mary in *Agnes of Sorrento* (1862). In this historical romance of fifteenth-century Italy, the "prayerful maiden"

Agnes is rather too insistently offered—both pictorially and morally—as a latter-day Madonna.

Deemed "as beautiful as the Madonna" and "pure as Mary herself,"[30] Stowe's Italian virgin had long been sequestered from men and from most of the profane world by her grandmother. Like Hawthorne's Hilda, she even dwells physically above the populated world, beside the great gorge of Sorrento, where she tends a shrine of the Madonna and Child. Her uncle, an itinerant Dominican friar of San Marco in Florence, sees in her an inevitable model for his artistic rendering of the Blessed Lady. What is more, when the glamorous cavalier Agostino descends upon Agnes to plead for her prayers of intercession, he bears "a tall stalk of white lily . . . such as one sees in a thousand pictures of the Annunciation" (92). No wonder her uncle Antonio surmises that the agent of this dreamlike apparition must have been none other than "the holy Gabriel" (114).

Agnes, then, images the Madonna as young maiden rather than as matron. Yet she does not remain perpetually celibate. Because she is destined to become the sanctifying angel in Agostino's house, the mystique governing her virginity has at least as much to do with the ideals of Victorian America as it does with those of late medieval Europe. At the same time, her youth, beauty, and innocence reflect a version of Mary consonant with Romantic ideals of womanhood.[31] In any case, the author's hagiographic treatment of Agnes's sexually charged innocence sounds cloying today. Neither is Stowe persuasive in the way she narrates Agnes's abrupt conversion in Rome to an antipapal movement presaging "our enlightened Protestantism" (132).

But if *Agnes of Sorrento* is a decidedly antipapal novel that betrays condescension mixed with selective suspicion of Roman Catholic culture, it is scarcely on balance an anti-Catholic book. It is even less an anti-Marian pronouncement. Curiously, in fact, Stowe exploits to the full European traditions of Marian piety in order to set the purity of her Sorrento Madonna against the corruptions of papal Rome. It is under vow to Mary, and presumably through the Divine Lady's empowerment, that Agnes undertakes the pilgrimage to Rome that finally reveals to her the heinous character of Pope Alexander VI (Borgia) and his kin.

That the cultus of Mary and the saints rested on pagan precedents did not vitiate its Christian worth for Stowe, any more than it did for Hawthorne. Both had a chance to see physical confirmation of this evolution in Italy. Thus, in *Agnes of Sorrento,* Stowe makes a point of telling her readers that the convent of "saint Agnes, the guardian of female purity," had been built "out of the wrecks and remains of an ancient temple of Venus" (48). Antonio likewise assures stonecutter Pietro that by chiseling ruins of "naked nymphs" into "holy virgins" (153), he can construct a marble shrine fit to shelter the image of Mary.[32]

Even Stowe's Savonarola, who is characterized as a prototypical Puritan seeking to restore the church's "primitive apostolic simplicity" (257, 259), accepts the cultus of Mary. Although he had urged the destruction of paintings depicting harlots as models of the Blessed Lady, this reformer is no iconoclast in the style of Cromwell. Instead, according to Antonio, Savonarola encouraged artists "to give their pencils to Christ and his Mother, and to seek for her image among pious and holy women

living a veiled and secluded life, like that our Lady lived before the blessed Annunciation" (91).

To be sure, the narrator in *Agnes of Sorrento* sometimes looks down on the iconic
ritualism practiced by Europe's Catholic peasantry, regarding it as a concession to
preliterate evangelism or as a spirituality peculiarly suited to "Southern races." "Let
us not," she urges, "from the height of our day, with the better appliances which a
universal press gives us, sneer at the homely rounds of the ladder by which the first
multititudes of the Lord's followers climbed heavenward" (96–97). Yet the book
registers a fully appreciative response to the statuary and liturgical ceremonial presented by the cathedral in Milan. For a Protestant work, it also projects surprising
sympathy toward the nonworshipful invocation of saints. Such appeal in prayer to
"saints of the Church Triumphant" acknowledged them as a "ministering agency"
through which Christ's "mediatorial government on earth was conducted" (248).
And this address to intercessors, among whom Mary reigns supreme, carried great
affective power.

As living saint and Madonna, Agnes is, of course, designated the book's chief
intercessor and agent of regenerative inspiration. For several men, including Antonio, Francesco, and Agostino, she provides visible revelation of divine love. Thus
Agnes's spiritual director, Francesco, finds her a blessed woman indeed, for "It was
only in the heart of a lowly maiden that Christ had been made manifest to the eye
of the monk, as of old he was revealed to the world through a virgin" (191). Yet for
Francesco, a former man of the world, loving the beautiful Agnes also provokes
anguishing sexual conflict. Less sympathetic than Hawthorne to the notion of sacramental confession, Stowe exposes in Francesco's torment familiar Protestant fears
about the pastoral ministry exercised by celibate Catholic priests.[33]

In her portrait of Agostino Sarelli, however, Stowe sustains her earlier faith that
grace enables some souls to ascend successfully the ladder from profane to sacred
love. As his name suggests, Agostino is initially another Augustine, an appealing
though seductive natural man. While remaining something of a cavalier reprobate,
his noble ancestry, idealistic and poetic temperament as reader of Dante, and history of nurture by a saintly mother all evidence his ripeness for full conversion. Like
George Harris, he has suffered enough injustice and abuse of family members that
he has good reason for wondering "Is there a God?" (158).

Only the intercession of Agnes enables Agostino to advance beyond righteous
anger toward mature Christian faith, reverence, and inner calm. He testifies that
her face has mediated to him both earthly and heavenly love, that it "has been even
as a sacrament to me," while Father Antonio concurs that there are some "on whom
our Mother shed such grace that their very beauty led heavenward" (160). For her
part, Agnes, too, senses that "something within" her "continually intercedes" (130)
for the salvation of this disreputable but vital young man. Significantly, in this later
story Stowe shows her half-skeptical Agostino attaining at last the fully assured
conversion that had eluded her other Augustine (St. Clare).

But if Agnes becomes mother of at least one conversion, the narrative's concluding remarks do not suggest that she ever knows actual, physical maternity after
her marriage to Agostino. Unlike Virginie and Mary Scudder, then, this Mary marries

but does not mother. The author accepts unreservedly, as her Puritan forebears would not, the notion that Agnes's marriage is a sacrament. Yet Stowe seems reluctant to let matronly duties modify the prevailing image of Agnes as alluring yet pristine virgin. Though this novel invokes maternal metaphors, picturing the church as "a tender nursing-mother" (275) or Jerusalem as "mother of us all" (199), it supplies no model of domestic maternity for the direct emulation of American readers. Accordingly, *Agnes of Sorrento* comes closer than any other Stowe fiction to supporting familiar Roman Catholic views of Mary as consecrated virgin.

The unsatisfactory resolution of the novel suggests that Stowe was uncertain just how to dispose of her heroine. Wedded to Agostino, Agnes first retreats with him to France. Eventually, after the defeat of the infamous Borgias, she returns to Rome, where she fills the office of saintly princess. Yet despite the author's fondness for Latinate punning on Agnes' name as Agnus Dei, she does not allow this lamb to share in the heroic martyrdom of Savonarola and his company. Neither did history allow Stowe to portray Agnes and Agostino as leaders of a new and successful religious reform movement in Italy. Though presumably revered for her "sanctity of life and manners" (376), Agnes in her final static position as princess reverts to an earlier posture in which she "'looks like some choice old picture of Our Lady'— not a drop of human blood in her" (5).

It is worth noticing briefly, though, that two other evangelistic heroines in Stowe's later fiction do conclude their careers with "triumphant death" (277), ending in an apotheosis like that of Eva or of the legendary Christian Mary at her dormition. Even by name, both novelistic characters satisfy the role of New England Madonna. Mary Higgins, a Calvinist saint with charitable influence in *Poganuc People* (1878), radiates "invisible power" as household priestess and mother. The wider, sacerdotal scope of her maternity is suggested by the way her own husband, Zeph, addresses her as "Mother" when he approaches her deathbed. Inspired by the "beauty and purity of her character," stern-mannered Zeph had maintained an "almost superstititious confidence in her prayers and goodness, like what the Italian peasant has in his patron saint" (295).

In *The Pearl of Orr's Island: A Story of the Coast of Maine* (1862), young Mara embodies a more maidenly aspect of the Virginal Maternal. Still, this grandaughter of yet another Mary, Mary Lincoln, shows motherly solicitude for the Spanish orphan who washes onto the Maine shore. And the tale as a whole takes place in a matrifocal community focused on child rearing.[34] At first, Mara's biblical name and the early death of both her parents seem to brand her a child of bitterness. Yet ironically, it is this star of the New England sea who succeeds in drawing the child named Moses up from peril of damnation.[35] In her rescue of Moses, Mara exercises a peculiar intermixture of erotic, sisterly, and parental influences.

Typically, Mara dies of consumption in the process of birthing regenerative change for Moses and for her friend Sally. But Stowe reminds readers explicitly that just as Mary, the "only woman whom God ever called highly favored" (366), found this favor within a course of affliction and death, so also Mara draws her intercessory power from mortal sorrow. Her final status as pearl of the community is shaped largely from chafing and struggle. Only at the story's close does grandfather

Zephaniah Pennel enjoy a dream vision in which his lost pearl of great price reappears as a star shining on the forehead of Jesus (397). Yet on her deathbed, Mara assures Moses that he "will live to see many flowers grow out of my grave" (389), a prophecy that Sally both literally and figuratively helps to fulfill. And significantly, Stowe's narration links this promise of fruition to Marian iconography by recollecting "a beautiful legend which one sees often represented in the churches of Europe, that when the grave of the mother of Jesus was opened, it was found full of blossoming lilies—fit emblem of the thousand flowers of holy thought and purpose which spring up in our hearts from the memory of our sainted dead" (367).

Sacrament of Mother-Love, Compassion of the *Mater Dolorosa*

Overall, a distinctive mark of Stowe's treatment of divine womanhood is the way her fiction draws from Catholic antecedents but re-presents them in Calvinist instances—in characters like Eva St. Clare, Mary Higgins, and Mary Scudder, who are infused in turn with reminiscence of real-life New Englanders such as Sarah Pierrepont. For Stowe, this feminized amalgam of Calvinist rectitude and Catholic mythography attached itself, in addition, to Romantic notions of salvific womanhood and to Victorian glorifications of motherhood. Praising Goethe's great Romantic poem, Stowe observes that Faust is raised from sin not simply through the abstract force of "the eternal womanly" but through the particular intervention of Margaret, "who, like a tender mother, leads the new-born soul to look upon the glories of heaven." And, of course, many works published in nineteenth-century America, including Lydia Sigourney's *Letters to Mothers* (1838) and Charles Goodrich's *The Influence of Mothers* (1835), witness to popular faith in the power of a mother's sacred influence in home and community.[36]

Yet for Stowe, post-Calvinist piety supplied an essential continuity beneath all these elements. Thus, her reading of *Faust* credits Goethe not for articulating a Romantic vision but for displaying appreciation of Christian forgiveness and redemption. It is, after all, not through works but through the womanly mediation of grace that Faust is ultimately saved. And a conspicuous companion of Margaret in the "shining band" of purified women encircling him at his death is "Mary the mother of Jesus."[37] For Stowe, then, the archetype of divine maternity found its historic center in the conjoined Mother and Son of Nazareth—the unified epitome of mother love. So even the biblical text, which Stowe describes in *Oldtown Folks* as a "motherly book,"[38] yields definitive warrant for the sanctity of maternity.

In personal terms, though, the experience of motherhood seems to have yielded considerable bitterness as well as satisfaction for Stowe.[39] Accordingly, her theologizing imagination drew her persistently toward images of God as suffering servant rather than as superintending monarch, and toward a Jesus who learned something of that servanthood in the household of the *mater dolorosa*. Stowe could envision only such a woman, recalled in her several variants as Eva, Mary Scudder, or Mara with roots in the "salt, bitter waters of our mortal life," interceding on behalf of struggling humankind.

FOUR

THE SEXUAL MADONNA IN HAROLD FREDERIC'S
Damnation of Theron Ware

The Post-Romantic Madonna of the Future

By the close of the nineteenth century, the demographic profile of the United States showed drastic change from what it had been only a century earlier. As urban factory workers began to outnumber farmers, so also new swells of Atlantic immigration—first from Ireland in the 1830s, then from southern and eastern Europe with peak influx ending around 1910—qualified more and more the predominance of Anglo-Saxon Protestants within America's white population. Particularly between 1880 and 1890, a pronounced ethnic shift toward poorer Roman Catholic, Jewish, and Eastern Orthodox immigrants drew nativist reactions and threatened illusions that the United States might ever remain or become a solidly Protestant nation.[1] Meanwhile, the post–Civil War atmosphere of expansionism, political corruption, financial panic, and revisionist trends in science, religion, history, and philosophy encouraged literary Realism while nearly extinguishing Romanticism. The antebellum versions of Romantic religion that had stimulated engagement with divine womanhood in writers like Poe, Fuller, Hawthorne, Longfellow, Isaac Hecker, and James Russell Lowell no longer obtained.[2]

Not surprisingly, the changes overtaking American society in this era of pragmatism and Darwinism likewise proved inimical to the cult of true womanhood. As outlined by Barbara Welter, this cultural program emphasized the "four cardinal virtues" of "piety, purity, submissiveness, and domesticity."[3] Such ideals were jeopardized by the New Woman, who gained public view at the turn of the century as spirited, strong-willed, independent-minded, and possibly active in the cause of woman's suffrage. She was also apt to be educated, intelligent, and unmarried— or had been, at least, employed before marriage. In the Gibson girl image propagated by artist Charles Dana Gibson (figures 4.1 through 4.4), the free woman of the nineties appears in attractive good health, often in an athletic pose. Whereas that type of American girlhood identified by Martha Banta as the Beautiful Charmer had been culturally defined as chaste and more or less free of desire though eroti-cally alluring to others, the New Woman's sexual proclivities were seen as strong, though not often plainly directed.[4] The New Woman pursued her own career, with or without benefit of a paying profession, and she was rarely perceived as maternal.

Yet the image of an American Madonna had never been effaced. She had, in-stead, been reshaped to satisfy the spirit of her age. In Henry James's tale of "The

FIGURE 4.1. Charles Dana Gibson Sporting Number, *Life* (June 7, 1900).

FIGURE 4.2. Charles Dana Gibson, *Scribner's Magazine* (June 1895).

Madonna of the Future" (1873), a ruined painter named Theobald clings to the "transcendent illusions" that images of sanctified womanhood still inspire in his soul. Selecting an unlikely real-life woman as his model, the expatriate American artist aspires to succeed Raphael by once more turning a vision of Christianity's Magna Mater into his own magnum opus, though he recognizes there is "no demand" now for new Madonna icons.[5] Neither religious faith nor Theobald's more heartfelt belief in Romantic-Platonic forms of beauty and perfection quite survives his practical failure, but for James certain ideals of aesthetic integrity and of imagined womanhood apparently do. As Banta points out and as figures 4.5 and 4.6 illustrate, "idealized images of females" were "everywhere to be seen in the United States at the turn of the century"; yet men, particularly, felt considerable confusion about "whether they liked female images to be erotic or sanctified."[6]

FIGURE 4.3. Charles Dana Gibson, *Life* (April 4, 1901).

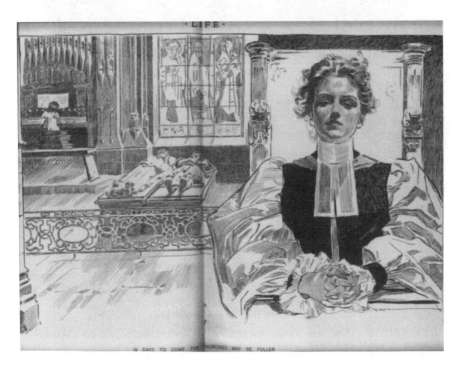

FIGURE 4.4. Charles Dana Gibson, "In days to come Churches may be fuller," *Life* (July 23, 1896).

Celia Madden: Catholic Madonna or Sex Goddess?

A revealing dramatization of this cultural confusion or conflation can be found in Harold Frederic's underrated masterwork, *The Damnation of Theron Ware* (1896). Though Frederic showed little concern with strictly religious meanings of the Madonna, or indeed with religion in general through most of his writing, he did record in his only first-rate novel a brilliantly ironic commentary on the ways in which eroticized Marian mythology reflected the cultural conflicts and ambiguities of his age. What might happen when an innocent male Protestant is drawn simultaneously into ethnic encounter with the newly emerging Catholic subculture, intellectual encounter with the New Science and New Religion, and psychosexual

FIGURE 4.5. Mary Cassatt, "Mother and Child" as engraved by Fran French. This form of Cassatt's painting was widely disseminated in *Harper's New Monthly Magazine* (1896). Throughout her career, Cassatt produced multiple versions of the secular Madonna image.

FIGURE 4.6. "Ere Christ, the Flower of Virtue Bloomed." Illustration by F. V. Du Mond for poem by Louise Morgan Sill, *Harper's New Monthly Magazine* (December 1898).

encounter with the New Woman? Or how, to personify the case, might an artless Methodist minister from upstate New York fare if thrown into the company of worldly sophisticates like Father Vincent Forbes, Miss Celia Madden, and Doctor Ledsmar? Such is the teasing proposition with which Frederic approaches his story of the Reverend Theron Ware.

Initially, Frederic leads us to regard his protagonist sympathetically. At this first stage of comic satire, we share Theron's ridicule of the small-minded, small-town philistines of Octavius who would ban his wife from wearing roses in her bonnet. Soon after Theron fails to land his expected appointment to upscale Tecumseh and ends up instead at the Methodist Church of Octavius, he learns just how oppressively parochial parish life can be. That glow of old Wesleyan piety still discernible in countenances of elder clergy gathered at the annual Nedahma Conference had long since departed this town, which resembles Frederic's native Utica.[7] Theron's Octavians can be stirred to hysteria by revivalistic fund-raisers, but their rigorist approach to the Methodist Discipline lacks true spiritual fervor.

No wonder Theron comes to loathe the town's mindlessly rigid social mores, bigotry, controlling personalities, and tightfisted pettiness. When Loren Pierce, an obnoxious church trustee, orders his minister to deliver a "straight-out, flat-footed hell" from the pulpit, Theron must be sorely tempted to comply with personal application to Pierce. It is hard to blame Theron for fleeing the benightedness of what one major character calls "this raw, overgrown, empty-headed place" or for seeking to grow beyond that version of himself he describes retrospectively as "the narrow zealot" and "country lout."[8]

Yet, as the story proceeds toward what Theron takes to be his "illumination," his character loses all sign of appealing innocence. Even as he fancies himself becoming a "new man" who has undergone a "metamorphosis" and "new birth" in his discovery of worldliness, what the Reverend Ware experiences is, in fact, a mock conversion. This pivotal irony shapes a second level of satire directed increasingly at the character whose perspective dominates the narration. Even the religiously skeptical Frederic eventually comes to ridicule Theron as more nearly damned— or, at least, monumentally self-deceived—than reborn. What Theron imagines to be his progress from innocence to experience figures instead as a fall or devolution. In idioms of the day, it might be called a degradation or, as Frederic's book labels it, borrowing what Larzer Ziff has called the "nineties' favorite word for its condition," a "degeneration."[9] Instead of expanding his moral sense with new knowledge, Theron swells with delusions of grandeur that render him unfit to work and unable to comprehend the rightful claims of his wife and others who surround him. Whatever becomes of him eventually as Seattle businessman or would-be politician, he is surely a sorrier creature at the story's close than he had been at the start of his pastoral career in Octavius.

Two members of the Irish Madden family deliver definitive pronouncements of Theron's ruin. Young Michael Madden, close to death, gives Theron clear word that he is "much changed" but not "for the good"—that he is, indeed, "entirely deceived" about himself (295, 298). But Michael's sister, Celia, delivers the palpable hit. After Theron abandons his wife, pursuing the ravishing Celia to New York in hopes of a rendezvous that will consummate all his worldly desires at once, she greets him first with a yawn, then with a witheringly Jamesian malediction: "We find that you are a bore" (321). Such a finish to Theron's new life is arguably more ignominious than the suicidal conclusion Frederic had originally considered.[10]

It is hard to date the precise moment of Theron's conversion to apostasy. His first encounters with the town's learned Irish priest, Father Forbes, and with Forbes's scientist friend, Dr. Ledsmar, certainly begin the process of his undoing. It is carried well along when he reads Dr. Ledsmar's copy of skeptic Ernest Renan's autobiography. Even as he becomes euphoric about discovering a brave new world of art, learning, and free-thinking epicureanism, so also he finds his old life as small-town pastor literally sickening after he is obliged to assist at the church's combined fund-raiser and love feast.

But it is Theron's encounter with Celia Madden that effectively seals his damnation. Theron himself dates his "new birth" (207) to that enchanted summer evening when Celia performs Chopin for him in her private chambers. By the time she invites him to kiss her during a forest walk several weeks later, he fancies he has completed his conversion and turned altogether from the darkness of his former life.

That Celia turns Theron's head—never, in truth, his heart—with her sexual allure is undeniable. Neither can one deny that Celia toys with his innocence, teases him with her coquettish charms. Frederic's tale thus incorporates elements of both Faustian and Adamic myth, yet it ends up assigning Celia a more complex role than that of the corrupting and seducing Eve.[11] It is not woman per se so much as Theron's faulty perceptions of womanhood that lead him to ultimate ruin. This misperception, rendered still more acute by rapid social change in the era of new womanhood, affects the representation of all three women who figure in Theron's life: Celia Madden, Alice Hastings, and Candace Soulsby.

Before examining the decisive interaction with Celia, one should notice that something is already wrong with Theron Ware when he first sets eyes on this Irish redhead.[12] Even as a beginning pastor, Theron's vocational commitment had been tainted by career ambitions and by vanity over his skill as pulpit artist. Though reportedly influenced as a young man by movements of religious enthusiasm, he gives no sign at the outset of sustaining any strong or deep personal faith. It is unclear how much the Reverend Ware ever worshiped God in his heart, though at the outset he had not hesitated to place his wife on "a glorified pinnacle" as "the most worshipful of womankind" (15, 18). As we shall see, this misplaced adoration prompts him to render ill service to his God, his wife, and himself.

Indeed, one must wonder whether *any* discrete character in this story—with the possible exception of Alice—is or ever had been an authentic believer.[13] Frederic does attribute earnest belief to those old clergymen occupying front places at the annual conference, but they produce no named spiritual progeny. Although Theron claims that the debauched New Yorkers he meets during his bout of despair "believe in God, those people," he also admits, "They're the only ones who do, it seems to me" (335). When Theron first walks on stage for this comic melodrama, he qualifies as culturally innocent but *not* as the thoroughgoing moral innocent both he and we might suppose him to be. Sister Soulsby gets this much right, pointing out that he is not "altogether bad" even in the posture of shameful degenerate—but neither had he been "altogether good a year ago" (336).

Translating this moral defect into psychological terms, one can endorse John W. Crowley's view of Theron as a sad case of arrested development. From the first, Theron shows himself to be a disintegrated personality suffering an Oedipal dysfunction. He therefore fails to develop mature relations to women or to confront his own sexual impulses.[14] Theron is already in bad faith when he suppresses his ever-tainted but shifting motives for buying his wife a piano or his unworthy reasons for planning a book project on Abraham—ironically, the father of faith. His bad faith already starts to sound ludicrous when we hear his eagerness to expunge all reference to his wife at the close of an early conversation with the glamorous Celia: "Well, then, I will bid you good-night here, I think. . . . It must be getting very late, and my—that is, I have to be up particularly early tomorrow" (100). And he stands all the more ironically and audaciously in bad faith by the end, when he protests disingenuously that his sneaking after Celia to New York "was an offence committed in entire good faith" (321).

Much of Celia's image, then, is reflected in this book through the immature and unreliable eyes of Theron Ware. As Crowley observes, Theron's psychic inability to distinguish between his own maternal and sexual longings leads him to regard women consciously in idealistic terms—as some version of the Madonna—but unconsciously as nude or lewd. Hence the telling juxtaposition of Madonna portraits with nude statues that impresses Theron in his perusal of Celia's room.[15] What is more, Celia's double image as sex goddess and Madonna bears important cultural import.

From Theron's point of view, Celia's Madonna image becomes associated with a mystique of covert sexuality. Celia strikes Theron and others as singular not only by virtue of "the bold luxuriant quality of her beauty, the original and piquant freedom of her manners," but also because of "the unlikelihood of her marrying anyone—at least any Octavian" (91). Although Theron is intrigued to learn later on that she is not or does not intend to remain physically virginal, she retains an independent bearing worthy, "one might say," of "a queen" (89; cf. 318). She is alone among all her sex in Octavius in her learning, her sophistication, and her refusal to honor conventional domestic expectations. She seems as provocatively capricious and imperious as a goddess. For deluded Theron, her singular wealth also lends her a transcendent allure. When alone with her in the forest, he is moved to see how "the glamour of a separate banking-account shone upon her," how the light playing on her hair reveals "the veritable gleam of gold" and "a mysterious new suggestion of power" (254).

At once alluring and unattainable, sexy and seemingly ethereal, she appears before Theron as in a vision—"a flitting effect of diaphanous shadow between him and the light which streamed from the casement" (185)—when he sights her standing before a distant window in the Forbes pastorate. At the close of his first encounter with her, he sees her as a woman clothed with the noontide sun that "made a halo about her hair and face at once brilliant and tender" (47). The celestial, apparitional quality of Celia's presence is reinforced by her name, while her unattainable, pseudo-transcendent image remains fixed in Theron's imagination to the last, when she sits near him in an "illusion" of proximity though she "was really a star, many millions of miles away" (324).

Insofar as Theron's Protestant world has largely suppressed recognition of a sacred Madonna or of most other versions of the feminine divine, Celia's Catholic exoticism urges him to project onto her the sort of all-surpassing devotion he supposes Catholics attach to Mary. Significantly, Theron says he was first drawn to enter Celia's church while she was playing the organ because he noticed outside on a stained-glass window the image of a woman's head with "a halo about it, engirdling rich, flowing waves of reddish hair, the lights in which glowed like flame" (77). "'I suppose it was the Virgin Mary,'" he tells Celia later, adding by way of explanation that "'She had hair like yours, and your face, too, and that is why I went into the church and found you'" (250).

Now a redheaded Virgin is fairly unusual in Marian iconography. So one might dismiss Theron's statement as yet another of his preposterous self-justifications. A stained-glass depiction might link Mary's head with Pentecostal flame and would commonly surround it with a halo—but few artists would presume to paint red hair on a Jewish mother. Yet when Theron gazes on that dimly perceived image in glass, he sees reflected there his own fixed image of Catholic womanhood identified now with Celia Madden, the desired personification of that image. He sees red. Though striving to discard old prejudices, he had long equated Catholicism with paganism in contrast with true Gospel Christianity. If anything, his acquaintance with Father Forbes's modernism encourages him in that association but saps it of condemnation. Perceiving his own inherited religious tradition as narrow and restrictive, he sees Celia's luxuriant hair flowing free; looking on his own marriage as colorless, he sees in the arresting tint of Celia's hair a passionate eroticism he desires. In Theron's imagination, then, a cascade of images runs from that familiar Protestant caricature of Roman Catholicism—the Scarlet Woman of Babylon—to Celia of Octavius, and from her to the Virgin Mary.

If Celia images for Theron a Catholic Madonna, she also represents an older spirit of the pagan Goddess in ways including yet surpassing her sexual appeal. Thus, he at times seeks in her a maternal solace proper to the Goddess as well as to the Madonna. And despite her worldliness, she evokes for him cognizance of primal forces in nature. After his forest kiss, Theron comes to idolize her as a moon goddess—prays, in fact, to the moon as "our God . . . Hers and mine" (263).[16] He also envisions her as a naiad rising marvelously from the "virgin bosom" of a secluded and verdant pool (264), an image recapitulated in John Henry Twachtman's advertising poster for the first edition (figure 4.7). As a version of ocean-born Venus, she even figures in Theron's fantasies of yachting pleasure: he thinks "of the sea—with Celia" (306). To Theron's bemusement, this Irish woman insists she is "an out-and-out Greek" and "as Pagan as—anything" (99). And having spoken before of the Chaldean Damkina or mother Earth (71), Father Forbes goes on to affirm Celia's spiritual maternity within the tradition of Irish paganism:

> "They brought with them at the outset a great inheritance of Eastern mysticism. Others lost it, but the Irish, all alone on their island, kept it alive and brooded on it, and rooted their whole spiritual side in it. Their religion is full of it; their blood is full of it—our Celia is fuller of it than anybody else. The Ireland of two thousand years ago is incarnated in her. They are the merriest people and the saddest . . . the most devout and the most pagan. These impossible contradictions war ceaselessly in their blood. When I look at Celia, I seem to see in my mind's eye the fair young ancestral mother of them all." (281)

Theron's bifurcated vision of Celia as Madonna and sex goddess becomes most striking in the crucial episode where he enters her room for a private recital of Chopin. In this mock seduction scene that occupies chapter 19, imagery of sacred ritualism combines with that of profane eroticism to captivate Theron's soul.

The erotic signals are plain enough. After a provocative offer to show Theron what is her "very own," Celia leads him behind closed doors and "heavy folds" of

FIGURE 4.7. John Twachtman, poster advertisement for Frederic's *The Damnation of Theron Ware*. Courtesy of Rare Book and Manuscript Library, Columbia University.

"thick curtain" into a darkened chamber (190, 189). Here Theron finds himself imbibing an atmosphere of sensual freedom heightened by several forms of sensory stimulation: the sight of Celia's deeply alluring eyes, bare arm, "shapely hand," jewels, "lustrous" apparel clinging to her body, and disarray of luxuriant hair released for exhibition; the aroma of cigarette smoke and perfume; the heady taste of alcohol; and the surging, wooing sound of Celia's music making that speaks "to him as with a human voice" (196). Once illuminated, the blue-and-yellow room discloses to the dazzled preacher curtains spread with "undulating radiance," four or five color prints adorning the walls, a glimpse of Celia's "sumptuous bed" in the adjoining chamber, and statues "mostly of naked men and women" standing in the corners (198, 202, 191). Theron discovers plenty here to stir an already-awakened libido.

At the same time, the scene is described in terms suggestive of sacred liturgy. As though presiding as priestess–celebrant for the rites of a new religion, Celia first leads Theron into a removed space equivalent to her sanctum sanctorum. After methodically applying her taper to illumine seven lights resembling vigil lamps, she then approaches and uncovers a mysterious structure—the instrument of her liturgy—that Theron mistakes at first for an altar, just as he perceives her imposing figure lit against the backdrop of an "altar-like wall" (196). Once she begins performing her sacred mysteries of sound, in a musical idiom more foreign to Theron than the Latin words he had heard her intone at an earlier deathbed scene, he stands "motionless in the strange room, feeling most of all that one should kneel to hear such music" (196). At times he even thinks this lyrical music sounds like "gently solemn chant" (195). Her playing, he testifies, comes on him with the force of "a revelation" (201).

In this new dispensation, the Reverend Ware stands as a mere catechumen receiving Celia's sacerdotal instruction and ministrations. Contrary to roles scripted by gender and ministerial prerogative, it is she who she assumes active presidency of the liturgy. It is she who offers up Chopin while he listens reverently, she who administers to him a cup of spirits—of pseudo-sacred Benedictine, in fact—prepared in "the inner room" (201). It is she who preaches to him the word of "absolute freedom from moral bugbears," impressing on her rapt auditor the Hellenistic virtues of bold hedonism and the pursuit of beauty as the summum bonum. He can only "gaze helplessly" after her when she moves with a candle to complete "the work of illumination" (202, 191). And after Celia is installed at the keyboard, he attributes to her an almost transcendent charism for mediating encounter with another realm: "He fancied her beholding visions as she wrought the music—visions full of barbaric color and romantic forms" (199).

By the end of the scene, Celia has become not only the celebrant but also the manifest object of Theron's worship. Imagining this Celia or Cecilia[17] canonized as a wonder-working saint, Theron sees her haloed in a "glowing nimbus of hair" (199), with a "veil of smoke" (192) rising above her head. No matter that the smoke comes from tobacco rather than incense or that she who once thought to take the veil as a Sister of Charity now devotes herself to serving her own pleasure and the religion of art. Once Theron is swept into the flow of her music, he forgets all disparity between the profane attraction of her sexuality and the apparently sacred—or, at least, singular—claims of her hieratic charism. Such distinctions dissolve in the rapturous mood that likewise dispels his anxiety at seeing her nude statuary set in scandalous proximity to her pictorial "variations of a single theme—the Virgin Mary and the Child" (191). Under the immediate spell of Celia's face and music, he stops worrying that there is "any such thing as nudity" (196).

Earlier, though, it is evident from the way Theron focuses simultaneously on these statues and on a large Marian portrait hanging nearby that this juxtaposition defines something essential about his perception of Celia. He is disturbed enough when he sees one marble figure, apparently a Venus with arms missing, robed only below the waist. He feels yet more threatened when he sees the other figures quite naked and considers the morals of modern womanhood that would welcome such a display:

> Theron stared at them with the erratic, rippling jangle of the waltz in his ears, and felt that he possessed a new and disturbing conception of what female emancipation

meant in these later days. Roving along the wall, his glance rested again upon the largest of the Virgin pictures—a full-length figure in sweeping draperies, its radiant, aureoled head upturned in rapt adoration, its feet resting on a crescent moon which shone forth in bluish silver through festooned clouds of cherubs. The incongruity between the unashamed statues and this serene incarnation of holy womanhood jarred upon him for the instant. Then his mind went to the piano.

From Maya and Mary to the New Woman

That Theron next "looked from the Madonna to Celia" (195) should by now seem a predictable progression. For some time, Theron's imagination has been reshaping Celia into an alluring stereopsis of Madonna and presumptive harlot. In her Madonna aspect, she stands as an exalted, revelatory goddess purged of threatening sexuality. In her other aspect as Venus or sex goddess, she is at once appealing and troubling. She is so troubling, in fact, that Theron will later picture her eyes dilating "like those of a Medusa mask" (247), a reptilian allusion that recalls in turn the study of serpent worship penned by her misogynist detractor, the sinister Dr. Ledsmar. This erotic version of Celia presses on Theron's subconscious in much the same way that he senses the presence of her naked statuary abiding at the room's margins throughout their meeting.

Conversely, several details link Celia with Theron's description of the Madonna portrait. The portrait's "full-length figure" clothed in "sweeping draperies" recalls the stature and dress of Celia. Mary's "radiant, aureoled head" corresponds to Celia's "glowing nimbus of hair," and traditional Marian blue reappears in the leather panels inside and curtains outside Celia's room, as well as in the fillet she wears. Celia's lunar affiliations, likewise prominent in Marian iconography, have already been noted. The "rose-tinted" beauty of Celia's face is "framed" (199) as though it belonged to a conventional Madonna painting. And to Theron, at least, the serene majesty represented in the Marian portrait looks a good deal like the urbane self-possession and queenly authority that Celia effuses.

What Theron does not report observing anywhere in this portrait is the Virgin's child.[18] In effect, Theron himself plays the role of child, albeit an unholy one. By the close of the ensuing camp meeting and picnic scene in the forest, we see him acting more like an insecure, puerile son than like a lover to Celia. As Crowley and others have pointed out, Theron betrays a regressive yearning for maternal solace, as well as an immature sexual identity. Hence Celia, during negotiations for the piano purchase in Thurston's store, responds to Theron's naive inquiries with "a comforting, friendly, half-motherly glance" (211). Lying beside her during their forest colloquy, Theron is moved to cling tearfully to her dress: "It was like being a little boy again, nestling in an innocent, unthinking transport of affection against his mother's skirts" (257). After Celia lectures him concerning "worship of the maternal idea," he pleases her immensely by disclosing that, for a moment, he felt "absolutely as if I were a boy again—a good, pure-minded, fond little child, and you were the mother that I idolized" (259).

Competing in Theron's disordered mind with this sense of Celia as maternal Madonna, however, is a fantasy of romantic intimacy with her that Frederic allows full play in the Hawthornian forest scene. During this wicked parody of erotic escape from the world, Theron toys suggestively with the ribbon of Celia's dress without asking himself too precisely what he dares to do with it or with her; and the episode reaches a fitting pseudo-climax when Celia invites a perfunctory kiss that Theron misinterprets as a pledge of enduring love. She might have proposed the kiss out of maternal pity or in playful jest but surely not from passion, as he wills to believe. So earnestly does Theron long to embrace his dreams of affluent, illicit, glamorous love with Celia that he fails to notice she has been talking the while on quite another plane. Whereas his fantasies are all about sex with her, her discourse in the forest is all about womanly autonomy (a life fulfilled *without* Ware) and matrifocal spirituality. Whereas he takes the kiss as declaring love for him, she articulates instead a personal "Declaration of Independence" (256).

Belatedly in the forest, Celia also gives Theron a revealing commentary on those pictures of the Virgin displayed in her room—and on how the divine womanhood they embody links them in spirit with her statues of naked women:

> "They get along together better than you suppose," she answered. "Besides, they are not all pictures of Mary. One of them—standing on the moon—is of Isis with the infant Horus in her arms. Another might as well be Mahanie, bearing the miraculously born Buddha, or Olympia with her child Alexander, or even Perictione holding her babe Plato—all these were similar cases, you know. Almost every religion had its Immaculate Conception. What does it all come to, except to show us that man turns naturally toward the worship of the maternal idea? That is the deepest of all his instincts—love of woman, who is at once daughter and wife and mother. It is that that makes the world go round." (258–59)

Celia commends the Greek spirit of "art and poetry and the love of beauty" as fostering this ennobling "worship of the maternal idea" within Christian tradition. By contrast, she indicts the early church fathers, particularly Latin fathers like Jerome and Tertullian, for imposing on the tradition a "Jewish" theology she deems misogynistic, legalistic, and dour. To recover the soul of religion and of life itself, she insists, one must reaffirm the primal mystery of feminine spirituality, expressed within the Christian mythos by "adoration of the Virgin." And she knows enough to credit Cyril, fifth-century patriarch of Alexandria accused of complicity in the murder of a pagan female philosopher and virgin named Hypatia,[19] with defending homage to the Virgin Mary as Theotokos:

> "In all the earlier stages of the Church, women were very prominent in it. Jesus Himself appreciated women, and delighted to have them about Him, and talk with them and listen to them. That was the very essence of the Greek spirit, and it breathed into Christianity at its birth a sweetness and a grace which twenty generations of cranks and savages like Paul and Jerome and Tertullian couldn't wholly extinguish. But the very man—Cyril—who killed Hypatia, and thus began the dark ages, unwittingly did another thing which makes one almost forgive him. To please the Egyptians, he secured the Church's acceptance of the adoration of the Virgin. It is that idea which has

kept the Greek spirit alive, and grown and grown, till at last it will rule the world. It was only epileptic Jews who could imagine a religion without sex in it." (258)

Not surprisingly, Celia's conception of religion as rooted in comparative mythology resembles that of Father Forbes, with whom she shares an enigmatic intimacy and who himself embodies "the great sex mystery" of the celibate priest (281). When this modernist cleric speaks casually of the Chaldean Damkina or mother earth in the same breath as "this Christ-myth of ours" (71), he scandalizes Theron with signs of rank unbelief. For his era, Forbes represents, indeed, an extreme case of priestly "liberalism": He is not only intellectual but epicurean, skeptical toward orthodox doctrine, and cynically pragmatic in his approach to religion. Father Edward Aloysius Terry, the prominent Utica clergyman upon whom Frederic modeled this character, shared Forbes's intellectual sophistication and "liberal" disposition but not his agnosticism. So far as one can glean from available public records, Frederic's friend Terry did not, despite his involuntary transfer from Utica to Albany, reject anything of essential Roman Catholic doctrine; neither did he, like Forbes, decline to preach. Terry was, on the contrary, an earnest believer renowned for his pulpit eloquence.

But Terry did show an unusually educated recognition of the ways in which Catholic Christianity had assimilated antecedent forms of pagan religion, including goddess worship. Hence, Frederic's frequent reports in the *Utica Daily Observer* of Terry's sermons, addresses, and involvement in doctrinal controversies are instructive. Such reports enlarge our understanding not only of the Forbes character but also of broader attitudes toward mythography and divine womanhood represented in the novel by Celia, Forbes, and the implied author. Forbes's sense of syncretistic recapitulation that sees all current mythology and religion "built on the ruins of something else" (71) owes something to Frederic's awareness of higher criticism and reading in historical studies such as those by William Edward Hatpole Lecky, William Frederic Farrar, and John William Draper.[20] Germs of this understanding also appear in Father Terry's discourse as reported in the *Utica Daily Observer* during 1879 and 1880, while Frederic was serving as news editor.

In May of 1880, for example, Frederic described a service at St. John's Church in which Father Terry spoke on St. Anastasia, a fourth-century female martyr, as well as on Marian piety. Frederic first observes that "the Month of May is specially dedicated in the Catholic Church to the honor of the Blessed Virgin Mary" and praises the sweet singing of child soloists that "accorded harmoniously with the spirit of reverence for the Mother of God that inspired the stately ceremonial." He then offers his newspaper readership a synopsis of Father Terry's eloquent discourse:

> Father Terry's address explaining the service was replete with information touching the origin of the Christian Church, which he traced from the Pagan inceptions through the first adoption by the early Church as a means of drawing the people into the true fold by humoring their habits and customs, until they were finally transformed into devout ceremonies, thoroughly imbued with the spirit of Christianity. Father Terry explained that the devotion to the month of May in the Catholic Church was originally a dedication to the Goddess Maya, the representation of the idea of maternity. The Christians kept up the observance, but changed it to a recognition

of Mary the Virgin, thus transforming what was with the Pagans an unlicensed indulgence in low orgies, into a manifestation of holy Love for the Virgin Mother as
an incarnation of the virtue of chastity.[21]

In a similar vein, Frederic's newspaper had reported an address given in New
York in which Father Terry "dwelt at length upon the object of the church in es-
tablishing festival days as a familiar human method of utilizing natural impulses and
national customs in the cause of religion," thereby bringing "God to us as a father"
and "the Virgin as a cherished mother." Extending "the idea of maternity" to his
own experience, Terry avers in another sermon (on "The Non-Exclusiveness of
the Catholic Church") that "next to God I worship in my inmost heart the mother
whom He gave to care for me in my helpless years."[22]

Enfolded within the maternal idea of Mary the Virgin, then, is humanity's re-
sidual memory of the "unlicensed indulgence" linked to worship of pagan Maya.
Some such perception on Father Terry's part parallels Theron's suspicion of lawless
pagan indulgence underlying Celia's radiant presence as Madonna. From Celia's
viewpoint, Maya and Mary, depicted in those icons of sexual woman and sacred
woman adorning her room, have ample reason to "get along."

Moreover, the terms in which Father Terry pursued a doctrinal dispute—over
the scope of salvation—with a General Assembly of the Presbyterian Church show
a peculiar sympathy with Celia's "Greek" disposition. In sermons reprinted by
Frederic for the *Utica Daily Observer,* Terry expresses repugnance toward Calvinist
doctrines of predestination, limited atonement, and the presumed damnation of
unbaptized infants. Confronting these teachings as well as more recent denials that
Roman Catholicism qualified as a true Christian church with valid baptism, Terry
responds with his own liberal polemic. He argues that God might "bring unto
Himself, some way, all who are of honest purpose and sincere desire," including
non-Catholics, and he explicitly denies that unbaptized infants are destined for hell,
though they might be excluded from "supernatural beatitude."

Now Terry's comparatively generous assessment of human possibility and God's
mercy does square with orthodox Catholic teaching of his day, as a supporting reference he makes to Pope Pius IX confirms. Yet, he concedes that St. Augustine and
some other Latin fathers of the church had taken a more severe position on infant
damnation. It is telling that Terry sides, instead, with "the Greek Fathers" who "all
dissented from the opinion of St. Augustine" in positing freer scope for God's salvation.[23] This appeal to the example and authority of Greek fathers over against Latin
ones bears an intriguing affinity with Celia's promotion of Hellenism contra Jerome
and Tertullian—even though for Celia, of course, the Greek spirit extends to a pagan
aestheticism that Terry cannot endorse.[24] It is true historically, at any rate, that the
Marian cultus first blossomed in a Hellenistic atmosphere. At the same time, Father
Terry's faith in a God of widely embracing compassion coincides inwardly with the
matrifocal spirituality to which both he and Celia are drawn.

But just who is Celia, really, beyond the various allegorical preconceptions she
reflects? In her own person, surely, she is neither the Madonna nor the wanton sex
goddess that Theron images her to be. As Frederic shrewdly illustrates, the ambiguity that seems to renders her one or both of these things—but little else—is fos-

tered in part by a cultural ideology that would limit drastically the range of what women might become. It arises also from personal deficiences in Theron that seriously impair his vision of her. In her own right, the Celia character is evidently a New Woman who remains somewhat elusive and capricious. She recalls some attitudes of late-nineteenth-century English culture—of Ruskin, Pater, and Arnold, of Aubrey Beardsley and *The Yellow Book* [25]—but combines these in original fashion with her own Irish-American, feminist temperament. Although Theron finally learns to his horror that she was not tempting him in earnest to sexual dalliance, it is never clear why she wished to stir his hopes and desires as far as she did.

Flaunting an independence befitting the New Woman, Celia keeps her own counsel. She betrays something of her attitudes in contrived speeches and in actions like the "swinging pirouette" she executes in front of the "gravely beautiful statue of the armless woman" after Theron leaves her blue and yellow room (203), but she avoids disclosing her innermost thoughts to anyone—including the novel's readers. We never learn for certain whether her intimacy with Father Forbes extends to sexual contact. For that matter, we can only speculate about the lines of sexual interaction hinted to flow every which way within the larger trio of Forbes, Ledsmar, and Madden. Even when Theron thinks he knows that Ledsmar and Madden, at least, are sworn enemies, Ceila reminds him—with an arresting collective pronoun—that he is only an ignorant outsider: "*we* find that you are a bore" (321, emphasis supplied).

What can be reliably discerned of Celia's character does not, however, present an altogether flattering portrait of the New Woman. Bereft of her own maternal guidance but spoiled in a material sense, she emerges not only as talented and attractive but also as vain, self-centered, and even a bit callous and manipulative. Judith Fryer calls her an "outspoken hedonist who has never known what it is to suffer."[26] Yet Frederic never quite condemns Celia. Neither does he glamorize her. Instead, he dramatizes her resistance to any man's outside control, including his own managing presence as author. Above all, Frederic shows her resisting what Theron, as the book's center of semiconsciousness, wants to make of her. Theron constantly misreads her while trying to satisfy his own cravings and fantasies.

Thus, misinterpreting Celia's rejection of traditional moral standards, Theron suspects she has jettisoned ethics and discretion altogether in her own sexual conduct. He supposes—and ultimately wishes—that an exponent of "female emancipation" would consider herself free to do anything at all. For the sensualist unbeliever, there must be no limit to licentiousness and no such thing as immorality. So he concludes, erroneously as it turns out, that Celia's main purpose for traveling to New York is to enjoy a tryst there with Father Forbes. More absurdly, he thinks she might abandon Forbes on the spot to take up an affair with him once he shows up to stage a plaintive confrontation at her hotel room! Theron does not understand that Celia is more of an ethical antinomian, who follows a law of her own, than a lawless nihilist. Although she does what she pleases, it does not please her to gratify Theron's sexual desires, particularly at the cost of disgracing her family and ethnic community.

Theron's misperception of Celia and finally of all womankind shows itself also in his compulsion to worship and to possess women instead of appreciating their variable humanity. Adoration and acquisition seem, in fact, to be his chief modes of relating to women. Thus, he betrays his urge to possess Celia as an abstract albeit precious commodity when he characteristically apprehends her through language of statuary. He is entranced by her "statuesque, dreaming face" (200), by her apparel of "statue-like drapery" (198); seeing her angry, he perceives her neck becoming "as white, it seemed to him, as marble" (248). During her forest declaration of independence, Celia attacks this sort of Pygmalion delusion squarely. Refuting the "old-fashioned idea" that "women must belong to somebody, as if they were curios, or statues, or race-horses," she insists that she is herself and belongs to herself "exactly as much as any man" does. She denounces as "preposterous" the notion that "any other human being could conceivably obtain" by marriage or other means "the slightest property rights" over her (254–55). Yet Theron, as usual, misses the point and fails to grasp its relevance to his own wishes. As a figure sculpted to derive life from his fondest dreams, Celia has come to abide in his mind as a more active extension of the statues already stationed in her room.

Theron also purports to worship Celia. In what passes for a love speech in his final meeting with her in New York, he professes adoration at the same time he disingenuously claims to give ownership rights now to *her:* "'No other man in all the world can yield himself so absolutely to the woman he worships as I can. You have taken possession of me so wholly, I am not in the least master of myself any more . . . I am not worthy of you, I know. . . . But no one else will idolize and reverence you as I do'" (319). As if this protestation were not embarrasssing enough, Theron then justifies stalking her to New York by invoking biblical language from the book of Ruth and the sanction of a religion he is freshly zealous to abandon: "'Whither thou goest, I will go, and where thou lodgest I will lodge . . .'" (319). Aptly, Celia responds by shrugging her shoulders and moving away from him.

Celia is not the only woman toward whom Theron has professed adoration. Alice Hastings, too, he had once imagined standing by virtue of her bearing and wealth "on a glorified pinnacle far away from the girls of the neighborhood" (15–16) before he came to possess her as his wife. Earlier in his marriage, he had meditated on "the vast unspeakable marvel of his blessedness, in being thus enriched and humanized by daily communion with the most worshipful of womankind" (18).

After the move to Octavius, though, Theron finds Alice gradually losing her glorified position. No longer an appealing Madonna, she reverts now to the character of drab housewife and farmer's daughter. She becomes obtuse and uncooperative, failing now to "understand and make allowances" as a wife should for the "big, ambitious thoughts and plans" with which her husband is burdened (205). She fails also "to maintain a hold upon his interest and imagination" (291) as he expands his intellectual horizons. She "had had her chance" to do so but "had let it slip." She seems to have lost her energy and former intelligence. How, Theron wonders, did Alice become so dull?

Yet Alice and Celia, as Frederic hints by using the same five letters in both names, are not so radically different as Theron supposes. Both play the piano, like flowered hats, associate with roses, and, on occasion, become fiercely annoyed with Theron Ware. Both might be considered attractive. And though Theron grows contemptuous of his wife and says he feels fettered in a dreary marriage, the ironic accents of Frederic's narration make it clear that the fault lies rather in his solipsistic misperception of her.

It is Theron who becomes so consumed by narcissistic dreams and male arrogance that he loses all recognition of Alice's vivacious wit, brightness, and steadfast love. Though he thinks he admires womanly independence in the shape of Celia, he treats Alice condescendingly because he considers it "a wife's part to understand" (205) and to bend her will to his whim. "Wives, with their limited grasp of the realities of life, were always expecting their husbands to do things which turned out not to be feasible for them to do" (214). Theron therefore considers it his right if not his duty to surround himself as best he can with women smarter, more attractive, more intellectually stimulating than Alice Hastings. He comes to treat her, she complains, as though she were a blockhead with "absolutely no mind at all" (289). Yet his evening with Celia in the blue-and-yellow room has taught him, he believes, "how a wife ought to be handled" (206).

Beneath her posture of outward acquiescence, Alice retains a dignified autonomy in the face of Theron's abuse and her own struggle with depression. She never claims Celia's open independence, but this woman Theron once recognized as a "serenely self-reliant girl" (15) still sustains something of an inner life, to which Theron is oblivious, once her husband destroys their common life. After recognizing her inability to restore Theron's conjugal commitment, she learns instead to cultivate her own garden—literally, of course, with the help of church trustee Nelson Gorringe. Theron scorns even the kindness and chaste affection Gorringe bestows on Alice in her isolation, preferring to suspect his wife of infidelity so as to justify his plan to possess Celia. No sooner has Theron knocked Alice from her "glorified pinnacle" as his Madonna than he wants to ensure her ignominy as a whore. And whereas Nelson Gorringe reaches an adult admission that he had earlier been inclined to mistake his erotic desires for sacred ones, Theron Ware never gets this far.

Though Alice scarcely qualifies as a New Woman, she does not quite conform to the submissive, simple-minded profile of True Woman, either. She endures, without wholly accepting, her husband's vagaries. She sees and understands more than he realizes. She also preserves as much inward self-reliance as her circumstance permits, though she intimates at the end that Theron has beaten down her spirits more or less permanently. All the way through the story's final paragraph, with a new life expected in Seattle, she lodges a gentle protest against Theron as a man unlikely to start treating her more equitably than he has in the past. "'Most probably,'" she remarks, "'I'd be left to amuse myself in Seattle'" (344) if Theron ever decides to revisit the East. Even toward her God, Alice protests that she gets "no assistance," and she dares to express—albeit with affecting Marian humility—a fear that God has forgotten "His poor heart-broken hand-maiden" (288).

That Frederic treated *his* unsophisticated wife, Grace Williams, rather shabbily both before and after he set up a separate household with Kate Lyon in England does not soften the bite with which he satirizes Theron's callous, condescending treatment of Alice. On the contrary, the author's scathing portrayal of his protagonist faces some of his own personal failings. As a personality, Frederic could be arrogant, ambitious, truculent, self-indulgent—even dishonest, if one notices his earlier publication of plagiarized work. Yet, as a writer, he displayed keen moral insight. Theron, then, is aptly described in Stanton Garner's words as "the Harold Frederic who might have been."[27]

The novel's third embodiment of late-century womanhood, Candace Soulsby, shows no hesitation about taking control of her life, her career, or her man. As Gorringe wryly observes, Sister Soulsby "wears the breeches" (120) when it comes to managing the Soulsby debt-raising business. Having supported herself "for a good many years" (177) through enterprises ranging from comic opera to fortune telling, she has evidently mastered the American art of adaptability. In her independent resources, self-confidence, and rejection of domestic occupations, she claims attention as yet another version of the New Woman. As such, she puzzles Theron, who does not expect a woman to talk as much and as freely as she. Sister Soulsby's class origins and personality also set her apart from usual images of new womanhood in the nineties. She is less Easternized, less genteel, and more conversant with populist sentiments than most other fictional representions of the type. Yet Candace is arguably the novel's freest woman in her capacity for fiscal self-reliance. Looking at her and Celia together indicates how far divergent personality traits can fit within the cultural category of new womanhood.[28]

Like Alice, though, Candace bears more resemblance to Celia than first appears. John Crowley gives a discerning account of the connection:

> Plain, candid, tough-minded, and shrewd, Sister Soulsby seems the antithesis to Celia Madden. Yet they are linked in Theron's unconscious. Sister Soulsby has been a mistress to a married man, a dance-hall actress, a confidence operator, and one vote shy of criminal conviction. Like Celia, she is sufficiently disreputable to be sexually alluring. Further, Sister Soulsby understands the evocative power of Chopin, whose melodies she uses to seduce the tight-fisted Methodists as Celia uses them to tantalize Theron. But scarred by his illness, Theron represses the idea of Sister Soulsby as a nude and regards her instead as a madonna.[29]

The Unsettling Character of Soulsby and the Undoing of Ware

Particularly after the disgrace of his final rejection by Celia, Theron turns to Soulsby for maternal solace. He adopts a posture at once infantile and worshipful, casting himself "on his knees at her feet" and burying his head in folds of her skirts while she consoles him with "a soothing, motherly intonation in her voice" (331). Theron thinks of Sister Soulsby by turns as a mother whose guidance he craves, as a "most attractive-looking woman" whose seductive powers he consents to see applied to fleecing his congregation, and as a "good fellow" (183) whose friendly vulgarity places him at ease. He also notices that she projects a queenly power, albeit one exercised mainly through acting and scheming, that begets results. Like a character in Stowe's *The Minister's Wooing,* she bears the "quaint and unfamiliar old Ethiopian name" of Candace (137), a name associated with ancient queens and with epochs of matriarchal rule.

The "good fellow" epithet, which Sister Soulsby first applies to herself, suggests yet another aspect of cultural change captured in this novel: a growing sense of instability in gender definitions and in the sex-based determination of social roles.[30] Thus, Sister Soulsby reflects a number of conventional masculine traits with her toughness, business sense, and unsentimental zeal for manipulation, whereas Brother Soulsby displays his capacity for motherly sympathy with the same expression—"I've been a mother myself" (329)—that Frederic himself once used in corresponding with an editor.[31] Ledsmar studies hermaphroditism in plants. Settled in an increasingly "feminized" clerical profession,[32] Theron acknowledges that "'I suppose people really do think of us as a kind of hybrid female'" (112). He, in turn, marvels at the androgny presented in Father Forbes, at once a figure of commanding male "virility" and an aesthete who wears a long black gown "with the natural grace of a proud and beautiful belle." In Forbes's presence, he feels "as a romantic woman must feel in the presence of a specially impressive masculine personality" (67, 281). He is also taken aback to learn that the George Sand who had lived openly with Chopin was female.

Confronted with such unsettling ambiguities and beset with confusion about his own identity, sexual and otherwise, Theron instinctually tries to fix both Alice and Celia within the unquestionably female categories of Madonna or harlot. Yet Candace Soulsby presents a more variable, elusive impression of womanhood that he cannot resolve into any single image. She does not think, speak, or look quite like any other woman—or man, either—he has met before. Soulsby remains very much her own woman.

Whether Frederic intends to privilege Sister Soulsby's pragmatic, nominalistic philosophy over other positions articulated in the novel remains doubtful, however. In the single plank of Soulsby's religion, sheep get separated from goats only on Judgment Day—if there is a Judgment Day. For practical purposes within this mortal sphere, Soulsby's outlook erases all distinction between good and evil, between authenticity and fraud. It recognizes no such thing as visible damnation. There is only effective "machinery, management, organization" (179), on the one hand, or dysfunctional characters or groups on the other. Soulsby helps render Theron functional once again by the story's end. For her, the question of Theron's moral standing either before or after his "fall" is irrelevant.

Yet even more textual evidence can be found to support a contrary assessment of Theron as morally culpable and willfully deluded, as one who has wandered in decidedly goatish paths whatever his eternal fate. Despite the amoral assumptions usually attached to Frederic's protonaturalistic realism and Forbes's parting reminder that "the truth is always relative" (326), it is hard to escape the judgment that Theron has degenerated, indeed, into a foolish and blameworthy character.

It is likewise hard to feel entirely sanguine about the sort of redemption that Theron ends up anticipating, thanks to Sister Soulsby's intervention, at the story's denouement. The ex-preacher may well "thrive in Seattle," as Candace predicts, but one suspects he will do so without scruples about method and at somebody else's expense. Despite Alice's geographic relocation, she will find little new satisfaction in marriage to Theron Ware, who appears less than fully rehabilitated even after his chastening recovery from disintegration. Theron's old arrogance revives as he fantasizes about the multitudes who will now applaud the sound of his voice. "'Talk is what tells,'" he declaims, so "'I may turn up in Washington a full-blown Senator before I'm forty'" (344). As the story ends, Theron is heading into the prosperous realm of real estate, not the damnation of hell, but he has yet to encounter real "illumination." His delusions persist, though they now take another shape.

Beyond Illusion: The Grace of Critical Realism

What kind of statement, then, does *The Damnation of Theron Ware* finally make about how a resurgent mythology of the Madonna colored perceptions of women in American society at the turn of the century? For one thing, Frederic shows that the masculine mind will not easily sustain its penchant for idealizing and elevating real-life women into Madonna figures in an age of naturalistic skepticism. Theron's career dramatizes the folly of inscribing preconceived romantic images of holy womanhood, harlotry, or both onto actual women. Women like Candace Soulsby or Celia Madden, having developed their own voices and public personae, will not permit this outworn cultural mythology to define them. They will belong to no man. Even if Theron never understands the point clearly, Frederic's reader presumably can. The New Woman is here to stay.

But if Frederic's book demolishes the cultural mythology that created a latter-day secular Madonna, what view does it take of the corresponding religious mythology or of the truth claims of religion in general? Answering this question is trickier. The book's critical realism exposes several competing belief-systems, both religious and irreligious, to skeptical trial. It satirizes the narrowness and superficiality of Theron's original faith, as well as the self-centered pride of his final agnosticism. The primitive piety of Methodism's elder leaders is shown to be admirable but nearly extinct. Although Theron's naive Christianity cannot survive the intellectual challenges of modernity, the alternative of Ledsmar's scientific rationalism is portrayed as even more repellent. And though Celia condemns Ledsmar's "heartless, bloodless science" (97), her epicurean approach to life carries a heartlessness of its own. Sister Soulsby's pragmatic atheism yields some worthy results, but its manipulative methods and cynicism toward the prospect of truth finding remain troubling. Forbes's pragmatic exploitation of his clerical position, conjoined with his belief in agnostic aestheticism, raises similar questions of integrity. By the close of the novel, it is unclear whether Alice's beleaguered religious faith will remain tenable in Seattle, but that faith cannot be regarded as less admirable than the worldly materialism to which Theron thinks he has progressed.

It is safe to say that this novel exposes several forms of religious belief, as well as religious skepticism, to skeptical scrutiny. Frederic's characterization presents us with irreligious hypocrites as well as religious ones. The novel at least allows, then, that a feminine aspect of divinity *might* exist as a cosmic force beyond or despite Theron's deluded attempt to identify the Madonna with Celia. At the key moment when Theron looks "from the Madonna to Celia," he projects onto Celia several sorts of repressed needs—at once sexual, maternal, and religious. That is what it means, ultimately, for him to idolize her as his Madonna.

By way of religious deprivation, Our Lady Celia seems to show Theron elements of beauty and sacred femininity mostly absent from the emphatically patriarchal tradition of Protestant piety that has sustained him thus far. "Puritanism," asserted the author of a chief scholarly source Frederic consulted for the novel, "is the most masculine form that Christianity has yet assumed." By contrast, Catholicism, despite its tendency toward superstition and the weakening of human character, retained a reverence for the Virgin that sustained aesthetic appeals to "modes of feeling" and imagination, elevating ideals, and "that kind of moral beauty which is peculiarly feminine."[33]

Celia evokes a realm of poetry, mythology, and music that strike Theron—perhaps accurately, in this case—as spiritual revelations indeed. Such elements are also lacking in the modern rationalistic temper displayed by Ledsmar, the insane Darwinian scornful of beauty and religion. Ledsmar is a nonpracticing physician whose aggressive scientism involves the "heartless, bloodless" pursuit of knowledge without benefit of feminizing compassion or the disposition to heal. His sense of science as a form of conquest coincides with the zeal of Western powers in the same century to pursue a new economic imperialism directed toward regions such as China and Latin America. Only a few decades after the infamous Opium War, Ledsmar exploits a Chinese man for his sadistic opium experiments.

"He looked from the Madonna to Celia"—but lamentably, Theron never looks in the opposite sequence, from profane Celia toward the possibility of authentically divine womanhood. He is therefore frustrated by expectations that Celia raises yet cannot deliver. Theron commits a grave error when he tries to make Celia his goddess—that is, capture in the flesh "the lady of his dreams" (293) or his "Madonna" in something like the word's literal sense. The Madonna of God could never be captured or possessed, and at least this trait she holds in common with the New Woman.

Admittedly, though, Frederic's novel affirms no single position about the validity of metaphysical or religious beliefs beyond the order of social observation. The chief aim of its comic irony is negative: to destroy old romantic illusions; to expose the limitations of newer beliefs and doubts; to critique the myth of progress in its several scientific, moral, or social formulations; and to dramatize the extent to which long-standing cultural myths of femininity or masculinity no longer define American women and men of the nineties. *The Damnation of Theron Ware* affords no blinding "illumination" as to who the New Woman really is at this time of profound social dislocation, but it reveals unmistakably who she is not.

FIVE

HENRY ADAMS

The Virgin as Dynamo

The Woman Unknown in America

Of the six authors who occupy chapters in this book, only Henry Adams is well known for having sustained an interest in the cultus of Mary. A pivotal chapter in *The Education of Henry Adams*, the autobiographical work that supports his current literary reputation, juxtaposes medieval Mariology with the new technology of the dynamo. The Virgin of Chartres had likewise occupied center stage in his earlier *Mont Saint Michel and Chartres* and in the highly personal verses he called his "Prayer to the Virgin of Chartres."

In *The Education*, Adams nonetheless made a point of denying that the Virgin had ever meant much in the United States: "The Woman had once been supreme; in France she still seemed potent, not merely as a sentiment but as a force; why was she unknown in America?"[1] He thus locates divine woman mainly in the past and in the traditional-minded culture of southern Europe; conversely, he declares her quite absent from the present-minded culture of America shaped by Puritanism. Predictably, she fills no role within the all-male preserve of Adams's nine-volume *History of the United States during the Administrations of Jefferson and Madison* (1890). So far, Adams's own preoccupation with Mariology seems purely idiosyncratic. It might be just the sort of oddity one expects to see displayed in a well-heeled American historian and aesthete absorbed in matters centuries removed from the popular zeitgeist.

At some level, though, Adams had to have known that his interest in the Virgin Mother was shared by other Americans. By the turn of the century, even Boston had accumulated plenty of Catholics and some Protestants who knew Mary.[2] Adams also had to know that his portrayal of the United States as a unified, post-Christian,

Anglo-Protestant culture represented no less a fiction than his description of medieval Europe as flowering in a "thirteenth-century unity" of art and thought. He may have tried to ignore American Catholics and other new subcultures to the extent that he felt personally threatened by population shifts in New England, for as Peter Gardella observes, "In the 1870s, Irish Catholics assumed the supremacy his family had held since colonial times in Quincy, Massachusetts."[3] But his overassertion of Mary's absence from America, like many other such statements in *The Education,* also serves a rhetorical end relevant to the intellectual and spiritual challenge of his era. The heartless new age of technology called forth a prophetic assertion: that the United States needed to qualify its pride of mastery as a global economic and military force by discovering deeper access to those "feminized" forces and values symbolized for Adams in the Virgin Mother.

Adams's Mariology deserves to be analyzed, then, not only as personally idiosyncratic but also as culturally symptomatic. The main worth Adams's texts hold today, after all, derives from the author's ability to make his own life and sensibility symptomatic of his age. To be sure, the later writing loses authority as cultural prophecy to the extent that it suffers distortion from various of the author's character defects.[4] Such defects include Adams's proclivities toward cynical melancholy and false modesty, his self-absorption, and his inability to admit his craving for public recognition. He also could not resist the urge to construct grand theoretical schemes on the shaky base of an underdeveloped understanding of science and theology.

In works like *The Education,* Adams nonetheless articulated the essential problem of twentieth-century modernity—in its several moral, spiritual, and intellectual dimensions—as trenchantly as any other witness we have. Searching for values that might sustain and center the human psyche in this age of decentered consciousness, Adams returned again and again to an ideal of eternal womanhood symbolized by the figure of Mary.

The Adamic Quest for New Eve

Many of the values Adams attached to the Virgin he also attributed more broadly to womankind and associated, in turn, with Romantic conceptions of the mystical and redemptive woman. Adams maintained an intense conviction of women's worth, albeit in his own mostly nonfeminist terms. He also displayed a marked preference for female companionship. In *The Education,* he asserts hyperbolically that "no woman had ever driven him wrong; no man had ever driven him right" (798). Accordingly, his writing gives implicit testimony that the Virgin does, in fact, sustain symbolic relevance even for twentieth-century Americans. Despite the author's apparent relegation of Mary to the past, she remains a vital rhetorical presence both in *Chartres* and in parts of *The Education.* She is, if anything, more emphatically *alive* than the dynamo. After analyzing the rhetoric Adams deploys when he sets the image of Mary as medieval woman against that of the dynamo as modern machine in *The Education,* I hope to show that this comparison yields something closer to a polarity, carrying several lines of continuity, than an absolute contrast. Symbolically, Adams's comprehensive ideal would be to see Virgin wedded to Dynamo.

It might be helpful at this stage to identify five distinctive characteristics of the Virgin that persist across the span of Adams's writing about her. She is *divinely personal, redemptive, transhistorical, potent,* and *self-subsistent.* Some of these features are more or less consonant with Christian orthodoxy; others are peculiar to Adams's outlook.

Thus, Adams's depiction of Mary as a *personal* female face of God is not particularly novel. Neither is his portrayal of her as the most unfailingly sympathetic form of personal divinity accessible to ordinary folk in the Western world. In the context of Adams's own intellectual agnosticism, however, his attraction to the emotional intimacy of Marian devotion is arresting. Despite Adams's enduring distaste for credal theism and his denial of a life beyond death, part of him shrank from the void, from the idea of the cosmos as heartless mechanism. His resisting self embraced Marian devotion as the most plausible version of a religious belief that for Henry Adams never advanced beyond the hypothetical. In effect, Adams's writing expresses the self-contradicting view that there is no God—but that Mary might truly be God's mother.

In confirming that the *morally redemptive capacity* of the Virgin extends to women generally in a corrupt world, Adams reflected something of earlier nineteenth-century cultural attitudes associated with true womanhood.[5] But he did not equate this saving influence of womanhood with qualities like domesticity, submissiveness, asexual bearing, intellectual weakness, or conventional piety. Regarding women as superior to men in several senses, he held to an almost mystical faith that woman might yet save the world—that is, restore wholeness—not only morally but also spiritually and philosophically. As archetypal woman and *alma mater,* the Virgin symbolized humanity's best hope to recover from that individual and corporate crisis of soul precipitated by the cultural triumph of Cartesian rationalism.

For Adams, *sexuality* had a good deal to do with the mystery of the Madonna. His treatment is distinctive in emphasizing not the sexual purity of the Virgin but her potency and fecundity, the unseen erotic force she contains and channels beyond herself to sustain the creative life of her prolific offspring in the human race. Adams portrays her as a kind of inspirative life force that is at once sexual and pneumatic. Hers is the motivating power that erects great cathedrals. Adams's Virgin reveals herself, above all, in force rather than sentiment.

Adams's broadly mythic delineation of the Virgin Mother's identity as axis of generativity immediately suggests a fourth characteristic of his portrait: Mary as a *composite, transhistorical manifestation of the universal Goddess.* Adams's Virgin, "the last and greatest deity of all" (523), subsumes the multiple personalities of divine womanhood including Venus, Diana of the Ephesians, Isis, Demeter, and Astarte. Our Lady embraces Eve and archaic woman; she also recognizes as kin all queenly women of the world, including three French rulers to whom Adams devotes a chapter of his *Chartres.*[6] The author never envisions her as belonging exclusively to medieval France; still less does he fix her historically in the biblical world of ancient

Nazareth. This expansive sense of Mary as a figure who had assimilated the import of mother goddesses from many different archaic and ancient cultures doubtless owed something to Adams's cognizance of recent discoveries in social anthropology, folk-lore, and comparative religion. From his reading, he had learned how precedents for the Marian cultus had developed in ancient Egypt and elsewhere. As Ernest Samuels points out, Adams found an important articulation of the maternal prin-ciple in archaic society when he read J. Bachofen's *Das Mutterrecht* in the course of researching his 1876 *Essays in Anglo-Saxon Law*.[7] That same year saw him lecturing on "Primitive Rights of Women" at the Lowell Institute. Later on, his 1890–92 travels in the South Seas enabled him to encounter for himself the decaying rem-nants of an archaic maternal culture, an experience mirrored in his private printing of *Memoirs of Marau Taaroa, Last Queen of Tahiti* (1893).[8]

A fifth characteristic of Adam's Virgin, doubtless influenced by preoccupation with her pagan lineage, is her *radical autonomy* in relation to other persons of the Trinitarian Godhead. For Adams, the Virgin of Chartres is a self-subsistent mon-arch who owns and rules the place. It is her shrine. She reigns in defiance of patri-archal authority, whether exercised on a divine or an ecclesiastical plane. In read-ing Mary's primacy from the architectural and literary record of cathedral culture in medieval Normandy, Adams rightly observes the disparity between extravagant popular piety and limits posed by official doctrine. Taken strictly as medieval his-tory, his description of this case in *Chartres* is marred by overstatement. Taken as personal narrative, however, *Chartres* simply mirrors its author's imaginative predi-lections when it overlooks the integral relation between Mary and her Son—or between God's mother and the Divine Trinity—that others have found displayed in the art of Chartres Cathedral.[9] Adams celebrated the autonomy of the eternal woman as symbolized by Mary of Chartres or other figures described nostalgically from the past. But, as Kim Moreland suggests, he could not accept so readily the idea of powerful women assuming public positions in his own day. In fact, he largely rejected the political and social claims of the New Woman as antithetical to quali-ties he believed essential to ideal woman.[10]

Across the range of these responses to the Marian mystery and particularly in *Chartres,* it is telling that Adams characteristically adopted for himself the persona of pilgrim. Combining the more venerable role of pilgrim with that of avuncular historian, he visited Mary's shrines without denying the prospect of discovering there sustenance of soul. He could not help shading the pilgrim role with irony, sometimes exchanging it for lesser parts as wanderer or globe-trotter. His unchurched skepticism demanded as much. But, to a surprising degree, he retained the pilgrim's sense of heartfelt homage and genuine spiritual quest. In large part, this search of Adams for a new Eve, this urge to know and preserve connection with the Divine Woman, seems to have been impelled by the suicide of his wife, Marian, in 1885. No wonder the Marian personality he encountered at Chartres bore a striking resemblance to Marian Hooper, whom he still mourned.[11]

Beyond whatever compensation it provided for personal loss, Adams's descrip-tion of the American pilgrim returning to seek divine womanhood in the Old World also presented a symbolic statement about the new nation's culture. As William Decker says in general of Adams's global voyaging in widowerhood, "His travel motive may have been at first simply recuperative, but from the start choice of itinerary and travel terminology make his movements an ironic commentary upon the broad patterns of Puritan and American emigration." The pilgrim role becomes all the more ironic in view of the "long New England genealogy" constituting Adams's own lineage.[12] Like the reverse migration of Christopher Newman to Europe set forth in James's *The American,* Adams's physical pilgrimage implied that even affluent America might lack something important—perhaps something obtainable elsewhere in the world. If the Pilgrim separatists sought to purge religion of paganism, to escape from the sort of Catholic idolatry represented in Mariolatry, Adams wanted to discover what they might have lost on the way to realizing their dream in Massachusetts.

Some slippage must have occurred when religious passion, "the most powerful emotion of man, next to the sexual" (751), had disappeared from Boston by the time of Adams's boyhood, leaving behind only "mild Deism" and a Unitarian establishment from which Adams expected nothing but comfortable moralism. America's contemporary worship of commerce—a faith shaken by the economic panics of 1893 and 1907[13]—and of steam engines scarcely promised more. "If only I still knew a God to pray to, or better yet, a Goddess," he confessed in a letter of 10 November 1891, "for as I grow older I see that all the human interest and power that religion ever had was in the mother and child, and I would have nothing to do with a church that did not offer both."[14]

Of course, Adams would have nothing to do with a church in any case. Certainly, he had no intent of reversing the tack of Protestant pilgrimage to the extent of personally embracing Roman Catholicism. Only a Catholic church made over to suit his syncretistic and matrifocal tastes might draw his assent, were he disposed toward faith commitment in the first place. Moreover, he knew that modern Americans, particularly Protestants, could not return permanently to medieval Normandy. They could never give their hearts to a thirteenth-century Virgin in quite the way villagers of Chartres once had.

Yet, for Adams, what the Virgin Mary symbolized of eternal womanhood remained relevant to the needs and aspirations of humanity even into the twentieth century. Whatever new shape the feminine divine might now assume beyond the figure of Mary, it belonged to the optative future as much as to the past. Discussing issues of literary audience in a letter to poet George Cabot Lodge in 1903, Adams mixes sociological and mythical predictions when he reveals that his "instinct rather turns to the woman than the man of the future." "What will the woman turn out to be?" he asks. "Read me that riddle aright, and art will conform to the answer," for "what she will become is known only to the Holy Virgin."[15]

"The place has no heart":
Preserves of Womanly Grace in *Democracy* and *Esther*

Although it culminates in *Chartres* and *The Education,* Adams's preoccupation with womankind surfaces much earlier in his writing. The novels Adams published in

1880 and 1884 both feature female protagonists whose gender has much to do with their character and destiny. In *Chartres,* he would declare that "the proper study of mankind is woman, and by common agreement since the time of Adam, it is the most complex and arduous." And he would link this enterprise directly with "the study of Our Lady," which, "as shown by the art of Chartres, leads directly back to Eve, and lays bare the whole subject of sex" (523). The fictional studies of women in *Democracy* and *Esther* confirm the complex and problematic—yet essential—nature of womankind in Adams's eyes.

Part of what makes these studies complex is the character of Adams's personal identification with women. Adams took pains to mask the maleness of his authorship by publishing *Democracy* anonymously and *Esther* under the female pseudonym of Frances Snow Compton. And, though the central characters of Madeleine and Esther reflect a good deal of Marian Hooper Adams, they also embody something of Adams's own "womanly" disposition and circumstance.[16]

For Adams felt keenly the awkwardness, as well as the privilege, of his position as male member of a distinguished family dynasty. Seemingly destined for leadership in America's ruling patriarchy, as the grandson of one U.S. president and the great-grandson of another, Adams nonetheless failed to play his assigned part as political actor on the public stage. Instead, he assumed the characteristic posture of observer, of one who contemplated the public scene and the inner life of things from another sphere. This scholarly sphere of reflection intersected with that separate sphere of presumed rectitude occupied by American women. Of course, Adams never disappeared from public view so thoroughly, or in the same domestic manner, as true womanhood dictated. During his lifetime, he would gain several sorts of public recognition as journalist, editor, lobbyist, Harvard professor, lecturer, and author. In proportion to his own expectation and sense of alienation, however, Adams remained obscure. Aside from the *History,* which attracted little notice in its own day, almost all writings for which he might be known today were first published either privately (*Chartres* and *The Education*), not under his name (*Democracy* and *Esther*), or not at all ("Prayer to the Virgin of Chartres").

For Adams, women retained a redemptive vocation in society even, or especially, in the face of modernity. He acknowledged that some women, including authors and queens, might function effectively in public roles. But only insofar as women sustained contact with secret reserves of the eternal feminine might they offer the world a force superior to corruption, cynicism, and sterile rationalism. Even when the woman managed to extend her saving influence toward individuals, she would likely be destroyed by the world before she succeeded in reforming it. Women should therefore not aspire to reform, to undo immediately that corruption endemic to the public order, but only to preserve for humanity a refuge of integrity accessible for future healing.

Such is the sober conclusion suggested, for example, by the career of Madeleine Lee in *Democracy*. Initially drawn to the nation's capital to observe the operation of political power, this affluent young widow becomes fascinated with the Washington drama even as she is repelled by the shameless dishonesty of its leading actors. Soon she finds herself tempted to take an active part in the scene she observes by marrying Senator Silas P. Ratcliffe, a "high priest of American politics" (20) from Illinois who admits to having engineered vote fraud to ensure his state's support for the Union cause while he was serving as governor. Never scrupulous about the means by which he achieves his ends, Ratcliffe has consolidated a power base in Washington even firmer than the president's.

It is scarcely clear at first why Madeleine should consider marrying such a man. The character John Carrington, though he is Ratcliffe's romantic rival for Madeleine, accurately describes him as "only a coarse, selfish, unprincipled politician" (132). Certainly Madeleine is not enchanted by Ratcliffe's physical attributes or the refinement of his bearing. His capacity to wield political power interests her considerably more, for she had come to Washington in the first place "to see with her own eyes the action of primary forces" and "to measure with her own mind the capacity of the motive power." Again, Carrington is right when he fears "the evident attraction which Ratcliffe's strong will and unscrupulous energy exercised over her" (7).

Yet Ratcliffe errs when he supposes that Madeleine will marry him because she shares his lust to possess and apply power for herself. If she comes perilously close to marrying this scoundrel, it is not because she dreams of holding sway as first lady. It is rather because she aspires to save Ratcliffe from himself—and, thereby, to help save the nation by wedding the power he represents to moral virtue. The "indescribable" (10) Madeleine preserves a mystique of archetypal womanly virtue even though she is unable to discern, in abstract analytic terms, any alternative to "accepting the Ratcliffian morals" (98). In short, Madeleine is tempted to think she can reform American democracy by reforming Ratcliffe.

Several circumstances heighten this temptation. Adams tells us "she had a woman's natural tendency towards asceticism, self-extinction, self-abnegation" (90). After the deaths of her husband and baby, she has lost all urge to secure her own happiness. She suspects that by sacrificing herself now for Ratcliffe she might benefit not only him, by way of moral amelioration, but also her sister, Sybil, by transferring to her the prospect of marrying Carrington.

As Sybil recognizes, Ratcliffe himself encourages Madeleine's misplaced urge toward self-sacrifice by "trying to make her think she can reform him" (112). Toward this end, he confronts her with a shrewdly aimed personal appeal: "'In politics we cannot keep our hands clean. I have done many things in my political career that are not defensible. To act with entire honesty and self-respect, one should always live in a pure atmosphere, and the atmosphere of politics is impure. Domestic life is the salvation of many public men, but I have for many years been deprived of it'" (153).

Madeleine also renders herself vulnerable when she brings to Washington an untested confidence that "surely something can be done to check corruption" (37) within a democratic polity. Such virtue might survive Washington but never subdue it. Men like Ratcliffe simply cannot be motivated by virtue, but only by self-interested expediency; for them, the issue of governance is "not one of principle but of power" (81). Madeleine cannot bridge the great gulf fixed between what Adams portrays as the essentially masculine domain of politics and the feminized precinct of ethics. Only when Carrington, another self-abnegating personality and feminized male, intervenes to supply her with a secret letter exposing Ratcliffe does she accept the futility of that hope. Eventually, she grants that she should not presume to purify politics or, indeed, to "reform anything" (178). In seeking to infuse American democracy with virtue, she had nearly been destroyed by the "massive machinery" of the governmental engine.

Foreshadowing the dynamo, Adams's mechanical imagery seems apt because in the power world of the machine era, distinctions between virtue and vice often give way before the debased pragmatism of "what works."[17] Adams's novel shows American government to be corrupt not only despite but also partly because of its democratic character. For in a complex, postagrarian society like the United States, the people's majoritarian will can be registered only through a vast, impersonal machinery of governance. In the contemporary process of electing democratic leaders, Jeffersonian ideals of natural aristocracy and consent of the governed are supplanted by Darwinian precepts of natural selection and struggle.

Thus, in reply to Madeleine's demands to "know whether America is right or wrong" and whether democracy represents "the best government," shrewd Nathan Gore from Massachusetts will affirm only his faith in "human nature," in "science," and in "the survival of the fittest" (39, 40, 41). Madeleine admits she does not much understand the volume of Darwin she borrowed from the Library of Congress, but Ratcliffe, ironically, scorns what he presumes to be the book's assertion of human descent from monkeys. What he could more plausibly urge her to believe from the authority of his own experience is that, in the masculinized ethos of social Darwinism, values of aggressive achievement and self-aggrandizement bespeak power rather than corruption. Both the individual figure of competition and the social paradigm of government as massive machine lie beyond good and evil. By marrying Ratcliffe, Madeleine would not change him; neither would she alter the inexorable course of government power. Democracy's great machine would instead grind her to death.

Marriage likewise looms as a mortal threat before Adams's female protagonist in *Esther*. Esther Dudley presents herself from the first as a spirited, artistic, independent-minded woman not unlike Marian Hooper Adams. Her name, a variant of Hester,[18] derives from the Babylonian fertility goddess Ishtar. Her forceful personality recalls as well the biblical Esther, Jewish wife of a Persian king who saved her people from slaughter. Although Adams's Esther is drawn to marry by social, emotive, and presumably sexual motives, she cannot do so without compromising a certain virginal autonomy essential to her integrity. And to marry the Reverend Stephen Hazard is so hazardous to her spiritual and psychic health that it promises to be, in effect, suicidal. "You are killing me," she (304) cries in protest of his final bid to possess her.

Yet personal independence is not the only ideal Esther's nature drives her to fulfill. She cannot rest satisfied as the lonely goddess because she craves human sympathy as well as some medium of expressing her creativity and natural fecundity. Significantly, she ends up painting in St. John's Church because even here, in a New World Episcopal edifice with a high-church priest, no image of the Madonna has survived the Reformation. When Esther and Catherine Brooke arrive, their presence starts to fill this absence. The artist Wharton tells Esther he wished she had come to paint earlier but that he "would like now, even as it is, to go back to the age of beauty, and put a Madonna in the heart of their church" because "the place has no heart" (234).

Although John's Gospel emphasizes love, St. John's of New York—in its architectural as well as its fellowship body—lacks the sort of heart supplied by the Madonna's presence. Its presiding spirit is not Christly love or maternal compassion but the intensely masculine will of Stephen Hazard. Hazard's apparent devotion to the softer beauties of music, art, and mysticism cannot hide for long the obdurate, pugnacious temper of his inner nature. "Hazard's grasp of all subjects," announces the narrator, "though feminine in appearance, was masculine and persistent in reality" (218). Neither the combative, "masculine work" of Wharton's art (247) nor the stark materialism of George Strong's science confront Esther so aggressively. That same force, carrying an almost sacred violence, with which Hazard appeals to Esther also threatens Esther.

Despite his elegant manners, Hazard presses her to yield herself—and her beliefs—against her will. Adams extends his unflattering and not quite persuasive depiction of Hazard's proselytizing zeal to the point of clergy caricature. Clearly, Hazard approaches courtship as an imperative of conquest, at once sexual and ideological. And though Hazard outwardly denies the Cartesian claim of ego-centered authority, he tries to dominate Esther in a manner plainly intended to confirm his own faith and ego strength. In fact, when he assures her that "she had but to trust herself to him" (274, 330), he is urging what amounts to an idolatry focused on him rather than faith in the Spirit of God. No wonder she ends up attacking his churchly commitment as "all personal and selfish," as a faith devoid of "spiritual life" (332, 333).

A central irony of the novel is that Esther, though incorrigibly agnostic, embodies more of the Madonna's spirit and heart than any of the art displayed in St. John's Church. And there is evidently more godliness in her—or, for that matter, in her atheistic cousin Strong—than in Hazard. Hazard belies the self-abnegating identity of his namesake, St. Stephen, when he shows himself to be less martyr than persecutor. He presumably shares some temperamental traits with Esther, whose character is marked by "a vein of mysticism running through a practical mind" (265). Yet, even Hazard notices that Esther is animated by "a soul stronger and warmer than his own" (270), by a spirit force that likewise inspires Wharton to regard her as a kind of "new deity" (200) despite her amateur artistry.

Esther reflects toward her trio of male admirers a radiance reminiscent of the absent Madonna—not through her unsublime portrait of St. Cecilia, but in her own person. If the youthful beauty and innocence of Catherine Brooke, Esther's artistic model, suggest a fanciful image of "the new Madonna of the prairie" (222), Esther appears in Wharton's view as the new Madonna of the pagan future. As Wharton confides to Hazard, "There is nothing medieval about her. If she belongs to any besides the present, it is to the next world which artists want to see, when paganism will come again and we can give a divinity to every waterfall" (200). Strong, too, describes Esther as "the sternest little Pagan I know" (196). Yet, her innate spirituality is such that she ironically pictures Hazard, in his liturgical function, as though he "were a priest in a Pagan temple, centuries apart" from her (332).

If paganism can locate divinity in waterfalls, then Esther discovers something comparable at the famous cataract of Niagara. Weeping at the sound of mighty waters whose "manners are divine" (314), she hears in Niagara a masculine countervoice to Hazard's importunity. She is awestruck at facing the "huge church which was thundering its gospel under its eyes" (315). Although the Niagara episode represents a turning point in Esther's struggle to refuse marriage, it offers her not a supernatural theophany so much as an occasion of self-revelation. The "secret" from the "great reservoir of truth" (314, 321) that Esther confronts here is an interior one, previously hidden from herself. Catherine expresses quite another reading of the cataract.[19] By 1889, only five years after publication of Esther, another Adams—banker Edward Dean Adams—would begin organizing the capital to support hydro-electric development at the falls. To regard Niagara as a site of religious revelation would become more difficult once its waters had been harnessed to power the dynamo.[20]

For Esther, though, the falls do at least open a wider perspective from which she can more clearly perceive the strength and value of her virginal autonomy. In the solitude of Niagara, she also confirms her connection to elemental reality, deepening that sense she had already confronted in her father's death. She accepts at last the impossibility of willing herself into a state of faith; she admits openly that she finds Hazard's Christianity neither tenable nor attractive. Yet, she accepts also the insufficiency of critical skepticism to satisfy her heart's desires; she shares Adams's longing for sustaining absolutes.

When Hazard leaves, Esther feels desolate—an awful silence, a peace of despair rather than of repose. Unlike Hazard, who could imagine no "stopping-place between dogma and negation" (289), Esther resolves to preserve her anomalous autonomy without embracing the worldview either of Hazard or of Strong. At the novel's close, Adams does not specify the ultimate outcome of Esther's struggle with despair. He leaves us uncertain if or how her life might bear fruit in the world. But he implies she has the strength to survive in a way that Marian "Clover" Adams, tragically, would not.

It is scarcely hopeful, in any event, that the female protagonists of both novels come to look on marriage as at least spiritually if not physically suicidal. Only by withdrawing from the public marketplace can Madeleine and Esther preserve their sanity and integrity. After escaping Ratcliffe, Madeleine says she wants to withdraw for "rest" all the way to Egypt, whose ancient society Adams had earlier praised for its unsurpassed promotion of the social position and "primitive rights" of women.[21]

As Adams's hopes waned for seeing the absent Madonna reincarnated in actual women of the United States, he drew his attention more and more toward the Virgin Mother who ruled in another time and place. On the biographical plane, his sense of loss and longing for feminine presence was sharpened immeasurably by his wife's suicide. He was also deeply moved, as he testifies in The Education, by the horrid death of his sister Louisa from tetanus in 1870. His love for the beautiful but unattainable Elizabeth Cameron, young wife of Senator Donald Cameron, rendered more acute his sense of alienation at encountering a new cultural era in which he counted himself a failure. All of this personal history stands behind three of Adams's well-known later works: "Prayer to the Virgin of Chartres," *Chartres,* and *The Education.*

Mary of Chartres as Personal Presence and Romantic Ideal

On its outer, objective face, *Mont Saint Michel and Chartres* mirrors the art and thought of medieval France. Having largely trained himself by 1870 to begin teaching courses in medieval European history at Harvard, Adams first responded intensely to the Gothic structures of France—at Bayeux and Coutances, then at Chartres—during a summer tour with Henry and Anna Cabot Lodge in 1895. As a guidebook to the physical and intellectual landscape of medievalia, *Chartres* remains instructive, though open to correction. But later critical interpretation has emphasized, instead, the work's character as a subjectively rendered poem in prose.[22] In this light, it reveals at least as much about the impression of fin de siècle modernity on an American author's sensibility as it does about medieval France. In fact, as Michael Colacurcio suggests, *Chartres* is even more personal than Adams's supposed autobiographical record in *The Education.*[23] As *Chartres* unfolds, its portrayal of Mary of Chartres merges more and more with an Adamic fantasy of eternal woman. Enfolded within Adams's discourse on the medieval Virgin is an indirect commentary on the current state of the United States, as well as an existential plea for meaning, inner wholeness, and love.

Adams was drawn toward Chartres, as Robert Mane has ably shown, by several persons and circumstances. The nostalgic medievalism of James Russell Lowell and his poem "A Day in Chartres" may have played a role; but even more decisive, according to Mane, was the aesthetic influence of John La Farge and H. H. Richardson, combined with Brooks Adams's ecstatic view of the Gothic imagination. Brooks Adams's corresponding melancholy about the "decay" of a later Western civilization in which bankers gained power while artists lost imaginative influence enlarged his brother's disposition to adopt similar views. Unhappily, Henry Adams's way to Chartres was even paved with racist and anti-Semitic views, as the author pursued an escapist myth of his own Norman ancestry while minimizing his association with presumably less pure English forebears, including Puritans.[24]

Yet, standing plainly above the jumble of motives that inspired *Mont Saint Michel and Chartres* and the array of medieval topics, places, and personalities this book addresses is its leading character: the Virgin Mother. A relatively brief opening account of Mont Saint Michel as image of militant masculinity leads directly—through the portal imagery of chapter 5—toward a corresponding but fuller commentary on the feminine sovereignty embodied in Mary, Queen of Heaven. After discussing Mary's presence in the architecture of Chartres, Adams goes on to link divine womanhood not only to writings concerned with "Les Miracles de Notre Dame" but also to the literature of courteous love and the sensibility of pre-Enlightenment

male mystics such as St. Francis and Adam of St. Victor. The book concludes with
a chapter outlining the rational system of the great thirteenth-century philosopher,
St. Thomas Aquinas. Yet, even in this third section, where masculine rationality
regains prominence, Adams stresses the "feminine" elusiveness of final truth and
the role played by the artistic anima in Thomas's grand creation.

If *Mont Saint Michel and Chartres* is, indeed, structured according to a triptych
scheme in which three chapters on St. Michael's Mount in Normandy occupy the
first panel and three chapters on St. Thomas and the church intellectual fill the last,[25]
the matter of Mary evidently holds a central position in more ways than one. Mary
lives at the heart of things; in *Mont Saint Michel and Chartres,* her universal church
affective subsumes the church militant and church intellectual. For Adams, the book's
main architectural symbol, the cathedral, comes alive in the Virgin Mother, whose
body is likewise a sacred temple enclosing all humanity and the cosmos (figure 5.1).
"The Trinity had its source in her,—*totius Trinitatis nobile Triclinium,*" Adams writes

FIGURE 5.1. *Notre Dame-de-la-Belle-Verrière* at south transept of Chartres Cathedral, France
(Foto Marburg / Art Resource, New York).

by way of summarizing views of the mystics, "and she was Maternity" as well as "poetry and art." More than that, "in the bankruptcy of Reason, she alone was real" (642). To enter Chartres is to enter her shrine, the "Court of the Queen of Heaven" (407). Not surprisingly, Adams referred to *Chartres* as his "great work on the Virgin."[26]

AMONG THE BOOK'S most striking passages are those in which Adams gives heartfelt witness to his personal fascination with the Virgin Mother. At such moments, the speaker abandons his professorial pose as objective historian. He even steps beyond his fictive role as the easygoing uncle on vacation. Mary assumes more than antiquarian interest: She becomes a living spirit, a presence, a figure with distinct personality. Adams portrays her as by turns willful, quirky, endearing, intellectual, "peculiarly gracious and gentle" (407), and iconoclastic in the face of ordained authority. She is majestic but, even more, merciful toward her supplicants. Her mercy surpasses not only justice but also all human standards of clemency. At Chartres, Adams finds Christ "identified with his Mother, the spirit of love and grace" (407). She is the very "mother of pity and the only hope of despair" (600). She is illogical, unreasonable, and irrepressibly familiar with common mortals. Though exalted with celestial power, she is also "the most womanly of women" (408). In the book's most emotively charged expositions, Adams suggests that her presence inspired not only the art of Chartres cathedral in the twelfth and thirteenth centuries but also the artistry of his own literary creation in the twentieth.

To be sure, the uncle sometimes relegates Mary's presence and influence to the past. Once, to those who designed Chartre's portal, the "Virgin in her shrine was at least as living, as real, as personal an empress as the Basilissa at Constantinople"; watching the play of light on glass of the western rose, however, the speaker laments that "unfortunately she is gone, or comes here now so very rarely that we never shall see her" (408, 473). More often, though, Adams's extravagant descriptions of Marian piety overflow to present tense. Remarking on Mary's power in late-sixteenth-century France, for example, he affirms that "the Virgin still remained and remains the most intensely and the most widely and the most personally felt, of all characters, divine or human or imaginary, that ever existed among men." "Nothing," he says, "has even remotely taken her place" (578).

Often recalling for his readers the mythical antecedents and universal scope of Mary's appeal, Adams is inclined to number himself among her subjects: "In the center sits Mary, with her crown on her head and her son in her lap, enthroned, receiving the homage of heaven and earth; of all time, ancient and modern; of all thought, Christian and Pagan; of all men, and all women; including, if you please, your homage and mine, which she receives without question, as her due; which she cannot be said to claim, because she is above making claims; she is empress" (408–9).

The sense of Mary's immediate presence at Chartres remains strong for Adams despite his skepticism toward the faith she represents. "One sees her personal presence on every side," he confirms, and "anyone can feel it, who will only consent to feel like a child." After absorbing the cathedral's sensory stimuli, "you or any other lost soul, could, if you cared to look and listen, feel a sense beyond the human ready to reveal a sense divine that would make that world once more intelligible, and would bring the Virgin to life again, in all the depth of feeling which she shows here" (505). Even now it is "not altogether easy . . . to resist the rapture of her radiant presence" (441). So definitively has the Virgin "concentrated the whole rebellion of man against fate" that "we, although utter strangers to her, are not far from getting down on our knees and praying to her still" (596).

In *Chartres*, the Virgin remains a vital personality even when Adams pictures her "looking down from a deserted heaven, into an empty church, on a dead faith" (522). The evidence of inspired art still "proves the Virgin's presence" (438). It is she who creates and sustains the art of Chartres as well as of Adams's *Chartres*. The glory of her artistically mediated presence remains so overwhelming, in fact, that one can become "a little incoherent talking about it" (459).

Several of the legendary miracles that Adams recounts, including apparitions before an acrobatic tumbler at Clairvaux monastery or on the deathbed of an indigent peasant woman, serve more to dramatize the Virgin's presence than to advertise worldly benefits of her intervention. For Adams, these miracles demonstrate not so much Mary's suspension of natural law, in terms defined by Hume and subsequently debated by New England Unitarians and Transcendentalists, as her overturning of social conventions. Above all, the art concerning *Les Miracles de La Vierge* testifies to the immediacy and vitality of her presence.

What Adams sees fulfilled for humanity in medieval France by the Virgin Mother he typically finds wanting in his own nation and era. Hence, the commentary of *Chartres* everywhere implies—and sometimes specifies—a cultural critique of modernity. Its response to Europe likewise conveys a contrasting assessment of American culture, particularly in its Puritan origins. Rejecting the myth of progress, Adams laments what he takes to be a general decline in taste, primitive energy, intuition, and aesthetic and sensory sensitivity in his own age as measured against the high Middle Ages. He determines that "The twelfth [century] is, in architecture, rather better off than the nineteenth" and that "the thirteenth century knew more about religion and decoration than the twentieth century will ever learn." In an even more sweeping judgment, he complains, "Our age has lost much of its ear for poetry, as it has its eye for color and line, and its taste for war and worship, wine and women" (373, 498, 368).

Adams's judgments against the spirit of his age and against presumptions of progress reflect, in turn, an essentially Romantic myth. Robert Mane points out that the first citation in *Chartres* comes not from a medieval source but from Wordsworth and that Adams's sense of the Gothic was colored by Romantic conceptions.[27] The book's central values may actually derive less from the twelfth and thirteenth centuries, or even from the twentieth, than from the early nineteenth. Throughout, Adams validates Romantic urges to recover the child's purity of perception, to remove the film of custom, and to celebrate the organically unified life of the world. "Unless you can go back to your dolls," he warns the niece, "you are out of place here," but "if you can go back to them, and get rid for one small hour of the weight of custom, you shall see Chartres in glory" (424).

Thus, the principle of "unity" that Adams attributed to thirteenth-century culture owes as much to Romantic ideals of unified perception as to the fiction of intellectual uniformity and convergence he purported to locate in the medieval mind.[28] If not illusory, the "organic unity" (693) of thought and will Adams assigned to the Gothic sensibility is belied by the "want of unity" he admits in Chartre's artistic design (506), as well as by substantive discord among intellectual leaders, illustrated in the case of Abelard versus William of Champeaux.

Within the larger symbolic argument of *Chartres,* the unity that Adams esteems by contrast with the fragmentation of modernity signifies not so much a coherent intellectual scheme as an ideal of psychic and social integration centered on the Virgin Mother. Thus, Adams cites a hymn of Adam de Saint Victor imploring the Virgin to "unite" in her fold those "separated" from her (430). Rather than a static uniformity, Adams's Lady of Perpetual Unity represents an organic vitality, a feminine presence and immediacy needed to offset what the author perceived to be the overmasculine, antiaesthetic, mechanistic mood of American culture following the Gilded Age. For Adams, the Virgin Mother embodied a unity that enclosed chaos without destroying it—for "the Mother alone could represent whatever was not Unity; whatever was irregular, exceptional, outlawed; and this was the whole human race" (584). She embodied an anarchy-in-unity that preserved tension between "pure Nominalism" (621), on the one hand, and an absolute coalescence founded in philosophic Realism, on the other. Adams, one suspects, would have been receptive to analogous formulations of paradox in the chaos theory developed by scientific thinkers today.

In Adams's view, the Puritans failed to appreciate the psychic and spiritual value of a unity that embraced the mystical domain of the unruly, the unknown, the liminal and subliminal. Instead, they enforced a cerebral uniformity as unyielding as New England granite. By contrast, St. Thomas is shown to have developed at least a plausible philosophic theory of "Multiplicity in Unity" (680). Adams charges the Puritans with hostility toward the mythic symbology of womanhood, as well as toward actual women. They not only "excluded" the Virgin "from their society" but also sought to "renew the quarrel with Eve" so far as to "abolish the woman altogether as the cause of all evil in heaven and earth" (580, 597). In so doing, they initiated what Adams regards as a pattern of repression that continues to provoke existential questions: "Why did the gentle and gracious Virgin Mother so exasperate the Pilgrim Father? Why was the Woman struck out of the Church and ignored in the State? These questions are not antiquarian or trifling in historical value; they tug at the very heart-strings of all that makes whatever order is in the cosmos. If a Unity exists, in which and toward which all energies centre, it must explain and include duality, Diversity, Infinity,—Sex!" (582–83).

Pointing especially to nineteenth-century scientists such as Michael Faraday and James Clerk Maxwell, Adams argues that science, too, has characteristically aimed "at nothing but the reduction of multiplicity to unity" (689). And insofar as "the scientific mind" supports the disjunctive tendencies of rationalism, it remains "atrophied, and suffers under inherited cerebral weakness, when it comes in contact with the eternal woman,—Astarte, Isis, Demeter, Aphrodite, and the last and greatest deity of all, the Virgin" (523).

Throughout *Chartres,* then, Adams exposes his own disposition toward philosophic skepticism—that is, toward disbelief in the capacity of human reason to resolve ultimate questions. As Adams recognizes, philosophic skepticism is scarcely identical to religious skepticism. He declares, in fact, that "religious minds prefer skepticism" and that "the true saint is a profound sceptic; a total disbeliever in human reason, who has more than once joined hands on this ground with some who were at best sinners" (639). If Adams certifies his own disbelief as regards philosophic skepticism, he reflects a more variable blend of unbelief, agnosticism, and tentative fideism as regards religion.[29] "Without Mary, man had no hope except in Atheism," he insists—or, perhaps, in that "modern sort of religion" based on the thought of one's "own importance" (574, 515).

But the author of *Chartres* cannot, after all, quite consent to live without the Virgin Mother. He will not deprive himself, at least, of her imagined image. And his sense of her as rescuer of shipwrecked souls, epitomized in verses by Adam de Saint Victor, retained strong existential appeal for someone inclined to lament his own peril, failure, and loss. In addition to Mary's power of rescue, *Chartres* invests considerable credence in her capacities as universal *genetrix.* Adams discusses at length St. Thomas's conception of God as the "Prime Motor which supplies all energy to the universe" in a system comparable to that of the modern dynamo (686–87).[30] Yet the book as a whole attributes generativity still more directly to the Virgin, who inspires movement and distributes energy well beyond the plane of materiality. Again, it is she who moves the hearts and minds of artists to create Chartres; and she, evidently, is the dynamo who energizes the feeling and expression Adams displays in his writing.

Adams's *Education*: The Unknowable and Generative Woman

First printed just three years after *Chartres,* that peculiar blend of personal narrative and cultural history titled *The Education of Henry Adams* does not focus so steadily on the theme of divine womanhood. Yet, most commentators agree that Adams's meditation on "The Dynamo and the Virgin" in chapter 25 fills a pivotal role in *The Education.* Moreover, the author presents his later work as integrally and dialogically related to *Chartres.* Though the Virgin appears only briefly in *The Education,* she becomes a chief point of symbolic reference within the narrator's search for meaning, coherence, and the trajectory of historical change.

Beyond a quest for intellectual understanding, the "education" of Adams engages him in a broader moral, psychological, and spiritual struggle to apprehend the world. And that world changes rapidly, from the surviving eighteenth-century ethos of orderly confidence that shapes the author in childhood to the twentieth-century "chaos" he confronts in his later years. In response to the instability of his environment, Adams shows the subject of *The Education* involved in a process of perpetual self-instruction and self-fashioning. But the more Adams learns, the less satisfied he becomes with the amplitude and relevance of his knowledge.

In fact, the main spiritual import of this "education" is to lead Adams toward an existential recognition of his ignorance and insufficiency. Starting from the Baconian presumption that knowledge is power, *The Education* moves toward acceptance of the Socratic wisdom that "ignorance is learning." Along the way, Adams comes to appreciate the vanity of political diplomacy, the futility of his own bid for a public role in Grant's government, and the unfathomable intricacy of life adumbrated by modern scientific and historical theories. Even in accepting Darwinism, the author experiences more negation than affirmation because he cannot share with other Darwinists the belief that natural selection might supply the equivalent of "religious hope" or an evolutionary "promise of ultimate perfection" (931). Like Adams's "failure," Adams's ignorance is presented as culturally emblematic rather than personally idiomorphic. What Adams eventually "knows," therefore, is "that no one knows" (1098). The pilgrim's progress of Adams as latter-day "Adam"[31] follows a course of unknowing that reveals the limits of rational understanding. At the end point of this secular *via negativa,* the Virgin stands for the elusiveness of the eternal feminine—and for everything the new learning and incipient modern America were *not.*

In *The Education,* then, Mary defines for Adams a positive residue of hope on the far side of negation. She embodies longing for a personal presence in the void, for affirmation of a center that might lend meaning to the otherwise chaotic dynamic of forces made manifest by science. To be sure, her presence becomes less immediate and palpable in *The Education* than it had been in *Chartres.* The celebratory mood of *Chartres* yields in *The Education* to a more apocalyptic and ultimately elegiac sense of things. Yet, for Adams, even the dynamo, with its arresting display of unmeasurable force at the Great Paris Exposition of 1900, does not supersede the Virgin. Her latent potency remains unsurpassed. As "symbol or energy, the Virgin had acted as the greatest force the western world ever felt, and had drawn man's activities to herself more strongly than any other power, natural or supernatural, had ever done" (1075). Though largely unrecognized by American culture, she represented "the highest energy ever known to man" and that which had created "four-fifths of his noblest art, exercising vastly more attraction over the human mind than all the steam-engines and dynamos ever dreamed of" (1071).

Accordingly, the terms of opposition between "The Dynamo and the Virgin" presented in chapter 25 range well beyond the bounds in which Adams consciously frames them. Ostensibly, the Virgin symbolizes a twelfth-century unity antithetical to twentieth-century multiplicity, as figured in the dynamo. A chasm presumably divides the age of faith and order that Adams discovered at Chartres from the era of technology and chaos that confronts him at the Great Paris Exposition of 1900. While pondering these "two kingdoms of force which had nothing in common but attraction," Adams finds his "historical neck broken by the sudden irruption of force totally new" (1070, 1069). Within the logic of Adams's stated equation, the Virgin should not figure as more than an outdated token of an antique sensibility.

Yet the symbology in chapter 25 reaches beyond the author's surface statement of antithesis between medievalism and modernity. Imaginatively, the cultural symbols of Virgin and dynamo relate not only as antithetical but also as parallel and even complementary figures.[32] Their association is dialectical. Moreover, in *The Education,* Mary refuses to cede primacy to the machine, despite a sequence of historical change that would seem to render her irrelevant.

Coincidentally, Adams meets both Virgin and dynamo in France. He understands both to mediate powerful forces of nature—yet in each case these unseen forces suggest something transcending commonsense apprehension of nature. Hence "to Adams the dynamo became a symbol of infinity," its chief value having been attributed not to its utility but to "its occult mechanism" (1067). Electricity and invisible radiation, closely considered, resembled religious faith more than empirical fact, for "the rays that Langley disowned, as well as those which he fathered, were occult, supersensual, irrational; they were a revelation of mysterious energy like that of the Cross; they were what, in terms of mediaeval science, were called immediate modes of the divine substance" (1069). The almost reverential helplessness Adams feels before the dynamo, the disposition to pray before a manifestation of "silent and infinite force" (1067)—all of this sounds close enough to responses provoked by his encounter with Mary at Chartres.

The generative capacity of the Virgin, though, far surpasses that of the dynamo. The dynamo represents a channel of force that remains not only decentered and impersonal but also incapable of generating art, beauty, or sexual energy. It is dynamic but lifeless, powerful but impotent. By contrast, the Virgin's fecundity extends beyond biology and religion to art, emotion, and imagination. Her influence touches even artists, including the American Saint-Gaudens, who lack conscious understanding of the womanly "force that created it all" (1073). It is telling that Adams's rhetoric comes most alive when he expounds on the vitalizing influence of divine womanhood: "She was Goddess because of her force; she was the animated dynamo; she was reproduction—the greatest and most mysterious of all energies; all she needed was to be fecund" (1070).

Within Adams's gendered construction of the Virgin-dynamo duality, "the female energy" (1074) of the woman receives stronger validation than the implicitly masculine, industrial, unartistic force of the machine. A biographical corollary of this emphasis can be detected in the self-justifying tone with which Adams describes effeminate tendencies in his own bodily and mental development. Growing up with a shorter and lighter physique than his brothers displayed, he finds that "his character and processes of mind seemed to share in this fining-down process of scale." He discovers he is "not good in a fight," distrusts "his own judgment," and possesses nerves "more delicate than boys' nerves ought to be" (726).

Yet insofar as chapter 25 affirms the common force and polar connection of Virgin and dynamo, it also affirms a psychosexual ideal of wholeness. As "the animated dynamo," the Virgin represents not only an apotheosis of femininity but also a synthesis of beauty with the prodigious force customarily linked to masculinity.[33] Her potency is such that it at least begins to dissolve the chapter's conceptual dualities of feminine-masculine, medieval-modern, Europe-America, and Virgin-dynamo. In the Madonna's "mystery of Maternity," as the author reflected earlier in his prayer-poem, lies "Soul within Soul,—Mother and Child in One!" (1207). Adams's sym-

bol of the Venusian Virgin likewise conjoins several gender values that contemporary critical theorists are apt to regard as antithetical. Thus, Priscilla L. Walton's
recent poststructuralist reading of Henry James identifies "femininity" with plural
signification, otherness, unknowability, and absence; conversely, Walton links
"masculinity" with logocentric singularity, availability, textual coherence, and presence.[34] Yet Adams's Virgin, who is at once present and absent in chapter 25, refuses
to plant herself clearly in either camp of this radical dualism.

Lamenting that in America the idea of the Virgin "survived only as art" (1071),
Adams nonetheless portrays divine womanhood as the inspirative origin of most
visual art, music, and literary discourse. And if Adams regards the Woman as a
preverbal and transverbal mother of language by virtue of her "attraction over the
human mind" (1071),[35] he also seems (particularly in *Chartres*) to credit her with
inspiring much of his own expression, perhaps including his colorful description of
the dynamo. More profoundly than the "barely murmuring" sound of the dynamo
(1067), the mystical silence of the Virgin reverberates beyond the limits of language,
of Adams's critical skepticism, and of death.

Despite all that Adams had tried to make of himself, to say for or about himself,
and to achieve visibly for himself in the world, the Virgin embodied a contrary
principle of passive acceptance and receptivity to silent, invisible powers. For him,
she signified what might be salvaged positively from a rigorously skeptical, negative education. If the God who seemed to torture his sister before her death "could
not be a Person" (983), then the person of the Virgin at least supplied an image of
presence occupying the void. If Marian's suicide helped to enforce a famous twenty-
year hiatus in the *Education* after 1872, a silence mimed by the hooded memorial
figure that Augustus Saint-Gaudens crafted for Rock Creek Cemetery,[36] Blessed
Mary stood in that chasm as well.

At the close of *The Education,* though, Adams gives no sign that the Virgin's
existential presence enters the silence—or relieves the loneliness—of his old age.
Two chapters before the end, in "Vis Nova," he describes a 1904 return visit to
Marian shrines in France, where he again feels the force of his "adorable mistress"
penetrate "to the last fibre of his being" (1148). This time Virgin rules machine to
the extent of forcing Adams to buy an automobile to pursue her. Yet, if "the Virgin had not even altogether gone" (1149), Adams could not see her grace affecting
the bloody chaos of twentieth-century history. In 1918, the year he died, poster
artist A. E. Foringer envisioned the American Madonna in a pietà posture that
contained—but scarcely averted—the sacrificial horrors of World War I (figure 5.2).
Yet already by 1905, with Adams's dear friends John Hay and Clarence King both
gone, he blends elegiac sadness with a stoic recognition that for him, too, "It was
time to go" (1181). His labors, his attachments, his absorption in the Virgin—all
seem to lie in the past. Having described himself throughout in the guise of a
detached, third-person object of narration, he cannot avoid ending on a plaintive
note that betrays the extremity of his personal distress.

By this time, then, the Virgin has receded from immediate view. Having earlier
tried to define her spirituality almost exclusively under the rubric of force,[37] Adams
cannot sustain a confirmation of her presence beyond the hypothetical. Adams

FIGURE 5.2. A. E. Foringer, "The Greatest Mother in the World" (poster, 1918). From the Library of Congress.

remains a "Unitarian mystic" without benefit of mystical experience, a "conservative christian Anarchist" (1151) without Christian commitment.[38] His "heart's hope," as R. P. Blackmur discerned, "was his soul's despair" for "he had no faith, but only the need of it."[39] Similarly, in the author's composite "Prayer to the Virgin of Chartres" and "Prayer to the Dynamo" composed in 1900 (1202–7), he had offered less a full-blown prayer and testimony of faith than a lament that "ourselves we worship" in the new age of technocratic unbelief. Although Adams here addresses the "Gracious Lady" with a claim to "feel the energy of faith / Not in the future science, but in you," he does not quite profess to invest himself in this faith. Neither does faith relieve the pain of waiting "for what the final void will show" or render meaningful "the futile folly of the Infinite." It is hard to tell just where this "prayer" shades into an effusion of nostalgic fantasy.

Nonetheless, the earnestness with which Adams presents his poetic appeal to Divine Maternity is arresting. Contrasting his own "mocking art" with the Virgin's spirit of beauty, which passes rational understanding, he seeks here a stoic peace beyond the strivings of ambition. In this ideal dispensation, Adams would dwell for once not on the egotistical problem of his own failure but on the all-encompassing, tragic mystery of "the failure of the light" that Mary bore:

> Help me to see! not with my mimic sight—
>   With yours! which carried radiance, like the sun,
> Giving the rays you saw with—light in light—
>   Tying all suns and stars and worlds in one.
>
> Help me to know! not with my mocking art—
>   With you, who knew yourself unbound by laws;
> Gave God your strength, your life, your sight, your heart,
>   And took from him the Thought that Is—the Cause.
>
> Help me to feel! not with my insect sense,—
>   With yours that felt all life alive in you;
> Infinite heart beating at your expense;
>   Infinite passion breathing the breath you drew!
>
> Help me to bear! not my own baby load,
>   But yours; who bore the failure of the light,
> The strength, the knowledge and the thought of God,—
>   The futile folly of the Infinite! (1207)

ELIOT'S ARCHETYPAL LADY
OF SEA AND GARDEN

The Recovery of Myth

Myth, Modernism, and Lady Mary

In the first quarter of the twentieth century, a critic reviewed a major literary work, penned by an author born to New England Unitarianism, that abounds in irony and cosmopolitan skepticism. Self-consciously addressing the problem of modernity, the work under review highlights images of discontinuity and cultural fragmentation. Clearly, the reviewer finds much to dislike—as well as some things to admire—about this expression of malaise, alienation, and "dissolvent" disbelief coming from "a sceptical patrician." Was such a critical response provoked by T. S. Eliot's *The Waste Land*? One might suspect as much. In fact, the review in question was written *by* Eliot, not about Eliot, and its object is *The Education of Henry Adams*.

Even as Eliot here admits his kinship with Adams, another melancholic patrician once inoculated with the "Boston Doubt," he attacks that Prufrock-like shadow of himself who "could believe in nothing."[1] Eight years before announcing his conversion to Christianity and three years before publishing *The Waste Land,* Eliot bemoans the uncentered skepticism, verging on narcissism, into which he thinks Adams had been drawn. (Adams's flirtation with Mariolatry, which never develops into full-blown existential commitment, apparently fails to impress this reviewer enough to qualify his judgment that Adams "could believe in nothing.") Already Eliot resolves to find beliefs capable of sustaining spiritual life beyond the wasteland of modern Western civilization. Influenced by F. H. Bradley's philosophy of the Absolute and James G. Frazer's anthropological theory of monomyth, he is also driven to search for some unifying scheme of reality beyond—or antecedent to—specters of fragmentation.

What deeper roots of love and spiritual meaning might survive the aridity of modern culture? Where might they be found amid the "stony rubbish"[2] of a post-Christian world, and how might their fruits be cultivated? This larger search, whose character Eliot eventually understands to be religious, involves for him the recovery of myth and revalidation of "the mythical method."[3] In an age of analysis and demythologizing rationalism, Eliot looked retrospectively toward the symbolic expression of myth for hints of continuity between the inner worlds of archaic and contemporary humanity. Thus, his notes on *The Waste Land* underscore his debt to Jessie Weston's account of the Grail legend and to James Frazer's view of archaic vegetative myths in *The Golden Bough*. As Jewel Spears Brooker points out, a distinctive trait of Eliot's international "high modernism" is the impulse "to move forward by spiraling back and refiguring the past."[4] *The Waste Land*, a prominent literary instance of the case, refigures several dimensions of the past; yet it appeared in print only a year after the human race was supposed to have advanced—according to Henry Adams's scientific theory of history—beyond its ethereal phase to the very limits of thought.[5]

In time, of course, Eliot's personal response to his studies in comparative religion, anthropology, and mythography contributed to his movement toward a public profession of Christian belief in 1927. This decision is often discussed in relation to Eliot's conservative social and political views. Yet two other points are worth amplifying here with regard to the particular, Anglo-Catholic version of Christianity he embraced. First, the understanding of "tradition" prevalent within this historic branch of the church catholic incorporates ritual and ceremonial forms not unlike those anthropologists had been discovering in archaic religion. Instead of rejecting all pagan and mythological elements as antithetical to Gospel faith, Anglo-Catholic piety tends to subsume them—to baptize them, as it were—into Christian theology. Eliot came to perceive the old myths intersecting with history, gaining new veracity and transfigured meaning in the light of the Incarnation.

The second salient point involves an application of this principle. From Anglo-Catholicism's general willingness to see religious truth conveyed through mythopoeic forms, it follows that Marian devotion in particular finds much greater acceptance in this High Church atmosphere than in mainstream Protestantism—or, for that matter, in Broad Church sectors of Anglicanism.[6] Such a disposition can be seen, for example, in William Force Stead, the Anglican clergyman and writer who performed Eliot's baptism. In a testimony of spiritual search titled *The Shadow of Mount Carmel: A Pilgrimage,* Stead reveals his highly emotional response to the shrines of Notre Dame of Paris and Our Lady of Lourdes as symbols of "something deep and true in our hearts."[7]

By reflecting on how Eliot envisions the Virgin Mother artistically, through Dante, one can deepen understanding of the peculiar feminine symbology that pervades his poetic corpus. If divine womanhood, represented mostly in pre-Christian or non-Christian figures, remains a subordinate concern in *The Waste Land,* it can nonetheless be described as an essential element in the mythic substructure of that poem, whereas in "Ash-Wednesday" and parts of the *Four Quartets,* specifically Marian material rises to unmistakable prominence.

On balance, Eliot's poetry identifies the Marian Madonna—in contrast to the Belladonna—with an ideal of beauty, love, and fecundity rarely embodied in contemporary life. The fecundity in question is at once sexual and procreative, emotional, aesthetic, and spiritual. Of course, insofar as Eliot's Madonna corresponds to a gendered ideal of womanhood, it is hard to view her without a certain critical skepticism—or apart from the biographical circumstances of personal and sexual anxiety involved in Eliot's first marriage and presumably mirrored in earlier poems like "Prufrock." Such skepticism may be compounded by the observation that, apart from Madonna women, wanton or Belladonna women represent a fair proportion of the female presence in Eliot's poetry.[8] Read in sociological terms, then, Eliot's Madonna can be an embarrassment.

Yet in mythic terms, the Virgin Mary represented for Eliot the coalescence of a traditional and orthodox, yet deeply personal and affective faith. Symbolically, Eliot's verse evocations of the Virgin also conveyed a critical judgment of modern culture. Fully aware of the mythic roots of Marian piety beneath Christian orthodoxy, Eliot emblematized the Madonna as a garden oasis of solace and spiritual sustenance amid the mythopoeic desert of current civilization. What is more, the poet's anomalous position as Unitarian American turned Anglo-Catholic Englishman focuses the oxymoronic tension inherent in the cultural development of an American Madonna.

The Sibyl and Belladonna of *The Waste Land*

In *The Waste Land,* the prospect of a redemptive female presence is raised at several junctures but never fully realized. Neither, for that matter, does the poem ever realize that broader prospect of renewal, salvation, and resurrection implied by Eliot's title for part 1, "The Burial of the Dead," within the context of Anglican funeral liturgy. Although the epigraph to the published version directs attention from the very start to a prophetic goddess, the Sibyl of Cumae, this former guide of Aeneas is represented in the citation from Petronius as withered, despondent, imprisoned in a bottle.[9] And the poem's subsequent reliance on mythical allusions to dead and dying male gods, the heroic grail quest, and the associated plight of the Fisher King seems heavily dominated by masculine symbology. In one sense, then, the saving influence of divine womanhood looks conspicuous here mainly by its absence; as Grover Smith says of *The Waste Land,* "It sacrifices along with love the feminine image which in a more nearly Dantean pattern would betoken salvation."[10]

In subtler ways, however, the poem does evoke the essential feminine side of its governing mythology. For though the wound of the Fisher King describes an aggregate failure of sexuality, fecundity, love, and spirituality, his recovery of wholeness and health would issue symbolically from exposure to the Holy Grail. The Grail, in turn, not only blends Christian and pre-Christian narratives but also evokes psychosexual meaning as a feminine mother-symbol in contrast to the phallic import of the lance. In some versions of the legend, a maiden is designated to guard or bear the Grail. Jessie Weston specifies plainly that the Grail, in conjunction with vegetation ritual, "represents the Female, reproductive energy."[11] Moreover, traditional mythography images the land, that face of physical nature dominated by the Fisher King and affected by his blight in Eliot's poem, as feminine. Joseph Bentley has pointed out how the wasteland fables support a gender division in which "the king is the guilty male, and the land is the woman whose health is impaired, whose fruit-fulness is lost."[12] So also in Eliot's *Waste Land* the portrayal of women, which here is often shaped by mythology, stresses either their elevating, divinely redemptive capacities or the desolation that ensues from their corruption.

In this gathering of both blessed and sinister women, the hyacinth girl of part 1 presents an enduring image of the first type. She inhabits the garden, an original antithesis of the wasteland. Particularly by association with the erotic and fecund hyacinth, she qualifies as a mother of life—in effect, as an Eve allied to the free-spirited "Marie" named in the opening verse stanza.[13] According to Grover Smith, she satisfies also the mythic role of "the Grail-bearer, the maiden bringing love."[14] But she embodies a life and erotic promise to which the speaker seems unable to respond, for she offers him flowers:

> —Yet when we came back, late, from the Hyacinth garden,
> Your arms full, and your hair wet, I could not
> Speak, and my eyes failed, I was neither
> Living nor dead, and I knew nothing,
> Looking into the heart of light, the silence.
> Oed' und leer das Meer. (38)

Laden with water and bathed in bright light, the hyacinth girl stands in memory not only as Lady of the Garden but also as Lady of the Sea. In her primal fluidity, she fulfills Frazer's description of "the goddess Istar (Astarte, Aphrodite) [who] descends to Hades to fetch the water of life with which to restore the dead Thammuz."[15] As such she mirrors inversely the archetype of "Belladonna, the Lady of the Rocks." This Belladonna recalls, in turn, the woman surrounded by rock and sea in Leonardo's famous painting (figure 6.1).[16] The Lady of the Sea abides as a still point of transcendent peace (a true *maris stella*) even when the questing speaker cannot spot her in the wasteland or in the oceanic emptiness of loss and death by water. By contrast, Belladonna is the endlessly opportunistic "lady of situations" whose name betrays her identity not only as shadow or anti-Madonna but also as poisonous plant and as seductive, deceptive bearer of cosmetics.[17]

Artificially conjured to life from a pack of cards by another maimed sibyl, Madame Sosostris, Belladonna becomes a composite figure of lovelessness both ancient and modern. She serves as presiding spirit not only of the desert with its rubble of broken images, including "Dead tree" and "dry stone," but also of the "Unreal City." She reflects the deracinated desperation of today's secular city as well as the degraded, manipulative forms of sexual interaction familiar throughout other phases of postarchaic Western civilization.

Such degradation pervades part 2, "A Game of Chess." Here a glittering Cleopatra figure, a Belladonna enthroned in her boudoir, reveals the charms of "her strange synthetic perfumes" rather than the force of her passion for another. Here, too, a more vulgar account of loveless sex in marriage issues in Lil's abortion. In lines Eliot

FIGURE 6.1. Leonardo da Vinci, *Virgin of the Rocks*. From the Louvre, Paris (Giraudon/Art Resource, New York).

removed from part 4, the goddess Fresca pursues self-indulgent narcissism to the point of preferring food, clever books, a "steaming bath," and "dreams of love and pleasant rapes" to real-life encounters.[18] And as a case of unenduring love, the apparently glamorous affair of Elizabeth and Leicester (part 3) bears more resemblance than one might suppose to the mechanical intercourse between typist and carbuncular clerk—or even, in some measure, to King Tereus's brutal violation of Philomel.

That Eliot links his Belladonna figure so persistently with prostitution, seduction, and lust does not mean, however, that he attaches chief blame to womankind for the general desolation he portrays. Clearly, afflicted characters like Lil and the typist—to say nothing of Philomel and Ophelia—are as much sinned against by men as they are sinners. Moreover, the consciousness of Tiresias, who functions as an androgynous sibyl, presumably bridges the great divide of gender. But insofar as that divide still stands, the poem's underlying mythic pattern would make male guilt and impotence primarily responsible for the ruin of the land.[19] Extending the poet's contention that "all the women" in this poem "are one woman" (p. 52, n. 218), Philip Sicker suggests that even Belladonna must be seen as but a fallen or corrupted version of the hyacinth goddess: "Thus, in Eliot's eyes, Philomel and Persephone, Cleopatra and Venus and all the other legendary women of our tradition are, at best, mere incomplete reflections of that original, single woman, Marie, the hyacinth goddess, who was neither victim nor seductress, but an equal, eager constituent in the act of love."[20]

It is telling, though, that after "the nymphs are departed" in part 3, the Lady of Sea and Garden never reappears at the poem's close. Despite references to fishing, rain, and the sea, the sign of her presence in a coalescence of rock, water, spring, and pool remains unfulfilled. Instead of the beatitude that would mark her return, the poem concludes with images of "maternal lamentation" in Eastern Europe and a ruined Grail chapel full of dry bones. There is no final word of regeneration from divine womanhood to offset Sibyl's opening word of death wish. Beyond the final Sanskrit incantations and the shoring of fragments against ruin, only Eliot's citation from the *Purgatorio* does much to qualify this gloom.

Even here, in alluding to a hopeful speech of Arnaut Daniel before his plunge into refining fire, the poem does not re-present the blessed woman overtly. One must seek her at several removes from the arid plain, starting with Eliot's subtextual note (n. 428, 54) that extends citation from the Provençal speech in *Purgatorio* 26.148: "'Ara vos prec per aquella valor / que vos guida al som de l'escalina, / sovegna vos a temps de ma dolor.'"[21] Ultimately, of course, that guiding virtue is God—but it is visibly embodied in Beatrice, who is about to replace Virgil in leading Dante's ascent and whom Virgil addresses as "donna di virtù" in Inferno 2.76. Daniel's speech points toward the pilgrim-narrator's imminent arrival in the earthly paradise (*Purgatorio* 28),[22] a verdant refuge of water and flowers inhabited by a mysterious "bella donna" (28.43).

Undoubtedly, this blessed woman, later named Matilda, anticipates Beatrice, whose revelation of love connects her in turn with the Blessed Virgin. By 1929, Eliot shows esteem for Christian theological values in the course of observing, "The system of Dante's organization of sensibility—the contrast between higher and lower carnal love, the transition from Beatrice living to Beatrice dead, rising to the cult of the Virgin, seems to me to be his own." But he admits it took him "many years" to appreciate Dante's characterization of Beatrice and portrayal of beatitude, in contrast to "what the modern world can conceive as cheerfulness."[23] Understandably, *The Waste Land* offers only hints of this recognition yet to come.

Toward Our Lady of *la Vita Nuova*

On the way to "Ash-Wednesday," Eliot revisits the desert landscape in "The Hollow Men" (1925). But he also introduces here a rose symbolism that will abide, bearing rich evocations of divine womanhood, in later poems. Exiled in a "hollow valley" with no hopeful eyes turned toward them, Eliot's stuffed men can only lean together:

> Sightless, unless
> The eyes reappear
> As the perpetual star
> Multifoliate rose
> Of death's twilight kingdom
> The hope only
> Of empty men. (58)

The beloved eyes recall those of Dante's Beatrice and, at the heights of paradise, those of Blessed Mary, "the perpetual star."[24] In addition to holding supreme honor among created beings in Dante's multifoliate rose of heaven, Mary herself traditionally figures as the rose of divine love who bears the flower of Christ. This topos of the rose as Mary's flower, which Dante likewise develops, gained prominence after Bernard of Clairvaux first articulated it in the twelfth century.[25]

In fact, the hollow men's corporate lamentation seems to echo that found in the traditional eleventh-century Salve Regina addressed to Mary. Suppliants in the prayer deem themselves banished children of Eve, exiles from paradise who stand "mourning and weeping" in this world's deathly "valley of tears" (*gementes et flentes in hac lacrimarum valle*). They implore Mother Mary, gracious Queen of Heaven, to turn her "eyes of mercy" on them (*illos tuos misericordes oculos ad nos converte*). In this place of desolation and bitterness, they crave the attention of one able to embody "our life, our sweetness, and our hope" (*vita, dulcedo, et spes nostra*).

Eliot's preconversion poem stops short of naming "The hope only / Of Empty Men" as Mary. Speakers in "The Hollow Men," oppressed by the shadow that still falls "between the conception / And the creation," witness no divine birth in their "cactus land." If the Salve Regina did influence this poem's language and imagery, as seems probable, its ironic presence never becomes so intrusive as that of the Lord's Prayer. But within a few years, several of Eliot's poems incorporate overt references to Marian material and liturgical texts. Such texts include not only the Salve Regina (invoked unmistakably in "Ash-Wednesday"), but also the Ave Maria (cited plainly though with ironically altered wording at the close of "Animula"), and the Angelus (in "The Dry Salvages").

In short monologue verses written between 1927 and 1930 and presented as "Ariel Poems," Eliot reflects his movement toward Christian faith. But the poet finds that conversion, instead of banishing his congenital melancholy, confronts him anew with the enigma of the cross. Neither the death of his mother in 1929 nor marital woes during this period helped to brighten his mood. Although the speaker in "Marina" does testify to the grace and joy realized in personal renewal, his counterparts in "A Song for Simeon," "Journey of the Magi," and "Animula" encounter more affliction than consolation. As Eliot enters his "new life," he is drawn to ponder more deeply the synergistic relation between life and death envisioned in Christian revelation. If Mary is the mother of new life and God's chosen vessel of beatitude, she is also the *mater dolorosa,* chosen to bear the anguish of her son's hideous death. Particularly in "A Song for Simeon" and "Journey of the Magi," Eliot expresses the travail that accompanies spiritual change. His male speakers even tend to identify with the labor pains that the woman of Nazareth endured at Jesus' birth and still more at his death.

In "A Song for Simeon," of course, the biblical narrative that Eliot adapted from Luke 2.22–35 already shows the aged Simeon identifying with Mary's predicted sorrow. As the infant Savior is presented for circumcision in the temple, Simeon prophesies that a sword will eventually pierce his heart—and the heart of his mother. For that matter, the new age will bring strife for many. Even as Eliot's Simeon prays collectively and individually for "peace" (in phrasing that anticipates the liturgical Agnus Dei), he foresees that God's peace will shatter the outward tranquility of believers for generations to come. For would not Jesus himself later declare that he came "not to send peace but a sword" (Matthew 10.34)?

Thus, the "certain hour of maternal sorrow" that Simeon predicts for Mary extends beyond that "time of cords and scourges and lamentation" marking the Passion of Jesus. The coming "time of sorrow" carries threats of apocalyptic crisis for other mothers as well: "But woe unto them that are with child, and to them that give suck, in those days! for there shall be great distress in the land . . ." (Luke 21.23).

Aged Simeon shows himself acutely aware of the intersection of birth and death set before him. On the one hand, decease is omnipresent. The poem situates Simeon's speech within the dying season of winter; laden with recollections and forebodings, Simeon also faces his own season of decline while "waiting for the death wind." As a twilight utterance, Simeon's Nunc Dimittis is traditionally recited or sung in the Anglican service of Evening Prayer. Yet, on the other hand, Simeon perceives signs of life in this "birth season of decease." He notices that "the Roman hyacinths are blooming in bowls," a sign of agonistic renascence that recalls the hyacinth girl in *The Waste Land*. And he recognizes the new promise for Israel presented in the Child as well as the birthing tribulations still to come for New Israel.

Eliot's octogenarian knows he will not live to help initiate the new order of God's kingdom. For that matter, it is uncertain whether he ever possessed the courage or charisma needed to become a Christian apostle, martyr, saint, or mystic. He no longer aspires to receive "the ultimate vision" of heaven on earth. Simeon does not excel or achieve. After his momentary encounter with the Child, he does not appear to accomplish anything more in the world. But he does accept. Although by nature a fearful, fretful, and slightly self-pitying old man, he is led by grace to declare his inner consent to God's will and ways. And that, as the Magus would say, is satisfactory. This simple yet profound act of consent enables him to pass graciously to what Eliot earlier termed "death's other kingdom."

A line heading the poem's final stanza can therefore be read as pivotal: "According to thy word." This direct citation of Luke 2.29 likewise repeats Mary's word of assent to the angel in Luke 1.38: "'Behold the handmaiden of the Lord; be it unto me according to thy word.'" Thus, Simeon's elliptical "According to thy word" amounts to more than a recognition of biblical providence. Its initial Marian context supplies the sense of existential commitment, with Simeon's first-person consent offered in spiritual anamnesis of Mary's crucial assent to divine life, assent that in turn brought forth "the still unspeaking and unspoken Word." Though hesitant, Simeon consents inwardly to the Word and brings his consent to speech (recreated in the poem) in a way that helps fulfill the Word.

In "A Song for Simeon," the subtle conflation of biblical texts involving both Simeon and Mary[26] underscores Eliot's growing sense of Mary's import as spiritual anima and vessel of divine grace. This perception, encouraged by the poet's increasingly religious response to Dante, becomes most manifest in "Ash-Wednesday." Yet in the darker mood of "A Song for Simeon," one senses the Blessed Mother's presence even more as *mater dolorosa* than as mother of saving joy. Only "Marina," among the Ariel poems, offers plainly joyous testimony to the grace made available to "empty men" (58) through blessed womanhood.

The circumstance of Marina in Eliot's poem, inspired by Shakespeare's *Pericles* and Seneca's *Hercules,* bears no direct relation to the biblical Mary. In fact, Shakespeare's story has Marina working as charwoman in a brothel at the time Pericles recognizes this lost daughter he had believed dead. Yet the dreamlike reunion dramatized in Eliot's monologue provokes something of a miraculous renewal for the speaker. As a half-forgotten realization of the speaker's anima,[27] Marina assumes a divine presence that for the moment of epiphany dissolves death and deadly sin. They "are become unsubstantial, reduced by a wind, / A breath of pine, and the woodsong fog / By this grace dissolved in place" (72).

For Grover Smith, "Marina's apparent restoration has conferred a grace, a life-giving and sin-purging benediction" that invests her "for purposes of the poem, with the characteristics of flesh clothing a divine emanation." John H. Timmerman likewise finds Marina mediating "the beatitude of grace" and absolution, for she is "the beatific figure who nonetheless, in the narrator's experience, obliterates the past horror and transforms the present in the recognition of grace."[28] As something of a goddess who transcends fleshly mortality, Marina is born at sea and linked to oceanic imagery. What is more, Eliot's poem places the speaker on a sailing vessel nearing landfall at the moment he senses her presence once again. Her form and face emerge from the subconscious depths "where all the waters meet"; they are limned by divine wind, by the odor of New England pine, by the song of woodthrush.

Like the beatific woman of the Ave Maris Stella, Marina offers a presence—"more distant than stars and nearer than the eye" to guide the speaker aright on his life journey. Marina inspires his effort to "life in a world of time beyond me," to resign his former life in favor of "that unspoken," to look confidently toward "the hope, the new ships." The lost child returns to him with the unexpected shape and spiritual authority of an adult. Though the speaker finally blesses Marina's recovery by acknowledging her as "My daughter," the poem also portrays the daughter as mother of his renewal. This paradox suggests how the new life reconstitutes all former relations. It anticipates as well the famous spiritual paradox we shall see represented by Eliot's citation from Dante—"Figlia del tuo figlio" (Mary as daughter of her Son)—in "the Dry Salvages."

Eliot's Soul Sisters: The Sacred and Profane Ladies of "Ash-Wednesday"

Manifestly born of Eliot's conversion to *la vita nuova,* "Ash-Wednesday" (1930) also shows a distinctive preoccupation with the Blessed Lady, an anima figure jointly evocative of Mary and of other soul sisters. The poem is central in several senses.

Falling between *The Waste Land* and *Four Quartets,* it lies roughly at the chrono-logical midpoint of a poetic career. It is also something of a midlife statement inso-far as it appeared in final form when Eliot was forty-two—or, in Dantesque spiri-tual terms, near the middle of the journey of his life. Appropriately, too, the Christian liturgy for Ash Wednesday confronts believers with their own mortality. Origi-nally dedicated to the poet's first wife, Vivienne, during a temporary reunion fol-lowing separation, the poem marks a turning point in the poet's hopes for personal transformation and rebirth.

More than any other poem Eliot wrote, "Ash-Wednesday" is permeated with the flavor of Marian devotion.[29] (Some sense of this devotion is conveyed by Murillo's famous image in Figure 6.2.) Accordingly, Louis Martz has wondered "why

FIGURE 6.2. Bartolomé Estaban Murillo, *Immaculate Conception.* From the Louvre, Paris (Foto Marburg/Art Resource, New York). This image hung in the bedroom of Eliot's parents in St. Louis.

Eliot, recently converted to the Church of England, should so insistently in this poem echo the Roman liturgy rather than the Book of Common Prayer." Martz sensibly concludes that Eliot's "choice is not ecclesiastical: it is thematic and poetical" as shaped in response to literary precursors such as Dante, Cavalcanti, and Petrarch.[30] Yet it is worth noting that even Roman practice accords no special role to Marian piety in the observance of Ash Wednesday. Initiating Lent, the church's liturgy (both Roman and Anglican) for Ash Wednesday highlights penitence, cognizance of mortality, and the spiritual nexus between sin and death. So one may yet wonder why Eliot's Lady, in her various forms, figures so prominently in a poem titled "Ash-Wednesday."

One explanation returns us to Dante. Eliot was powerfully drawn to Dante's vision of penitence as all-encompassing gift of personal renewal, rather than as somber duty or punishment. Although "Ash-Wednesday" betrays sentiments of guilt, regret, and uncertainty on the part of its monologic speaker, its Dantesque understanding of purgation is ultimately hopeful. The poem traces a contemplative search for salvation that leads from the desert's death-in-life toward the divine "Garden / Where all loves end" (62). And in this turning toward salvation, the Lady of the Garden fulfills multiple symbolic roles. She serves not only as lover and soul sister—that is, reflexive anima—to the poem's male protagonist but also as mother to his spiritual rebirth.

The shifting, variegated image of the Lady in "Ash-Wednesday" corresponds to the speaker's struggle to reconcile human and divine love. To complete the "turning" of conversion requires more than an about-face, more than a simple denunciation of evil and affirmation of good. For Eliot, influenced in turn by Dante, the process feels more like ascending a spiral stair from lesser to greater goods, with occasional stumbles and confusion along the way. The central line of escalation runs from profane to sacred love, with the beloved earthly lady rediscovered ultimately in the transfigured form of the Sacred Lady. But the soul, in its twisting path of ascent, must sort out the difference between elevating and debasing versions of desire, between salutary and destructive versions of profane eroticism.

Accordingly, our impression of the enigmatic woman in "Ash-Wednesday" evolves from superimposed images of the profane lady and the Sacred Lady. The profane lady, in turn, bears a dual identity. As a version of Belladonna shadowing the speaker's own insatiable lusts and shapes of deceit, she distracts and devours him in consort with the three white leopards. But for Eliot, as for Dante, the sexually alluring profane lady can also become an earthly icon of heavenly beauty. This lady of the rose and of sanctified desire retains some positive relation to the otherwise distracting eroticism evoked in part 3, with its Maytime imagery of lilac and sweetly dispersed brown hair. The more appealing sense of sexual womanhood stirs memory of the hyacinth girl.

So also Eliot's Sacred Lady appears in multiple guises—as lover, mother, and sister. As a beloved extension of the profane lady, she functions as a Beatrice. Charged with an erotic appeal but purely sub rosa, this lady projects goodness, loveliness at a distance, and contemplative repose. Particularly in part 2, her image blends into that of the Sacred Mother—identified preeminently with Mary as Mater Dei, Magna

Mater, and Womb of the Word. Finally, too, the speaker recognizes the veiled woman as "Blessed sister"—that is, as feminine kin to his own inner being. Because the Lady of Silences speaks to the veiled, recessive depths of the soul, the monologist honors her as his soul sister and guide in the contemplative journey.

The poem opens on a note of dissatisfaction and weariness verging on despair. Indeed, its litany of denials seems initially to deny the very prospect of conversion. The aging speaker insists he does "not hope to turn again," does "not hope to know again / The infirm glory of the positive hour" or "the one veritable transitory power." Though spiritually desiccated, he believes he "cannot drink / There, where trees flower, and springs flow, for there is nothing again."

Yet insofar as these negations confirm the vanity of worldly striving to possess "this man's gift and that man's scope," they prepare the way for spiritual renewal. The *via negativa* aspect of purgation first requires stripping away illusions about one's moral condition, ambitions, and mortality. Having confessed his destitution of spirit, the speaker intimates that he is yet disposed to hope again when he voices a decidedly undespairing prayer of petition:

> Because these wings are no longer wings to fly
> But merely vans to beat the air
> The air which is now thoroughly small and dry
> Smaller and dryer than the will
> Teach us to care and not to care
> Teach us to sit still.
>
> Pray for us sinners now and at the hour of our death
> Pray for us now and at the hour of our death. (61)

The closing refrain from the Ave Maria aptly follows the speaker's petition for engaged serenity of will. For at the Annunciation, God's Mother offers a paradigm of acceptance that settles her at the still center of Being. Though Mary carries within her the Word "within the world and for the world," this womb of the Logos remains "still," essentially silent yet centered. After enunciating the Magnificat, Mary, too, recedes from Gospel prominence to become a "Lady of silences." It is to such stillness of contemplative peace, beyond chatter and the anxiety of further turning, that the speaker aspires.

In part 1, the speaker tries to interpret the pain of separation from his beloved lady as a form of renunciation: "I renounce the blessed face / And renounce the voice." Yet the Salve Regina, which is invoked directly in part 4, supplies a context of allusion[31] in which such pain derives from provisional rather than permanent loss during "this our exile." Anticipating the new Magnificat he would sound at his return to the Mother's garden of love, the speaker repeatedly interrupts his opening lamentation with the telling word *rejoice*. If the main challenge of "Ash-Wednesday" is to reconstruct a disintegrated soul, the speaker can rejoice that he has come to know his elemental need of "having to construct something /Upon which to rejoice."

The sense of recognition is underscored in part 2, which Eliot first published separately in 1927 under the title of "Salutation." At one level, the salutation in question recalls Beatrice's greeting to Dante in the *Vita Nuova*.[32] But insofar as Eliot's Blessed Lady bears a composite identity, the "Salutation" must remind us also of Gabriel's famous greeting to Mary, or of Mary's reciprocated salutation to Elizabeth at the Visitation. In these biblical precedents, the dynamic of interchange typically runs from salutation through annunciation to verbal response. After Gabriel salutes Mary and announces the nativity, Mary pronounces her consent. And after Elizabeth hears Mary's salutatory voice (as does John, presumably, albeit in utero) and recognizes through the Spirit what it announces, she responds with her own Ave Maria. Mary, in turn, answers Elizabeth's response with the Magnificat.

Yet when the speaker in part 2 of Eliot's poem addresses his mysterious lady, she gives him no direct response or sign of recognition. In fact, the Lady remains speechless. In her initial bearing as a maidenly Beatrice or Matilda,[33] she "honours the Virgin in meditation" and shows herself silently "withdrawn / in a white gown to contemplation." When the speaker's vision of her deepens in the next stanza to reflect the recognizably Marian figure of Mother in the Garden, she remains a "Lady of silences" offering "Speech without word and / Word of no speech." Likewise the dream visitant of part 4, who walks in the "white and blue of Mary's color," appears as a "silent sister" who "spoke no word."

Although the Lady of silences does not speak or answer directly, for she carries "the Word without a word," she does inspire verbal responses from the depths of others. Thus, part 2 testifies that through the Lady's intercessory and purgative power, the speaker's dry bones are revivified to express songs of the soul. In effect, the poet recognizes the Blessed Lady as his muse in the *vita nuova*. If "the hollow round" of his skull first connotes a desert emptiness, the emptiness is one that purgative beasts—who devour the old Eliot—have prepared for a vital infusion.[34] So the former "hollow" becomes holy indeed. Eliot's salute to the Lady is animated by a life and grace that confirms her salutary inspiration in *his* life. Viewed in broadest perspective, the Marian rose contains Christ incarnate as both child and adult, as both resurrected and broken Savior; the Blessed Mother encompasses a life at once "Calm and distressed / Torn and most whole." Anxious souls can identify the more readily with a mother who has pondered sorrow in her heart. So even as the evocative song of the bones shows a distressed speaker identifying with the object of his praise, it revives cadences heard in traditional litanies to the Virgin:

> Lady of silences
> Calm and distressed
> Torn and most whole
> Rose of memory
> Rose of forgetfulness
> Exhausted and life-giving
> Worried reposeful
> the single Rose
> Is now the Garden
> Where all loves end
> Terminate torment
> Of love unsatisfied

> The greater torment
> Of love satisfied
> End of the endless
> Journey to no end
> Conclusion of all that
> Is inconclusible
> Speech without word and
> Word of no speech
> Grace to the Mother
> For the Garden
> Where all love ends. (62)

This glimpse of paradise regained identifies the rose, perennial emblem of both profane and sacred love, with the garden of creation. Just as the Lady of the Garden where love begins is Eve, so her biblical antitype in the garden "where all love ends" is (Ave) Maria. And just as Eve, the mother of all living, occupies an Eden where God walks "in the cool of the day," so Lady Mary becomes mother of the new creation and a paradise in person. Particularly in the Western mystical tradition, the book of Canticles is often read prophetically to envision Mary herself, or synecdochically her womb, as an enclosed garden. In Mary's womb, "The single Rose / Is now the Garden." The scattered bones sing "Grace to the Mother" in whom rests the encircled essence of creation. Recalling again St. Bernard's homage to Mary as rose in the *Paradiso,* Dominic Manganiello writes incisively on Eliot's response to Dante in this rose-garden sequence: "The Virgin's womb is itself a *hortus conclusis,* a sacred space; and, through her, Dante's hierarchical universe reverses into paradoxes which are reconciled by the Incarnation or the birth of the second Adam. This extraordinary event fulfils the fertile Word in Isaiah: 'Let the wilderness and dry lands exult / Let the wasteland rejoice and bloom' (35:1). Exodus similarly informs the central paradox of *Ash-Wednesday:* 'The desert in the garden the garden in the desert.'"[35]

Again, Eliot portrays the mother as silent because in the sacred space of her womb she contains the Word—because the Logos achieves its end, in her body, before it ever begins to address the world.[36] The preverbal power of maternity points toward the ineffable mystery of natural creation. In Eliot's poem, moreover, the divine mother affords desperate mortals hope of regeneration through the Word. Despite the new dispensation, this world remains largely a place of rocks and yew trees, aridity and death. But visions of the Lady hold out the prospect of a garden refuge for the soul even within the desert.

Beginning in part 4, Eliot draws increasingly on imagery of springs, fountains, and the sea to dramatize the rebirthing capacities of Our Lady. Within the bleak desert, she likewise makes "cool the dry rock" (64) and "firm the sand / In blue of larkspur, blue of Mary's colour."[37] Yet insofar as she shares humanity as a daughter of God, this Mother of Mercy can also be viewed as sister to every other human, including "those who walk in darkness" or "are terrified," those "who will not go away and cannot pray," those "who chose and oppose." She who once lived a human life in time can, in conjunction with her Son, better "Redeem / The time." And though the veiled sister may inhabit a dream landscape of time out of mind, this "higher dream" reflects only the depth of her continuing interior presence as soul sister or archetypal anima. Parts 4 and 5 suggest that the Holy Lady's fusion of maternal and sisterly roles only heightens her effectiveness as intercessor in prayer for the whole human race.

The poem's final section begins with telling variation on the original "Because I do not hope to turn again." A subtle substitution of "Although" for "Because" marks the shift in perspective. Although the speaker sustains his disenchantment with worldly prospects, he now subordinates this negation more clearly to spiritual affirmation. Signaled by verbs like *rejoices, renews, quickens,* and *recover,* the newfound hope emerges in a sequence initiated with an expansive picture of seascape:

> From the wide window toward the granite shore
> The white sails still fly seaward, seaward flying
> Unbroken wings. (66)

This brief relocation to an oceanic setting, particularly as contrasted with the desert, suggests new access to elemental rejuvenation for the "lost heart." To return to the sea is to revisit the archetypal cradle of life, of prenatal beatitude, of Venus; for the poet, it is also to revive fond personal memories of New England's coast. A psyche in ascension now appears in the beauty of white sails flying seaward with "Unbroken wings."[38] In "The Dry Salvages," Eliot will develop more or less explicitly the traditional nexus between ocean and Lady Mary as guiding spirit, or *Maris Stella,* of souls at sea. "Ash-Wednesday" never establishes so plain a connection. Neither does it resolve in a single clear image the multiple exposures we receive of the Lady as Beatrice, Matilda, or Mary, as Belladonna or courtly lover. But the poem does conclude with frank invocation—not merely description—of the Blessed Lady as spiritual director, intercessor, and soul sister with potent access to divinity:

> Blessèd sister, holy mother, spirit of the fountain, spirit of the garden,
> Suffer us not to mock ourselves with falsehood
> Teach us to care and not to care
> Teach us to sit still
> Even among these rocks,
> Sister, mother
> And spirit of the river, spirit of the sea,
> Suffer me not to be separated
>
> And let my cry come unto Thee. (67)

Significantly, some of the same petitions that the speaker directed to "God" in part 1 he now addresses unmistakably to the Holy Mother. Having already endured penitential exile from her blessed face and the paradise of natural love, he now locates in his vision of the Lady nothing less than a feminine face of God. Nothing less than the Holy Spirit renders her presiding spirit of fountain, garden, river, and sea. Yet it is in and through communion with the Son, rather than as independent goddess, that the Mother inspires such devotion. Hence the speaker aptly addresses his petition "not to be separated"—meaning, in ritual context of the Anima Christi prayer, not to be separated from Christ—to one who achieved singular unity with Christ both in spirit and in flesh.

It is likewise fitting that Dante's core belief in discovering "Our peace in His will" should be enfolded into the poem's intercessory prayer to Mother Mary. As Grover Smith observes, "the divine will, which Dante calls in the *Paradiso* (III, 86) 'that sea to which all moves,' is not only the destroyer of the old but the source of the new. It acts through the Virgin Stella Maris, the 'spirit of the sea.'"[39] Moreover, Christian teaching often sees Mary's reception of the Annunciation as exemplifying a self's ideal consonance with God's purpose. Her response expressed, indeed, in the language of Eliot's "Little Gidding," a "condition of complete simplicity / Costing not less than everything."

From one perspective, of course, Mary's readiness to resign her ego-centered will in favor of the divine will could seem an objectionable form of female submission. Yet for Eliot as for Dante, the self-renunciation in question applies equally to both sexes. Eliot believed that, far from betraying timidity, it engenders strength and freedom. Thus, he testifies to having experienced a singular impression of growth through self-surrender at his own first confession in 1928.[40] Such surrender affords strength of humility "not to mock ourselves with falsehood" as well as power of discernment "to care and not to care." Between "His will" and her spirit falls no shadow of separation. That the speaker, too, can pray at last "not to be separated" from "Thee" indicates that he has at least begun to know the peace that comes with full acceptance of death.

This hopeful finale to "Ash-Wednesday" is qualified by impressions that Eliot has yet to resolve all the tensions his poem exposes between sexuality and sacred love. Restoration of the soul's inner harmony remains incomplete. The phenomenal world remains a wasteland insofar as we are challenged to "sit still / Even among these rocks." But, like Emerson, who affirmed in his essay "Experience" that "yet is the God the native of these bleak rocks,"[41] Eliot perceives a green space surviving in the rocks. And when the rocks are made cool, and colored in Marian blue, they look less bleak. "Ash-Wednesday" points toward a coalescence of the mystical *via negativa* and *via affirmativa,* toward a unified sensibility able to encompass both the renunciation implied in the Marian title of "Virgin" and the affirmation of natural fecundity implied in "Mother." To be sure, this poem's penitential circumstance seems to weight its emphasis toward the *via negativa.* Yet, within the vast emotional and poetic range of *Four Quartets,* Eliot ends up developing a more integrative vision of the "one end" to which all inner journeying leads. It is therefore fitting to conclude with some remarks on Eliot's last great work.

"Best Dead Madonna this Side Atlantic": "The Dry Salvages" and the *Quartets*

Throughout most of *Four Quartets,* Marian motifs are sounded less conspicuously than in "Ash-Wednesday." Yet Eliot does invoke Lady Mary explicitly in Part 4 of "The Dry Salvages." And at several junctures of his meditative passage, he evokes impressions of divine womanhood—imagistically, in representing the rose garden and oceanic landscapes, as well as thematically, in probing the meaning of Incarnation.

At the start of "Burnt Norton," the epiphanic moment of beauty and love in the rose garden marks a rediscovery of natural beatitude that leads toward mystical transcendence. A mood of Edenic enchantment begins to arise as the speaker ventures past the gate into what seems an archetypal remnant of "our first world." The flower symbology also summons appealing thoughts of erotic love, though it seems Eliot tried to redirect his sexual feelings toward Emily Hale—with whom he shared the garden experience—into a safely ideal realm of hypothetical memory. Then, quite abruptly, a sense of encounter with deepest "reality" surfaces as the concrete pool fills "with water out of sunlight" (118). Combining Hindu, Buddhist, and Egyptian symbology, this encompassing vision of a lotus ascending "out of heart of light" has been related as well to Dante's *Paradiso* 12.28–29.

Yet another literary precedent for the episode Eliot describes might be found in *Paradiso* 23.70–83. There Beatrice calls Dante to turn his gaze toward a "fair garden" (*bel giardino*) with its rose—evidently the mystical rose of God's mother—that flowers in the shine of Christ's rays. He then sees "many hosts of splendours" illuminated suddenly from above by a light, streaming as through broken cloud, whose source remains unseen.[42] In any event, Eliot's rose and walled garden certainly recall traditional symbology of the Blessed Mother. Enclosing the Logos and the still center of the world, she contains in her Son the "one end, which is always present." "The point of intersection of the timeless / With time" (136) stands first upon the minute embryo she carries. It is fitting, then, that Dante should have St. Bernard address her as "the fixed point ('termine fisso') to which all things return."[43]

Only in the third quartet, though, does Eliot highlight Mary's role as the fixed star that guides souls through oceanic chaos to the "one end" of their voyaging. If each quartet focuses on a particular aspect of divinity in Christian terms, "The Dry Salvages" belongs, above all, to the Marian Mother of God.[44] The Blessed Lady emerges here from her natural mythic element: water. Despite its Trinitarian orthodoxy, then, the completed version of *Four Quartets* also shows some structural compatibility with Jungian images of a divine quaternary.

That the work's only explicit reference to Marian piety appears in "The Dry Salvages" might be surprising if, with Henry Adams, one regarded Mary as unknown in the United States. While the venerable English settings of "Burnt Norton," "East Coker," and "Little Gidding" stir reflection on the meaning of Western history and tradition, the landscapes inspiring meditation in "The Dry Salvages" mark this *Quartet* alone as unmistakably American. Eliot charges this poem's rhythms with American recollections of two great bodies of water: the Mississippi River, near his birthplace in St. Louis, and the Atlantic Ocean at Cape Ann, near his family's summer home in Gloucester.

Such memories are not purely nostalgic, though, because the poet brings to mind the destructive power of the Mississippi and Atlantic. Among the deities inciting these waters are "sullen, untamed and intractable" river gods, and sea gods who conceal their savage teeth—*les trois sauvages*—from unwary voyagers.

Among the "many voices" of the sea Eliot records are its heave, wail, howl, and whine, its bell tones of warning and of death. Despite other references to Asian religion, Eliot does not name the sea destroyer or choose to identify it with a devouring goddess such as Kali. Yet, in psychic terms, the same fluid, "feminine" element that contains these destroying energies contains also the creating, preserving influence personified in the lady who oversees the ocean in part 4. The sea creates starfish, whales, "the more delicate algae and the sea anemone" (130), even as it shatters lobsterpots, oars, boats, and sailors. Just as one can view "Time the destroyer" as a necessary complement of "time the preserver" (133), so also the poet can see both terrible anima and nurturing anima reflected in the elemental sea. The biblical Annunciation, an interruption of ordinary time declaring the renewal of life and time, is likewise a "calamitous annunciation" insofar as it leads toward death. It will sentence Mary also, with her Son, to a share in the Passion and demise of Emmanuel.

Throughout "The Dry Salvages," the sound of the tolling bell gains incremental force until in part 5 it becomes part of that "music heard so deeply / That it is not heard at all" (136).[45] The bell blends reminders of danger and death at sea with sounds that accompany devotional remembrance of the Annunciation in the Christian Angelus service. Eliot makes this connection plain in his lyrical petition to Mary in part 4:

> Lady, whose shrine stands on the promontory,
> Pray for all those who are in ships, those
> Whose business has to do with fish, and
> Those concerned with every lawful traffic
> And those who conduct them.
>
> Repeat a prayer also on behalf of
> Women who have seen their sons or husbands
> Setting forth, and not returning:
> Figlia del tuo figlio,
> Queen of Heaven.
>
> Also pray for those who were in ships, and
> Ended their voyage on the sand, in the sea's lips
> Or in the dark throat which will not reject them
> Or wherever cannot reach them the sound of the sea bell's
> Perpetual angelus. (135)

As A. M. Allchin remarks, the Angelus is "a form of prayer familiar throughout Catholic Christendom and certainly one which must have been often in Eliot's own heart and mind."[46] In its threefold structure marked at each stage with bell strokes, it recalls the angel's salutation to Mary, Mary's self-surrendering response,[47] and the fruit of that response as "The Word was made flesh and dwelt among us." It also calls worshipers to emulate Mary's responsiveness to God by responding themselves, in triple recitation of the Ave Maria. The ritual's concluding collect likewise appears as the liturgical collect for the feast of the Annunciation (March 25) in the *Book of Common Prayer*: "We beseech thee, O Lord, pour thy grace into our hearts; that, as we have known the incarnation of thy Son Jesus Christ by the message of

an angel, so by his cross and passion we may be brought unto the glory of his resurrection; through the same Jesus Christ our Lord."

Thus, the Angelus leads toward bittersweet recollection of Christ's Incarnation,
the central point of *Four Quartets*. It also dramatizes the human imperative to respond
to that "gift half understood" of Incarnation, a response that Eliot sums up as comprising "prayer, observance, discipline, thought and action" (136). The lyric in part
4 represents Mary's crucial position in the mystery of Incarnation by invoking her
at the start as the "Lady, whose shrine stands on the promontory." She stands, therefore, at the meeting point of sea and shore, at the elevated threshold of time and
eternity. The time of her Annunciation endures, in Allchin's words, as a "moment
which makes sense of all other moments" because it "is truly in time, not out of
time,"[48] though it brings an incursion of the divine Word from eternity.

One might suspect that the shrine Eliot portrays can be located on an actual site
in Gloucester where Our Lady of Good Voyage Church, on Prospect Street, overlooks the harbor.[49] According to Helen Gardner, Charles Olson even addressed a
postcard of the Marian statue on this site to Pound, identifying it as "my Lady that
Possum stole" and the "Best dead Madonna this side Atlantic." Yet, in a note that
Eliot attached to this card after it was passed on to him, he denies any knowledge
of the statue and insists that his long absence from Gloucester forced him instead to
image a shrine from imagination. "But I thought," he added, "that there *ought* to
be a shrine of the B. V. M. at the harbour mouth of a fishing port."[50]

At least in this case of landscape architecture, "what might have been" and "what
has been" (117) converge. The imagined Lady of Good Voyage is actual. One then
discovers another sort of incarnational concreteness in the homely appeals that Eliot's
speaker raises to the Virgin. Petition is made for those who fish or pursue other
maritime occupations, for women who await news of seafaring relatives, and for
those who have already reached their hour of death at sea. None of this poetry is
distinguished. The poet frames conventional petitions in strangely prosaic language.
How awkward of Mr. Eliot to write of those "Whose business has to do with fish,
and / Those concerned with every lawful traffic"! If this be prayer, it sounds like
common prayer indeed. Perhaps that is precisely the point.

Marian piety, after all, has always enjoyed more consistent favor from common
folk than from the educated elite. This populist ardor, which persists today among
Mexicans devoted to the Virgin of Guadalupe, fits the demographic profile of the
fisherfolk who figure in "The Dry Salvages." Although Eliot's writing rarely reflects
much working-class sympathy, the poet had in his youth at Cape Ann gained ad-
miration for the sturdy, salty New Englanders who labored at sea.[51] During his
American years, he also had more exposure than had other privileged compatriots
of Anglo-Saxon origin—Henry Adams, for example—to the sort of ethnic Roman
Catholicism that built the Lady's shrine. Many people of French and German Catholic origin had settled in St. Louis, his birthplace. There, too, lived Annie Dunne,
his devout Irish nurse who spoke with him of God. As regards Gloucester, he noted
in a 1928 book review the prevalence in New England, even outside cities, of "the
Portuguese in the fishing industry, and the Portuguese and the Italians in suburban
market-gardening."[52]

Both the men "forever bailing, / Setting and hauling" and the "anxious worried women" sustaining households in Gloucester (132, 131) could therefore make supplication to the Lady of Good Voyage as *Our* Lady. So could the learned poet. Though she reigns as Queen of Heaven from high above the harbor, she remains familiar and accessible to her people. Though exalted, she remains a human daughter of her son (*Figlia del tuo figlio*). This proletarian queen, acceptable even or especially in unregal America, will never disdain petitions concerning the business of fish, and the Mother of Sorrows must comprehend entreaties for those deceased or in peril. In sum, Our Lady offers humanity a feminine face of the Logos that qualifies, to apply Eliot's first epigraph from Heraclitus, as common to all.

For Eliot, of course, the supreme incarnation of the Logos appeared in Jesus. But its cosmic extension embraced all time and eternity; all love, beauty, horror, and affliction. Accordingly, the close of "Little Gidding" suggests a universal coalescence in which:

> . . . the tongues of flame are in-folded
> Into the crowned knot of fire
> And the fire and the rose are one.

The symbology of this unific vision draws together previously exposed figures of human and divine love, of love and destruction. Its Dantesque origins presume as well a beatific unity between Mother and Son. In the *Paradiso* (23.90), Mary is described not only as rose but also as fire—indeed, as "the greatest of fires" (*lo maggior foco*). Both in Dante's first vision of the Virgin and in St. Bernard's tribute to her in the climactic canto (31), images of rose and of illuminative blaze or warmth are conjoined.

Beyond the more familiar link with rose symbology, Mary's association with flame recalls her inspiration by the Holy Spirit.[53] It indicates, too, her engagement with the consuming fire of Love. According to the *Revelations of Divine Love*, Mother Julian of Norwich (an English medieval writer cited prominently in "Little Gidding") sees in the example of "our Lady Seynt Mary" not only a distinctive convergence of love and consuming pain but also a profound illustration of mystical "onyng" between Christ and humanity. As Mary watches her Son die, she who shared his flesh at the beginning becomes all the more *one* with him in spirit at the end: "Here I saw a part of the compassion of our lady Seynt Mary, for Christe and she were so onyd in love that the gretnes of his lovyng was cause of the mekylhede of hyr payne . . . for so mech as she lovid him more than al others, hir panys passyd al others; for ever the heyer, the myghtyer, the sweter that the love be, the mor sorow it is to the lover to se that body in payne that is lovid. . . . Here saw I a gret onyng betwyx Christe and us . . . for whan he was in payne, we were in peyne."[54]

Thus, the crowning love of Mary brings her unsurpassed pain yet knots her— and us—to Christ. To be sure, Our Lady St. Mary occupies but one unspecified strand among many in the lover's knot with which Eliot concludes the *Quartets*. Yet a poet who in later life prayed the Rosary daily[55] and valued immensely Dante's final canto of the *Paradiso* could scarcely forget Mary's place as singular bloom of grace and mercy within the celestial rose. "Little Gidding" demonstrates at least

that after the violent terror of part 4, the poet turns finally toward a God of motherly mercy and compassion to confirm the eschatological oneness of fire and rose.
Eliot further suggests a return to the primal assurance of divine maternity when he
intones Mother Julian's words from Christ that "all shall be well."

At Eliot's own beginning, Charlotte Champe Eliot apparently modeled an assurance of grace her son could not emulate. Whatever the complications of his adult
relation to her, he felt much more rejected by his father, who died thinking T. S.
Eliot a failure.[56] Moreover, Eliot often felt haunted by a sense of personal unwor-
thiness and, until his second marriage, by ambiguous attitudes toward women and
sexuality. All of these biographical circumstances would heighten the appeal to Eliot
of Marian devotion, which couples the promise of maternal solace with a measure
of displaced and idealized eroticism.

The cultus of Mary also figured in Eliot's ongoing search for a womanly muse.
If Vivienne helped to stir Eliot's creativity earlier in his career, others—particularly
Emily Hale and, less consequentially, Mary Trevelyan—later assumed versions of
this role. As model of the silent, ethereal, and unattainable virgin, Emily Hale
apparently played the most decisive role.[57] Yet, by the time Eliot composed "Ash-
Wednesday," the imaginative inspiration offered by English and American ladies
was merging more and more with that afforded by Our Lady St. Mary. The evocative beauty of "Ash-Wednesday" owes a good deal, I think, to the way in which
that poem claims access to the maternal power of the unspoken word, to its perception that springs of the poet's own speaking art arise from inner spaces of the
soul ruled by the lady of silences.

Eliot's attraction to a spirituality inclusive of divine womanhood reflects only
one dimension of a broader personal revolt against what he characterized as "the
intellectual and puritanical rationalism" enforced by his American upbringing.[58] But
ironically, the rebelliousness itself—and, as Henry James and others had taught him,
even the expatriate urge—lay in the American grain. Eliot ended up wedding his
innovative poetic style to an orthodox tradition of Christian faith. Within its tradi-
tionalism, though, this orthodoxy allowed space for a Marian piety that encom-
passed non-Christian mythologies—mythologies Eliot had earlier interrogated in
search of spirits adequate to confront modernity. Like Henry Adams, then, Eliot
believed something had been lost as well as gained in the new Reformation that
accompanied Anglo-Saxon migration to New England. The Reverend William
Greenleaf Eliot's grandson spent much of his adult life trying to repair that spiritual
and cultural deficit. It is altogether fitting that the twentieth-century poet thus committed to "restoring / With a new verse the ancient rhyme" ("Ash-Wednesday")
should have translated the Lady on the promontory from Marseilles to the American strand.

EPILOGUE

AT THE MOMENT, North Americans seem exceptionally preoccupied with the problem of gender. Debates about gender, sex, and psychosocial identity flourish in popular as well as academic culture; they surface repeatedly not only in talk shows and mass market publications but also in scholarly works representing a broad range of disciplines. So far, at least, the topic of this study engages current interests.

As an image of broader civic values, too, the American Madonna should interest social and cultural historians through her affiliation with familiar secular icons of national identity. Figures such as Dame Liberty and Daniel Chester French's queenly woman of "The Republic" (the latter who presided over the 1893 Columbian Exposition in Chicago) display the global import Americans have envisioned in and for their nation. By the era of electricity, Divine Woman also becomes a social icon of the need to preserve beauty and humanity in confrontation with the new impersonal, invisible forces driving technological progress. In the radically decentered, faceless world of the dynamo (or, in time, the Internet), the Virgin offers one symbolic address to the individual's craving for solace, stability, and bodily personality. In this regard, Henry Adams's Marian testament reflects widespread social anxieties. And social history, like gender studies, remains a proper subfield of interest within the literary academy.

Yet the religious aspect of the American Madonna is another matter. From the standpoint of cultural materialism, such a topic may look not just eccentric but irrelevant. By and large, postmodern theoretical approaches to literary scholarship diminish the role of religion in imaginative expression—or subsume religion into more acceptable categories marked by race, gender, class, and the pursuit of power. The intellectual world lately focuses more attention on T. S. Eliot's occasional though lamentable statements of ethnic bias than it does on the poet's all-encompassing religious vision. With few exceptions,[1] recent scholarly attempts to offer some expansive view of American literary culture give short shrift to institutional religion and even to less formalized versions of the interior life.

With Jenny Franchot, then, I think it fair to say that scholarship continues to underestimate the role of religion in American writing. Franchot's stress on this "studied neglect of religion" complements Stephen L. Carter's more political case for welcoming the reintegration of religious belief and discourse into the nation's public sphere. Both assessments argue against the tendency, in a "culture of disbelief," to marginalize religion by portraying it not simply as an illusion but—still more destructively—as a wholly private matter of consumer preference.[2]

Yet, as Carter knows, the "culture of disbelief" scarcely represents all of American culture, particularly in less privileged sectors of U.S. society. That a recent book about *Care of the Soul*[3] could make the best-seller list indicates the renewable force of a spiritual vocabulary prominent in America from the Colonial Puritans through the Romantic reformulations of Emerson, Dickinson, Whitman, Margaret Fuller, and beyond. Thomas Moore's testimony on behalf of soulful imagination, depth, and beauty finds a receptive audience even as Americans are crowded about with competing views of the self as psychic organism or mechanism, economic unit, or idiomorphic ego. Apparently the soul, like the search for ultimates, refuses to go away.

If, as the cases we have examined attest, Mother Mary likewise refuses to vacate even Anglo-Protestant spaces of the United States, I think her perseverance here owes much to her significance as a realized archetype of the soul. To be sure, she has often been reduced to an aesthetic artifact, trivialized in plastic, sensationalized in too many reports of "sightings," or eviscerated by the churches themselves. Still largely ignored in Protestant and Episcopal worship, she suffers other reductions of soul in Roman Catholic church culture when forced to model female docility or serve as a mouthpiece of moralistic authority—in the mold of what Garrison Keillor has pungently labeled "Our Lady of Perpetual Responsibility." She may be shunned as a déclassé spectacle in her familiar appearance as bathtub Virgin of the backyard, and, with the disintegration of some immigrant communities, she no longer symbolizes the sort of defining social presence she once did, for example, in the domus-centered society of Italian Harlem until the middle of this century.[4]

But it is hard to banish from sight the single most widely represented and enduring image of the feminine that Western aesthetics has displayed for more than a millennium. And the need to restore to psyche something of primal femininity remains manifest in American culture. Adams may have exaggerated when he claimed that the Virgin's power created "over four-fifths" of humanity's "noblest art," but clearly the broader imaginative influence of anima has been formidable even in the Adamic land of pragmatism and commerce. Indeed, the persistence of the American Madonna in a country where today just over half the population still identifies itself as Protestant owes much to her contrary disposition. In a positivistic age dominated by consumer capitalism, the Blessed Mother remains something of an affront to revered American values of utility, competitive exertion, and radical individualism.

That the Divine Woman contradicts the most emphatic assertions of American individualism is apparent in several of the instances considered here. Even Margaret Fuller, who was religiously heterodox compared with Harriet Beecher Stowe, recognized through her Marian and other feminine symbologies a need to revise Emerson's individualism toward a more communitarian sense of soul. Just as the icon of Mother and Child embodies a primal human connection, so also the Madonna-soul requires a community of faith to remain vital. Hence the ideal of the solitary soul, wedded only to American nature, has answered a mostly masculine desire. For Fuller, the faith community addressed in *Woman in the Nineteenth Century* is not a church but a compound of sisterhood and the national intelligentsia. Adams, though he admitted the crucial role of corporate symbology, carried his own effort to preserve a more-or-less private Mary fetish about as far as it could go. Much of the frustration and alienation that both Hawthorne and Frederic evinced toward the close of their literary careers likewise derives from their inability to locate a sustaining community of spirit either in America or abroad.[5]

Despite her mythological affiliations, the American Madonna also raises questions about the ahistorical, intensely present-minded sensibility of representative Americans as disparate as Emerson and Henry Ford. Of course, Emerson disavowed "retrospective" engagement with the past in favor of immediate experience while Ford, in his progressive optimism, waved history aside as "more or less bunk." For Emerson, the merely historical Jesus, to say nothing of Mary, ceases to matter. By contrast, Stowe insisted on the continuing force of Mary's past example. For her, Mary of Nazareth was not a lone goddess floating outside time but a mother embedded in history. As a committed Christian, Stowe perceived this mother's acquaintance with actual human loss as an essential inspiration for her own spirituality of maternity, which consequently informs the emotion and graphic timeliness of *Uncle Tom's Cabin*. Even Fuller, whose writing usually shows a much freer disposition to conflate Mary with (other) mythological goddesses, affirmed the distinctive position of Mary as an actual historical figure. Thus, the Madonna ends up occupying a peculiar status in imagination somewhere between history and archetypal mythology.

For this reason, I doubt that Mary can or will be wholly assimilated into the current revival of goddess religion in America, a revival that so far enjoys limited appeal and that reflects perforce a certain artificiality in our postagricultural culture. But the longing for an essential rebirth, and for a mother archetype to deliver it, persists in some form through all of the writers we have considered—at least as far forward as Eliot and, I should say, beyond. The impulse surely has its regressive aspects, in the more damaging as well as benign senses of regression. But if one legacy of Franklinian pragmatism and the Enlightenment is an American confidence in the self's endless capacity for reinvention, the American Madonna represents another, more intuitive locus of values. In the cases we have examined, adult authors in effect consent to assume in spirit and imagination the role of receptive child. Seeking more than a social reinvention of self, they witness to a perennial urge for rebirth. And surely *their* American tales about the return of the repressed Mother are not the last.

APPENDIX

I

Penitential Psalm

Virgin Mother, Mary Mild!
It was thine to see the child,
Gift of the Messiah dove,
Pure blossom of ideal love,
Break, upon the "guilty cross"
The seeming promise of his life;
Of faith, of hope, of love a loss
Deepened all thy bosom's strife,
Brow, down-bent, and heart-strings torn,
Fainting by frail arms upborne.

But 'tis mine, oh Mary mild,
To tremble lest the heavenly child,
Crucified within my heart
Ere of earth he take his part,
Leave my life that horror wild
The mother who has slain her child.

141

Let me to the tomb repair,
Find the angel watching there,
Ask his aid to walk again
Undefiled with brother men.
Once my heart within me burned
At the least whisper of thy voice;
Though my love was unreturned,
Happy in a holy choice;
Once my lamp was constant trimmed,
And my fond resolve undimmed.
Fan again the Parsee fire,
Let it light my funeral pyre
Purify the veins of Earth,
Temper for a Phenix birth.

II
Meditation

Virgin Mother, Mary Mild!
It was thine to see the child,
Gift of the Messiah dove,
Pure blossom of ideal love,
Break, upon the "guilty cross"
The seeming promise of his life;
Of faith, of hope, of love a loss
Deepened all thy bosom's strife,
Brow, down-bent, and heart-strings torn,
Fainting by frail arms upborne.

All those startled figures show
That they did not apprehend
  The thought of him who there lies low,
On whom those sorrowing eyes they bend;
  They do not feel this holiest hour,
Their hearts soar not to reach the power
  Which this deepest of distress
  Alone could give to save and bless.

Soul of that fair now ruined form,
Thou who hadst force to bide the storm
  Must again descend to tell
Of thy life the hidden spell;
  "Maiden, wrap thy mantle round thee"
Night is coming, clear cold night;

Fate, that in the cradle bound thee,
In the coffin hides thy blight;
　Angels weeping, dirges singing,
　Rosemary with hearts-ease bringing,
　　Softly spread the fair green sod,
　Thou escape and bathe in God.

　　Margaret! shed no idle tears;
　In the far perspective bright
　　A muse-like form as thine appears
As thine new-born in primal light.

　　Leila, take thy wand again;
Upon thy arm no longer rest;
　　Listen to the thrilling brain;
Listen to the throbbing breast;
　　There nightingales have made their nest
Shall soothe with song the night's unrest.

　　Slowly drop the beaded years;
Slowly drop the pearly tears;
　　At last the Rosary appears
A Ruby heart its clasp appears
　　With cross of gold and diamond
　　Like to that upon the wand.

　　"Maiden wrap thy mantle round thee"
Night is coming, starlit night,
　　Fate that in the cradle bound thee,
In the coffin hides thy blight;
　　All transfused the orb now glowing,
Full-voiced and free the music growing
　　Planted in a senseless sod
　　The life is risen to flower a God.

MARY AT THE CROSS

"Now there stood by the cross of Jesus his mother."

O wondrous mother! since the dawn of time
    Was ever love, was ever grief, like thine?
O highly favored in thy joy's deep flow,
    And favored, even in this, thy bitterest woe!

Poor was that home in simple Nazareth
    Where, fairly growing, like some silent flower,
Last of a kingly race, unknown and lowly,
    O desert lily, passed thy childhood's hour.

The world knew not the tender, serious maiden,
    Who through deep loving years so silent grew,
Full of high thought and holy aspiration,
    Which the o'ershadowing God alone might view.

And then it came, that message from the highest,
    Such as to woman ne'er before descended,
The almighty wings thy prayerful soul o'erspread,
    And with thy life the Life of worlds was blended.

What visions then of future glory filled thee,
    The chosen mother of that King unknown,
Mother fulfiller of all prophecy
    Which, through dim ages, wondering seers had shown!

Well did thy dark eye kindle, thy deep soul
    Rise into billows, and thy heart rejoice;
Then woke the poet's fire, the prophet's song,
    Tuned with strange burning words thy timid voice.

Then, in dark contrast, came the lowly manger,
    The outcast shed, the tramp of brutal feet;
Again behold earth's learnèd and her lowly,
    Sages and shepherds, prostrate at thy feet.

Then to the temple bearing—hark again
    What strange conflicting tones of prophecy
Breathe o'er the child foreshadowing words of joy,
    High triumph blent with bitter agony!

O highly favored thou in many an hour
   Spent in lone musings with thy wondrous Son,
When thou didst gaze into that glorious eye,
   And hold that mighty hand within thine own.

Blest through those thirty years, when in thy dwelling
   He lived a God disguised with unknown power;
And thou his sole adorer, his best love,
   Trusting, revering, waited for his hour.

Blest in that hour, when called by opening heaven
   With cloud and voice, and the baptizing flame,
Up from the Jordan walked th' acknowledged stranger,
   And awe-struck crowds grew silent as He came.

Blessèd, when full of grace, with glory crowned,
   He from both hands almighty favors poured,
And, though He had not where to lay his head,
   Brought to his feet alike the slave and lord.

Crowds followed; thousands shouted, "Lo, our King!"
   Fast beat thy heart. Now, now the hour draws nigh:
Behold the crown, the throne, the nations bend!
   Ah, no! fond mother, no! behold Him die!

Now by that cross thou tak'st thy final station,
   And shar'st the last dark trial of thy Son;
Not with weak tears or woman's lamentation,
   But with high, silent anguish, like his own.

Hail! highly favored, even in this deep passion;
   Hail! in this bitter anguish thou art blest,—
Blest in the holy power with Him to suffer
   Those deep death-pangs that lead to higher rest.

All now is darkness; and in that deep stillness
   The God-man wrestles with that mighty woe;
Hark to that cry, the rock of ages rending,—
   "'Tis finished!" Mother, all is glory now!

By sufferings mighty as his mighty soul
   Hath the Redeemer risen forever blest;
And through all ages must his heart-belovèd
   Through the same baptism enter the same rest.

Harriet Beecher Stowe, From *Religious Studies: Sketches and Poems* (896)

THE SORROWS OF MARY

Dedicated to the mothers who have lost sons in the late war

I slept, but my heart was waking,
  And out in my dreams I sped,
Through the streets of an ancient city,
  Where Jesus, the Lord, lay dead.

He was lying all cold and lowly,
  And the sepulchre was sealed,
And the women that bore the spices
  Had come from the holy field.

There is feasting in Pilate's palace,
  There is revel in Herod's hall,
Where the lute and the sounding instrument
  To mirth and merriment call.

"I have washed my hands," said Pilate,
  "And what is the Jew to me?"
"I have missed my chance," said Herod,
  "One of his wonders to see.

"But why should our courtly circle
  To the thought give further place?
All dreams, save of pleasure and beauty,
  Bid the dancers' feet efface."

.   .   .   .

I saw a light from a casement,
  And entered a lowly door,
Where a woman, stricken and mournful,
  Sat in sackcloth on the floor.

There Mary, the mother of Jesus,
  And John, the beloved one,
With a few poor friends beside them,
  Were mourning for Him that was gone.

And before the mother was lying
  That crown of cruel thorn,
Wherewith they crowned that gentle brow
  In mockery that morn.

And her ears yet ring with the anguish
   Of that last dying cry,—
That mighty appeal of agony
   That shook both earth and sky.

O God, what a shaft of anguish
   Was that dying voice from the tree!—
From Him the only spotless,—

  "Why hast Thou forsaken me?"
And was he of God forsaken?
   They ask, appalled with dread;
Is evil crowned and triumphant,
   And goodness vanquished and dead?

Is there, then, no God in Jacob?
   Is the star of Judah dim?
For who would our God deliver,
   If he would not deliver him?

If God *could* not deliver—what hope then?
   If he *would* not,—who ever shall dare
To be firm in his service hereafter?
   To trust in his wisdom or care?

So darkly the Tempter was saying,
   To hearts that with sorrow were dumb;
And the poor souls were clinging in darkness to God,
   With hands that with anguish were numb.

. . . .

In my dreams came the third day morning,
   And fairly the day-star shone;
But fairer, the solemn angel,
   As he rolled away the stone.

In the lowly dwelling of Mary,
   In the dusky twilight chill,
There was heard the sound of coming feet,
   And her very heart grew still.

And in the glimmer of dawning,
   She saw him enter the door,
Her Son, all living and real,
   Risen, to die no more!

Her Son, all living and real,
   Risen no more to die,—
With the power of an endless life in his face,
   With the light of heaven in his eye.

O mourning mothers, so many,
   Weeping o'er sons that are dead,
Have ye thought of the sorrows of Mary's heart,
   Of the tears that Mary shed?

Is the crown of thorns before you?
   Are there memories of cruel scorn?
Of hunger and thirst and bitter cold
   That your belovéd have borne?

Had ye ever a son like Jesus
   To give to a death of pain?
Did ever a son so cruelly die,
   But did he die in vain?

Have ye ever thought that all the hopes
   That make our earth-life fair,
Were born in those three bitter days
   Of Mary's deep despair?

O mourning mothers, so many,
   Weeping in woe and pain,
Think on the joy of Mary's heart
   In a Son that is risen again.

Have faith in a third-day morning,
   In a resurrection-hour;
For what ye sow in weakness,
   He can raise again in power.

Have faith in the Lord of that thorny crown,
   In the Lord of the piercéd hand;
For he reigneth now o'er earth and heaven,
   And his power who may withstand?

And the hopes that never on earth shall bloom,
   The sorrows forever new,
Lay silently down at the feet of Him
   Who died and is risen for you.

Harriet Beecher Stowe, from *Religious Studies: Sketches and Poems* (1896)

EXCERPT FROM "THE GOLDEN LEGEND" (SPEECH OF PRINCE HENRY)

This is indeed the blessed Mary's land,
Virgin and Mother of our dear Redeemer!
All hearts are touched and softened at her name,
Alike the bandit, with the bloody hand,
The priest, the prince, the scholar, and the peasant,
The man of deeds, the visionary dreamer,
Pay homage to her as one ever present!
And even as children, who have much offended
A too indulgent father, in great shame,
Penitent, and yet not daring unattended
To go into his presence, at the gate
Speak with their sister, and confiding wait
Till she goes in before and intercedes;
So men, repenting of their evil deeds,
And yet not venturing rashly to draw near
With their requests an angry father's ear,
Offer to her their prayers and their confession,
And she for them in heaven makes intercession.
And if our Faith had given us nothing more
Than this example of all womanhood,
So mild, so merciful, so strong, so good,
So patient, peaceful, loyal, loving, pure,
This were enough to prove it higher and truer
Than all the creeds the world had known before.

Henry Wadsworth Longfellow, from *The Poetical Works of Henry Wadsworth Longfellow* (Cambridge, Mass.: Houghton, Mifflin, 1893), 5:265.

NOTES

Introduction

1. Starhawk, *The Spiral Dance: A Rebirth of the Ancient Religion of the Great Goddess* (San Francisco: Harper & Row, 1979). The classic structural and psychological analysis of the archetypal feminine is Erich Neumann's *The Great Mother: An Analysis of the Archetype*, trans. Ralph Manheim (Princeton: Princeton University Press, 1955; 2d ed. 1963). Other notable treatments of the phenomenon include Robert Graves, *The White Goddess: A Historical Grammar of Poetic Myth* (New York: Farrar, Straus and Giroux, 1966); Edwin Oliver James, *The Cult of the Mother Goddess: An Archeological and Documentary Study* (New York: Praeger, 1959); Elinor W. Gadon, *The Once and Future Goddess: A Symbol for Our Time* (New York: Harper & Row, 1989); and David Leeming and Jake Page, *Goddess: Myths of the Female Divine* (New York: Oxford University Press, 1994).

2. *Woman in the Nineteenth Century* (1845) as cited in *The Essential Margaret Fuller,* ed. Jeffrey Steele (New Brunswick, N.J.: Rutgers University Press, 1992), p. 347.

3. From T. DeWitt Talmage's Introduction to A. Stewart Walsh's *Mary: The Queen of the House of David and Mother of Jesus, The Story of Her Life* (Pittsburgh: A. S. Gray, 1889), pp. xiii–xiv, xvi. In the central text, however, Walsh regards Marianism less conservatively as "seeded with the germs of revolutionary impulses"; indeed, he equates "the renaissance of Mary" during the Crusades with "the disenslaving of woman" (31, 46).

4. Mary Daly, *Beyond God the Father: Toward a Philosophy of Women's Liberation* (Boston: Beacon Press, 1973); Marina Warner, *Alone of All Her Sex: The Myth and Cult of the Virgin Mary* (New York: Alfred A. Knopf, 1976). See also Rosemary Radford Ruether, *Mary, the Feminine Face of the Church* (Philadelphia: Westminster, 1977); and Doris Donnelly, ed., *Mary, Woman of Nazareth: Biblical and Theological Perspectives* (New York: Paulist Press, 1989).

5. For a reliable summation of the strictly biblical issues, see *Mary in the New Testament: A Collaborative Assessment by Protestant and Roman Catholic Scholars,* ed. Raymond E. Brown

et al. (Philadelphia: Fortress Press, 1978). Beyond the essential material in Luke, other cru-cial Marian passages include the Johannine crucifixion narrative, wherein Jesus commits his mother to the beloved disciple (John 19.25–27), and mention of her presence amid the postresurrectional Jerusalem community of the upper room in Acts 1.14.

6. See, for example, Hilda Charlotte Graef, *Mary: A History of Doctrine and Devotion* (New York: Sheed and Ward, 1964); and, from a less orthodox standpoint, Geoffrey Ashe, *The Virgin: Mary's Cult and the Re-emergence of the Goddess* (London: Routledge and Kegan Paul, 1976). For a very recent, authoritative account of postbiblical developments in Marian piety and theology in relation to culture, see Jaroslav Pelikan's *Mary through the Centuries: Her Place in the History of Culture* (New Haven: Yale University Press, 1996).

7. See Barbara Newman, *Sister of Wisdom: St. Hildegard's Theology of the Feminine* (Ber-keley: University of California Press, 1987), esp. pp. 156–95.

8. See Neumann, *Great Mother,* p. 312. In *The Sexuality of Christ in Renaissance Art and in Modern Oblivion* (New York: Pantheon–Random House, 1984), esp. pp. 110–15, Leo Steinberg comments on iconographic representations of the Marian spousal motif in Renaissance art. In *Love and Death in the American Novel* (1960; 2d ed., New York: Dell, 1966), Leslie Fiedler attempts to trace into America the cultural and imaginative complica-tions resulting from Protestant suppression of erotic Mariolatry throughout Northern Europe in combination with traditions of courtly and sentimental love.

9. Cited in *The Divine Liturgy* (New York: Dept. of Religious Education, Orthodox Church in America), p. 28.

10. C. G. Jung, *Answer to Job,* trans. R. F. C. Hull (Cleveland: Meridian, 1954), p. 197.

11. For an excellent account of this tradition, see A. M. Allchin, *The Joy of All Creation: An Anglican Meditation on the Place of Mary* (Cambridge, Mass.: Cowley Publications, 1984).

12. Not to be confused (though it commonly is) with the doctrine of Jesus' virgin birth, the view that Mary was herself conceived without stain of original sin provoked opposition even from some prominent theologians within the Roman church—includ-ing Bernard, Bonaventure, and Aquinas—prior to its dogmatic promulgation in the nine-teenth century. From one point of view, this doctrine simply enlarges other affirmations of Mary's spiritual singularity; from another, it has been lamented as both unscriptural and theologically problematic, in part because it associates the transmission of sin with procreative sexuality.

CHAPTER 1

1. *Mosses from an Old Manse,* in *The Centenary Edition of the Works of Nathaniel Hawthorne,* ed. William Charvat et al. (Columbus: Ohio State University Press, 1963–87), 10:20, 8, 19, 5; future references to this edition are indicated parenthetically in the text. In addition to the Raphael (probably his *Madonna del Pesce,* figure 2.3) and landscapes by Sophia, the Hawthorne residence was evidently adorned throughout its several relocations with at least two other Madonnas by Correggio and Leonardo da Vinci, both gifts of Emerson. See Julian Hawthorne, *Nathaniel Hawthorne and His Wife* (Cambridge: Riverside Press, 1893), 1:279, 286, 367–69; and Rose Hawthorne Lathrop, *Memories of Hawthorne* (Cambridge: Riverside Press, 1897), pp. 51, 54, 185, 192. Sophia reported that visitors to the Old Manse were struck by "the pictures of Holy Mothers mild on the walls" (Lathrop, *Memories,* 65); antici-pating the family's subsequent return to Salem, she wrote her mother that she expected to find there "a very nice chamber, upon whose walls I can hang Holy Families" (Julian Hawthorne, *Nathaniel Hawthorne,* 1:286).

2. Leland S. Person Jr., *Aesthetic Headaches: Women and a Masculine Poetics in Poe, Melville, and Hawthorne* (Athens: University of Georgia Press, 1988), p. 1.

3. Lawrence Buell, *New England Literary Culture: From Revolution through Renaissance* (New York: Cambridge University Press, 1986), pp. 270, 279; the most thorough and incisive analysis of Hawthorne's engagement with New England Puritanism can be found in Michael C. Colacurcio's *The Province of Piety: Moral History in Hawthorne's Early Tales* (Cambridge: Harvard University Press, 1984).

4. Leonard J. Fick, *The Light Beyond: A Study of Hawthorne's Theology* (Westminister, Md.: Newman Press, 1955); Gilbert Voight, "Hawthorne and the Roman Catholic Church," *New England Quarterly* 19 (1946): 394–97; and Henry G. Fairbanks, *The Lasting Loneliness of Nathaniel Hawthorne* (Albany: Magi Books, 1965), pp. 185–202.

5. See Gloria Erlich in *Family Themes and Hawthorne's Fiction: The Tenacious Web* (New Brunswick, N.J.: Rutgers University Press, 1984), esp. p. 100; and, for a different assessment of the psychobiographical context, Nina Baym, "Nathaniel Hawthorne and His Mother: A Biographical Speculation," *American Literature* 54 (1982): 1–27.

6. Person, *Aesthetic Headaches,* esp. pp. 94–95; see also T. Walter Herbert's searching discussion of gender conflicts in Hawthorne's life and work: "Nathaniel Hawthorne, Una Hawthorne, and *The Scarlet Letter:* Interactive Selfhood and the Cultural Construction of Gender," *PMLA* 103 (1988): 285–95.

7. Louise DeSalvo, *Nathaniel Hawthorne* (Atlantic Highlands, N.J.: Humanities Press, 1987), p. 5.

8. James D. Wallace, "Hawthorne and the Scribbling Women Reconsidered," *American Literature* 62 (1990): 213.

9. Nina Baym, "Thwarted Nature: Nathaniel Hawthorne as Feminist," in Fritz Fleischmann, ed., *American Novelists Revisited: Essays in Feminist Criticism* (Boston: G. K. Hall, 1982), p. 59. In "Hawthorne's Fair-Haired Maidens: The Fading Light," *PMLA* 75 (1960): 250–56, Virginia O. Birdsall has also noted the decreasing significance of Hawthorne's fair-haired women in later writings.

10. Thus, Person, *Aesthetic Headaches* (pp. 100–3) discusses Hawthorne's view of Sophia in his correspondence as alternating between fair "Dove" and "naughty wife."

11. Nina Baym, "Thwarted Nature," p. 66.

12. The implications of this imagery are elaborated by Kent Bales in "Sexual Exploitation and the Fall from Natural Virtue in Rappaccini's Daughter," *ESQ: A Journal of the American Renaissance* 24 (1978): 133–44. See also Richard Brenzo, "Beatrice Rappaccini: A Victim of Male Love and Horror," *American Literature* 48 (1976): 152–64.

13. For a discerning analysis of the tale's spiritual epistemology, see Michael Colacurcio, "A Better Mode of Evidence: The Transcendental Problem of Faith and Spirit," *ESQ: A Journal of the American Renaissance* 54 (1969): 12–22.

14. See especially cantos 32–33 of the *Paradiso* with the vision of the celestial rose and Bernard's prayer to the Virgin. I would not want to push the Marian affiliations of Hawthorne's Beatrice too far, despite several casual references to the Virgin in his story's dialogue. Still, insofar as Hawthorne's story makes much of its ostensibly paradisiacal atmosphere, it is worth considering the author's possible response to the *Paradiso,* even though most critical commentary has remained fixed on the *Inferno.* And consistent with the larger tradition of Christian mysticism that assimilated courtly love themes, an erotic element does color expressions of spiritual devotion to the Lady in Dante's *Paradiso.*

15. Nina Baym makes a similar case in "Thwarted Nature," p. 60.

16. See Rita K. Gollin and John L. Idol Jr., *Prophetic Pictures: Nathaniel Hawthorne's Knowledge and Uses of the Visual Arts* (Westport, Conn.: Greenwood Press, 1991), 29; Lathrop, *Memories,* p. 64.

17. Erich Neumann, *The Great Mother: An Analysis of the Archetype,* trans. Ralph Manheim (Princeton: Princeton University Press, 1955; 2d ed. 1963), esp. 147–208. On the negative

side of the mother archetype see C. G. Jung, *The Archetypes of the Collective Unconscious*, trans. R. F. C. Hull (1959; 2d ed., Princeton: Princeton University Press, 1969), p. 82; and *Symbols of Transformation* (1956; 2d ed. Princeton: Princeton University Press, 1967), pp. 306–93 and passim.

18. Philip Rahv, "The Dark Lady of Salem," *Partisan Review* 8 (1941): 362–81.

19. The Hester-Hutchinson association is most fully explored by Michael Colacurcio in "Footsteps of Anne Hutchinson: The Context of *The Scarlet Letter*," *ELH* 39 (1972): 459–94; and by Amy Lang in *Prophetic Woman: Anne Hutchinson and the Problem of Dissent in the Literature of New England* (Berkeley: University of California Press, 1987). For instances of attention to mothering themes in *The Scarlet Letter,* see Baym's "Thwarted Nature," p. 74; Monika M. Elbert, "Hester's Maternity: Stigma or Weapon," *ESQ: A Journal of the American Renaissance*: 36 (1990): 175–207; and Shari Benstock, "*The Scarlet Letter* (a)dorée, or the Female Body Embroidered," in *Case Studies in Contemporary Criticism:* The Scarlet Letter, ed. Ross C. Murfin (Boston: Bedford Books of St. Martin's Press, 1991), pp. 288–303.

20. The pietà iconography is discussed by Hugh Dawson in "The Triptych Design of *The Scarlet Letter*," *Nathaniel Hawthorne Review* 13 (1987): 12–14. Dawson also connects Hawthorne's reference to "sinless motherhood" with mid-nineteenth-century Roman Catholic teaching on Mary's Immaculate Conception.

21. See also Robert E. Todd, "The Magna Mater Archetype in *The Scarlet Letter*," *New England Quarterly* 45 (1972): 421–29. In *Sexual Personae: Art and Decadence from Nerfertiti to Emily Dickinson* (New Haven: Yale University Press, 1990), Camille Paglia describes Hester variously as "the Catholic Madonna drummed out of Protestantism," as a "wandering goddess still bearing the mark of her Asiatic origins," and as as an affront to Puritan repression of "beauty, sex, imagination, art" (pp. 580–81).

22. For fuller discussion of the theological issues involved in interpreting the famous statement about "consecration" in chapter 17, see my essay on "The Apocalyptic End of *The Scarlet Letter*," *Texas Studies in Language and Literature* 32 (1990), esp. pp. 509–12.

23. The view of Hawthorne's Madonna and Child as essentially pictorial and statuesque is set forth by Gollin and Idol, *Prophetic Pictures*, pp. 50–51.

24. Literally, standing mother, referring to the iconographic motif of Mary standing in grief beside the cross as developed in medieval and later tradition out of the description in John 19.25–27.

25. Jessie Ryon Lucke, "Hawthorne's Madonna Image in *The Scarlet Letter*," *New England Quarterly* 38 (1965), 391–92.

26. Dawson, "Triptych Design," p. 14 n. 6; for a provocative modern exploration of Mary's portrayal across the tradition as mother, lover, and daughter, see Julia Kristeva's "Stabat Mater" in *Tales of Love,* trans. Leon S. Roudiez (New York: Columbia University Press, 1987), pp. 234–63.

27. For a review of how Hester's return and prophecy have been read, and an assessment of what the return in particular might mean in its fuller cultural implications, see Sacvan Bercovitch, *The Office of the Scarlet Letter* (Baltimore: John Hopkins University Press, 1991).

28. See Gatta, "Apocalyptic End," esp. 516–17.

29. Julian Hawthorne, *Hawthorne and His Wife,* 2:194. Nathaniel Hawthorne likewise wrote of a Perugino painting that "the Virgin, who holds the dead Christ on her knees, has a deeper expression of woe than, I think, can ever have been painted since" (*Works* 14:371).

30. Luther S. Luedtke, *Nathaniel Hawthorne and the Romance of the Orient* (Bloomington: Indiana University Press, 1989), p. 203.

31. Irving Howe, *Politics and the Novel* (New York: Horizon Press, 1957), p. 171; Nina Baym, "*The Blithedale Romance:* A Radical Reading," *JEGP* 67 (1968): 555.

32. Edward Gibbons, *History of the Decline and Fall of the Roman Empire,* ed. J. B. Bury (London: Methuen, 1909), 1:327. On Hawthorne's familiarity with these works, see Luedtke, *Nathaniel Hawthorne,* pp. 66, 196, 208.

33. George Ripley, "Introductory Statement to the Revised Constitution of Brook Farm," and Elizabeth Palmer Peabody, "Plan of the West Roxbury Community," in *Selected Writings of the American Transcendentalists,* ed. George Hochfield (New York: New American Library, 1966), pp. 385–96.

34. The exotic, Oriental appeal of Zenobia may again owe something to Curtis's *Nile Notes,* where the eroticism of a Middle Eastern dancing girl named Xenobi is compared to that of the houri, supernatural women who grace the Islamic paradise. Luedtke (*Nathaniel Hawthorne,* 203) stresses rather the way in which Hawthorne's Priscilla-Zenobia relationship resembles the one Curtis illustrates between his younger Xenobi and older Kushuk Arnem.

35. Fuller applied regal descriptions to herself; such titles were also bestowed on her sardonically by others. See chapter 2, n. 1.

36. Given the bizarre catholicity and anti-Puritan tenor of Morton's imagination, I would not even rule out his intending in the "ma-re" nomenclature a further subversive pun alluding to the Christian "goddess" of womanly fecundity—that is, Mary. On Hawthorne's own (probably indirect) acquaintance with Morton's account, see J. Gary Williams, "History in Hawthorne's 'The Maypole of Merry Mount,'" *Essex Institute Historical Collections* 108 (1972): 173–89.

37. Taylor Stoehr, *Hawthorne's Mad Scientists: Pseudoscience and Social Science in Nineteenth-Century Life and Letters* (Hamden, Conn.: Archon Books, 1978), pp. 196, 200–212, 291–92.

38. J. J. Bachofen, *Das Mutterecht* (1861) in *Myth, Religion, and Mother Right: Selected Writings of J. J. Bachofen,* trans. Ralph Manheim (Princeton: Princeton University Press, 1967). Although Bachofen's own research drew more directly on philology, history, and linguistics than on archaeological excavation, Bachofen did study ancient mortuary art and reflected on the symbolism he found there of egg and maternal womb. He also supposed that imminent advances in scientific archaeology would corroborate his discoveries (Introduction to *Mother Right,* p. 69).

39. In a chapter fittingly called "The Expression and Repression of Sophia" in *The Feminine Dimension of the Divine* (Philadelphia: Westminster, 1979), pp. 74–120, Joan Chamberlain Engelsman discusses how cultural and theological formulations first developed but subsequently diminished the divine power of Sophia-Wisdom. In this context, the name of Hawthorne's wife may be too coincidentally apt to need further comment, presuming one accepts the standard premise that Hilda was largely modeled on Sophia.

40. This aspect is fully elaborated by Milton Stern in the third and fourth chapters of his *Contexts for Hawthorne: The Marble Faun and the Politics of Openness and Closure in American Literature* (Urbana: University of Illinois Press, 1991), pp. 36–147.

CHAPTER 2

1. Cited in Julian Hawthorne, ed., *Nathaniel Hawthorne and His Wife* (Cambridge: Riverside Press, 1893), 1:257; and in *The Letters of Margaret Fuller,* ed. Robert N. Hudsbeth (Ithaca: Cornell University Press, 1983), 1:332.

2. Barbara Welter, "The Cult of True Womanhood: 1820–1860," *American Quarterly* (1966) 18:151–74.

3. In a journalistic essay on Christmas, Fuller expresses regret that "some of these symbols" associated with the Christmas festival and Marian piety "had not been more rever-

enced by Protestants" (*Life Without and Life Within,* ed. Arthur B. Fuller [Boston: Brown, Taggard and Chase, 1860], p. 251).

4. Cited in *The Essential Margaret Fuller,* ed. Jeffrey Steele (New Brunswick, N.J.: Rutgers University Press, 1992), p. 7. Subsequent citations from Fuller are, unless otherwise indicated, from this edition (hereafter identified as *EMF*).

5. Nancy Chodorow, *The Reproduction of Mothering: Psychoanalysis and the Sociology of Gender* (Berkeley: University of California Press, 1978); Dorothy Dinnerstein, *The Mermaid and the Minotaur: Sexual Arrangements and Human Malaise* (New York: Harper & Row, 1976); Julia Kristeva, *Desire in Language: A Semiotic Approach to Literature and Art,* ed. Leon S. Roudiez (New York: Columbia University Press, 1980), esp. pp. 237–70. Chodorow and Dinnerstein are particularly concerned to revise biologically deterministic theories of mothering; Kristeva's version of feminist psychoanalytic criticism adapts Lacan and Freud to focus on the maternal body, language, and the semiotics of prelinguistic communication between mother and infant. See also Jane Silverman Van Buren, *The Modernist Madonna: Semiotics of the Maternal Metaphor* (Bloomington: Indiana University Press, 1989), esp. pp. 1–24.

6. The textual analysis by Marie Mitchell Olesen Urbanski in *Margaret Fuller's "Woman in the Nineteenth Century": A Literary Study of Form and Content, of Sources and Influence* (Westport, Conn.: Greenwood Press, 1980) occupies an eighteen-page chapter within a book that establishes Fuller's context and the circumstances limiting her reputation as a writer. In addition to his penetrating commentary and notes in *The Essential Margaret Fuller,* Jeffrey Steele has produced several useful pieces, including "Freeing the 'Prisoned Queen': The Development of Margaret Fuller's Poetry" in *Studies in the American Renaissance,* ed. Joel Myerson (Charlottesville: University Press of Virginia, 1992), pp. 137–75.

7. Charles Capper, *Margaret Fuller: An American Romantic Life* (New York: Oxford University Press, 1992), esp. pp. 29–37, 70, 158–71, 256. See also Ann Douglas, *The Feminization of American Culture* (1977; reprint, New York: Anchor Doubleday, 1988), pp. 263–69.

8. Fuller's chief experience of religious awakening seemed to have taken place in Cambridge on Thanksgiving Day, 1831, following her quarrel with George Davis. But further episodes of spiritual renewal followed her father's death (1835) and her encounter with Emerson (1836). In 1837 she took her first Communion, and the emotional and spiritual challenges of 1839–40 stirred religious energies in this presumably irreligious woman that led toward the major creative expressions of 1844. See Capper, *Margaret Fuller,* pp. 126 and 246, together with selections in *EMF,* pp. 10–14; and Steele, "Freeing the 'Prisoned Queen,'" pp. 146–47.

9. *EMF,* p. xii; Steele, "Freeing the 'Prisoned Queen,'" p. 38.

10. See *Memoirs of Margaret Fuller Ossoli,* ed. Ralph Waldo Emerson, James Freeman Clarke, and William Henry Channing (Boston: Phillips, Sampson, 1852), 1:308–9; cf. Fuller's letter to Caroline Sturgis (26 September 1840) referring to "mighty changes in my spiritual life" (*Letters,* 2:158–59).

11. Nathaniel Hawthorne, *French and Italian Notebooks* in *The Centenary Edition of the Works of Nathaniel Hawthorne,* ed. William Charvat et al. (Columbus: Ohio State University Press, 1963–87), 14:157.

12. Caroline Wells Healey, *Margaret and Her Friends, or Ten Conversations with Margaret Fuller upon the Mythology of the Greeks and Its Expression in Art* (Boston: Roberts Brs., 1895), p. 77.

13. Capper, *Margaret Fuller,* pp. 303–04.

14. *Margaret Fuller, American Romantic: A Selection from Her Writings and Correspondence,* ed. Perry Miller (1963; reprint Gloucester, Mass.: Peter Smith, 1969), p. 97; Steele, "Freeing the 'Prisoned Queen,'" p. 163; *Letters,* 3:213; Healey, *Conversations,* p. 77; *EMF,* p. 234. The traditional invocation of Mary as virgin, mother, and queen likewise appears in the final canto of Dante's *Paradiso* and at the close of Goethe's *Faust.*

15. *EMF,* p. 232. I would suppose (see Capper, *Margaret Fuller,* p. 101) she first encountered the name in Goethe's *Wilhelm Meister*—see *Letters* 1:172 and n. 5. But as she knew, the name means "night," both in Hebrew and Arabic.

16. *Memoirs,* 1:99.

17. See Steele, "Freeing the 'Prisoned Queen,'" p. 163.

18. *Selections from Ralph Waldo Emerson: An Organic Anthology,* ed. Stephen E. Whicher (Boston: Houghton Mifflin, 1957), p. 56.

19. Ramifications of the snake-goddess association are discussed in Erich Neumann, *The Great Mother: An Analysis of the Archetype* (Princeton: Princeton University Press, 1963), pp. 143–46; Marija Gimbutas, *The Language of the Goddess* (San Francisco: Harper & Row, 1989), pp. 121–37; Gimbutas, *The Goddesses and Gods of Old Europe* (Berkeley: University of California Press, 1982), pp. 93–101 and 112–50; Merlin Stone, *When God Was a Woman* (New York: Dorset, 1976), pp. 199–214; and Adele Getty, *Goddess: Mother of Living Nature* (London: Thames and Hudson, 1990), pp. 13–14.

20. See Neumann, *Great Mother,* pp. 18–20; for Fuller's mention of the uroboros, see Healey, *Conversations,* pp. 84–87.

21. Steele, "Freeing the 'Prisoned Queen,'" p. 169.

22. *Memoirs,* 2:90.

23. *EMF,* 14. In unpublished notes on art works recorded around 1838–39, she likewise observed that Mary is "revered as the most pra[i]se[d] of her sex, for from early pagan antiquity were already virginity and maternity revered in this connexion." MS Am1086A, Box A at the Houghton Library, Harvard; publication is by permission of this library.

24. Both Steele and Capper have underscored the impact of Fuller's sustained, long-unresolved mourning for her father, which may figure in this poem by way of inverted elegy for the child; Steele ("Freeing, the 'Prisoned Queen,'" p. 168) also observes the relevance of Fuller's sympathetic mourning for the death of Emerson's first child.

25. *Letters,* 5:293. For Fuller's rather bizarre self-portrayal as Mary waiting by the sepulchre, in 1838 correspondence with Samuel Ward, see Capper, *Margaret Fuller,* pp. 278–79; and *Letters,* 2:91. Fuller also sounds a *stabat mater* theme in one of her letters to William Henry Channing (*Letters,* 2:215). After Ward marries Anna Barker in 1840, Fuller softens her distress with facetiousness and adapts yet another Marian figure when she writes Caroline Sturgis that she has received a letter from the newlywed couple she identifies as "Raphael and his Madonna" (*Letters,* 2:163).

26. It is intriguing to see that in her *New-York Tribune* essay, "What Fits a Man to Be a Voter?" (*EMF,* 401 and Steele's ["Freeing the 'Prisoned Queen'"] remark on 467 n. 1), Fuller offers another sense of Mary as Dark Madonna by portraying her as racially nonwhite.

27. *The Complete Poems of Emily Dickinsons,* ed. Thomas H. Johnson (Boston: Little, Brown, 1951), p. 115.

28. On the pictorial embodiment of coredemption in this painting, see James H. Beck's *Raphael* (New York: Harry N. Abrams, 1976), p. 108. I presume that Fuller based her poem on the Raphael painting in the Borghese Gallery commonly known as *The Deposition* in her time but referred to today as *The Entombment.*

29. "Magnolia" in *EMF*, p. 48; see also Fuller's "Autobiographical Romance" (*EMF*, 32); Steele's introductory remarks in *EMF*, p. xviii; and Charles Capper, *Margaret Fuller*, p. 21. Fuller develops further implications of rose imagery in her poem "Sub Rosa—Crux."

30. Emerson reported that Fuller "had a taste for gems, ciphers, talismans, omens, coincidences, and birth-days" and she "never forgot that her name, Margarita, signified a pearl" (*Memoirs*, 1:219).

31. Cited in Capper, *Margaret Fuller*, pp. 133, 250.

32. Cited in Steele's Introduction to *EMF*, p. xxxi.

33. As suggested by editors of *The Norton Anthology of American Literature* (New York: W. W. Norton, 4th ed., 1994), 1:1588 n. 3, the reference to Moses might also carry some irony as regards the status of women under Mosaic law. But within the relevant context, Fuller seems to me much more plausibly and simply interested in lamenting the unimaginative resistance and skepticism of Moses' desert followers (and, by extension, of complacent Americans) toward the visionary ideal set before them: "Yet, in this country, as by the Jews, when Moses was leading them to the promised land, everything has been done that inherited depravity could, to hinder the promise of heaven from its fulfillment"(*EMF*, 253). See also Exodus 14.11–13 and 16.2–12, together with Psalms 78 and 106.

34. On Fuller's use of sermonic and oratorical forms in *Woman in the Nineteenth Century*, see Urbanski, *Margaret Fuller's "Woman,"* pp. 128–145.

35. One recent account of circumstances influencing Fuller's revision in the full-length work is provided by Larry Reynolds, "From *Dial* Essay to New York Book: The Making of *Woman in the Nineteenth Century*," in *Periodical Literature in Nineteenth-Century America*, ed. Kenneth M. Price and Susan Belasco Smith (Charlottesville: University Press of Virginia, 1995). Reynolds stresses differences in presumed audiences for the two versions with regard to gender, class, and high versus popular culture.

36. Elaine Showalter, "Miranda and Cassandra: The Discourse of the Feminist Intellectual," in *Tradition and the Talents of Women*, ed. Florence Howe (Urbana: University of Illinois Press, 1991) pp. 320–21. Even more persuaded of Fuller's achieved artistry, Annette Kolodny sees *Woman in the Nineteenth Century* as the author's distinctive, quite deliberate experiment in feminist discourse. In "Inventing a Feminist Discourse: Rhetoric and Resistance in Margaret Fuller's *Woman in the Nineteenth Century*," *New Literary History* 25 (1994): 355–82," Kolodny suggests that Fuller based the spontaneous, open-ended, collaborative rhetoric of *Woman* on the "polyphony of conversation" (367) orchestrated in her own weekly meetings with other women. Kolodny argues that Fuller combined the spirit of this discussion format with study of Richard Whately's *Elements of Rhetoric* to achieve a noteworthy model of collaborative feminist rhetoric and critical inquiry.

37. Donna Dickenson elaborates the distinction between "rationalist" and "romantic" feminism in *Margaret Fuller: Writing a Woman's Life* (New York: St. Martin's Press, 1993), pp. 133–35. Dickenson also points out that "Fuller's attempt to state a vibrant and positive ideal of femaleness borrows from the dominant discourse, the cult of True Womanhood, but ultimately transcends it" (134).

38. Bell Gale Chevigny considers the import of Fuller's symbolic contrast between Minerva and Muse in *The Woman and the Myth: Margaret Fuller's Life and Writings* (Old Westbury, New York: Feminist Press, 1976), pp. 218–19.

39. Although the first citation in Fuller's opening pair is a famous line from *Hamlet*, the second remains unidentified despite its orphic ring of authority and summation of familiar themes within the work's literary mythology.

40. Nathaniel Hawthorne, "Drowne's Wooden Image," *Centenary Edition*, 10:309–10.

41. In an essay on Goethe, Fuller praises him for having always represented "the highest principle in the feminine form." Thus, she sees Goethe attributing saving influence to Margaret-Gretchen, who reappears at the close of *Faust,* part II, "not only redeemed herself, but by her innocence and forgiving tenderness hallowed to redeem the being who had injured her" (*Life Without and Within,* p. 41). Jeffrey Steele (*EMF,* p. 460, n. 116) points out Goethe's probable influence on Fuller's depiction of a secret realm of mothers. Fuller also showed a thorough acquaintance with Novalis, whose *Heinrich von Ofterdingen* and *Hymnen an die Nacht* testified to the redemptive power of divine womanhood through a peculiar blend of eroticism and neo-medieval Marianism. In addition, the sense Novalis develops in *Hymnen an die Nacht* of a pneumenal feminine presence abiding in nocturnal secrecy seems to me another likely source for Fuller's mythological portrayal of Leila. Fuller had almost certainly read *Hymnen an die Nacht,* for she wrote of Novalis that "His hymns are chiefly remarkable for their religious tenderness" (MS Am 1086, Box 4 at the Houghton Library, Harvard). A Marian revival associated with pietistic mysticism characterizes other German literature of this era, including writing by Wilhelm Heinrich Wackenroder.

42. *Letters,* 3:220. Fuller makes the biblical context of this Elizabeth and Mary reference still more explicit in a parallel journal entry for June, 1844; see "The Impulses of Human Nature: Margaret Fuller's Journal from June through October 1844," ed. Martha Berg and Alice de V. Perry, *Proceedings of the Massachusetts Historical Society,"* 102 (1990): 56.

43. *Memoirs,* 2:90.

44. Caroline Healey, *Conversations,* p. 98, 26.

45. Anna Jameson, *Legends of the Madonna* (1853; reprint, Boston: Houghton Mifflin, 1896), p. 140. Fuller had read various of Jameson's works, refers to her travel writing in *Summer on the Lakes,* and had once written to her. Albertenelli's *Visitation* (figure 2.2) is one of the works Jameson discusses in *Legends of the Madonna* (pp. 233–34).

46. *Memoirs,* 2:31–32.

47. An impression of Mary's youth and vitality around the time of the nativity was strengthened for Fuller by exposure to paintings such as Raphael's *Dresden Madonna,* a copy of which provoked her to remark: "That 'girl mother' somebody called her and the extreme youthfulness of her figure does give a peculiar and touching grace to the whole." MS Am1086A, Box A at the Houghton Library, Harvard.

48. On Fuller's response to the idea of the *improvisatrice,* the untamed, self-created version of womanhood made famous by Madame de Staël's character of Corinne, see *EMF,* pp. 127, 446, n. 6; and Margaret Vanderhaar Allen, *The Achievement of Margaret Fuller* (University Park: Pennsylvania State University Press, 1979), pp. 22–23, 29, 155.

49. As Jeffrey Steele observes, the Old Testament figure of Miriam, sister to Moses and Aaron, "held special attraction for Fuller" ("'A Tale of Mizraim': A Forgotten Story by Margaret Fuller," *New England Quarterly* 62 [1989]: 98). Miriam's assertive temperament and position of leadership are indicated in Exodus 15.20–22, Numbers 12, and Micah 6.4. In a story published in *The Token* for 1842 that Steele has attributed to Fuller, "the sternly beautiful Miriam" (p. 94) is a powerful presence. Her spiritual authority as "prophetess" here rivals that of Moses. See Steele, "'A Tale of Mizraim.'" At the end of this tale, the dignity of her mourning for a kinswoman resembles that of David for Absalom or of Mary for Jesus.

50. "*Al vero Dio sacrato, et vivo tempio / Fecero in tua virginita feconda,*" *EMF,* 352. The translation is cited from Robert M. Darling, *Petrarch's Lyric Poems: The Rime Sparse and Other Lyrics* (Cambridge: Harvard University Press, 1976), pp. 578–79.

51. *Memoirs,* 1:190.

CHAPTER 3

1. Elizabeth Ammons, "Heroines in *Uncle Tom's Cabin*," *American Literature*, 49 (1977): 161-79; Ammons, "Stowe's Dream of the Mother-Savior," in *New Essays on Uncle Tom's Cabin*, ed. Eric Sundquist (New York: Cambridge University Press, 1986), pp. 155-95; Dorothy Berkson, "Millennial Politics and the Feminine Fiction of Harriet Beecher Stowe," in *Critical Essays on Harriet Beecher Stowe*, ed. Elizabeth Ammons (Boston: G. K. Hall, 1980), pp. 244-58.

2. For a summary of views on Mary expressed in writings by Charles and Henry Ward Beecher, see Peter Gardella's *Innocent Ecstasy: How Christianity Gave America an Ethic of Sexual Pleasure* (New York: Oxford University Press, 1985), pp. 108, 128. In Charles Beecher's *The Incarnation; or, Pictures of the Virgin and Her Son* (New York: Harper & Bros., 1849), the author supposes that Mary's beauty of soul was matched by an "exquisite symmetry of physical development" (p. 53).

3. Letter to Sarah Beecher, November 11, 1853, at Stowe-Day Library; Harriet Beecher Stowe, *Sunny Memories of Foreign Lands* (Boston: Phillips Sampson, 1854), 2:343. For information concerning the inventory of Stowe's artworks, I am indebted to Kristen Froehlich at the Stowe-Day Library and to Renée T. Williams of the New Britain Museum of American Art for her detailed notes on file at Stowe-Day. Photographic evidence confirms that the detail reproduction of *The Madonna of the Goldfinch* was displayed during Stowe's residence.

4. I say "ostensibly" because Marian devotion also figures notably in Eastern Orthodox spirituality and to some lesser degree in the Anglican and Lutheran traditions, as Inge Leimberg reminded participants at the conference in Cologne where I presented an earlier version of this chapter.

5. Charles Foster, *The Rungless Ladder: Harriet Beecher Stowe and New England Puritanism* (Durham, N.C.: Duke University Press, 1954) p. 115.

6. The footsteps material is also available in the collection *Religious Studies: Sketches and Poems*, vol. 15 of the Riverside edition (Boston: Houghton Mifflin, 1896). Although Stowe produced many of these religious writings (which typically appeared first as articles in the *Christian Union*) considerably later than her best-known novels, the views they offer of theology generally and of Marian themes in particular show a consistent development from earlier brief statements such as her 1849 Introduction to Charles Beecher's book on *The Incarnation; or Pictures of the Virgin and Her Son*. The *Incarnation* volume includes as well an early printing of Stowe's poem "Mary at the Cross," which demonstrates the role Mariology already played in her thinking by 1849. "The Sorrows of Mary," another relevant poem collected (with minor revisions) in *Religious Studies* and reprinted in the Appendix, first appeared in the Supplement to the *Hartford Courant* for February 16, 1867.

7. *Religious Studies*, p. 31.

8. *Woman in Sacred History* (1873; reprint, New York: Portland House, 1990), p. 193.

9. *Religious Studies*, p. 36.

10. *Religious Studies*, pp. 33-36, 41; *Woman in Sacred History*, p. 181. Antedating Stowe's prose statements of this point, her lines on "Mary at the Cross" (1849) include a remark on the hours Mary must have spent "in lone musings" with Jesus, gazing into his eye and holding his hand (*Religious Studies*, p. 315).

11. *Woman in Sacred History*, pp. 183, 185-86, 198; *Religious Studies*, p. 36.

12. "For many years my religious experience perplexed me—I could see no reason for it—why God led me thus and so, I have seen lately, and I believe that He has a purpose for which He has kept me hitherto. I am willing to be just such and so much and be used

for what He wills—'Behold the handmaid of the Lord.'" Letter to Charles Beecher, now dated before October 13, 1852, at Stowe-Day Library and printed in *Stowe Day Foundation Bulletin,* 1 no. 2 (September 1960).

13. *Woman in Sacred History,* pp. 198, 183; *Religious Studies,* p. 70.

14. Reprinted in *Religious Studies,* p. 190, 70; *Woman in Sacred History,* pp. 183, 70, 190.

15. *Woman in Sacred History,* p. 190.

16. Joan D. Hedrick, *Harriet Beecher Stowe: A Life* (New York: Oxford University Press, 1994), pp. 190-91, 214, 254, 274-83. Written after Stowe had lost both Charley and Henry, "The Sorrows of Mary" exposes the poignance of her identification with the *stabat mater:* "Had ye ever a son like Jesus / To give to a death of pain?" (in *Religious Studies,* p. 353). However, her earlier verses on the same theme, published in 1849 as "Mary at the Cross," were composed before Charley's death. In Charles Beecher's *Plymouth Collection of Hymns and Tunes* (New York: A. S. Barnes and Burr, 1863), a Protestant work with which Stowe was closely associated, hymn 26 extends involvement of the *stabat mater* figure to any instance of oppression, grief, or terror.

17. *Woman in Sacred History,* p. 172; *My Wife and I; or, Harry Henderson's History* (New York: J. B. Ford, 1871), p. 39; *Religious Studies,* p. 31.

18. In addition to Berkson and Ammons, critics Alice Crozier (*The Novels of Harriet Beecher Stowe* [New York: Oxford University Press, 1969]) and Jane Tompkins (*Sentimental Designs: The Cultural Work of American Fiction, 1790-1850* [New York: Oxford University Press, 1985]) have stressed the central role of mothers in Stowe's novel.

19. *Uncle Tom's Cabin, or Life among the Lowly,* ed. and intro. Ann Douglas (New York: Viking, 1981), p. 63. Subsequent references, identified parenthetically, are to this edition.

20. Tompkins, *Sentimental Designs,* p. 142.

21. Hedrick, *Harriet Beecher Stowe,* p. 8.

22. *Woman in Sacred History,* pp. 174-75.

23. In her *Revelations of Divine Love,* which Stowe could not have read, the fourteenth-century English mystic Julian of Norwich envisions a similar connection between birth pangs and the Passion of Jesus.

24. Elizabeth Ammons ("Heroines," 175) aptly describes Legree as "a caricature, and a very serious one, of supermasculinity, which Stowe associates with the devil."

25. See Lawrence Buell, "Calvinism Romanticized: Harriet Beecher Stowe, Samuel Hopkins, and *The Minister's Wooing,*" *ESQ: A Journal of the American Renaissance*" 24 (1978): 121.

26. *The Minister's Wooing* (Hartford: Stowe-Day, 1988), p. 19. Subsequent references, indicated parenthetically, are to this edition.

27. I am grateful to my graduate student Kurt Heidinger for pointing out this significance of Candace's name. I have also benefited from discussion of this issue in an unpublished essay by Monica Hatzberger.

28. Julia Kristeva, "Stabat Mater," in *Tales of Love,* trans. Leon S. Roudiez (New York: Columbia University Press, 1987), p. 250.

29. On Stowe's fictive adaptations of the historical character of Hopkins, see Buell's "Calvinism Romanticized," the title of which inspired my titling of this chapter.

30. *Agnes of Sorrento* (Boston: Houghton Mifflin, 1896), pp. 325, 131. All subsequent references, indicated parenthetically, are to this edition.

31. On Mary as reflection of Romantic ideals, see Gardella, *Innocent Ecstasy,* p. 100. In *American Catholic Arts and Fictions: Culture, Ideology, Aesthetics* (New York: Cambridge University Press, 1992), Paul Giles emphasizes Stowe's rendering of Agnes in conformity with "the dictates of Protestant humanism" (p. 79). But like Jenny Franchot (in *Roads to*

Rome: The Antebellum Encounter with Catholicism [Berkeley: University of California Press, 1994]), I see Agnes as linked fairly directly to the Marian Madonna insofar as her "creative chastity draws on the celibate yet fertile Virgin" (253).

32. In the working journal (at the Stowe-Day Library, Hartford) from which Stowe developed the first part of her novel, she records the strangeness of seeing defunct shrines of pre-Christian religion extant in Italy, for example, of watching a mare with her foal pasturing in the temple of Ceres.

33. See Gardella, *Innocent Ecstasy,* pp. 25-32 and especially the illustrations following p. 102, for elaboration of these fears. Yet overall, Stowe certainly rejected the sort of virulent anti-Catholicism that her father, Lyman Beecher, tried to promote.

34. See Laurie Crumpacker, "Four Novels of Harriet Beecher Stowe: A Study in Nine-teenth-Century Androgyny," pp. 89-94 in *American Novelists Revisited: Essays in Feminist Criticism,* ed. Fritz Fleishmann (Boston: G. K. Hall, 1982).

35. *The Pearl of Orr's Island: A Story of the Seacoast of Maine* (1862; reprint, Ridgewood, N.J.: Gregg Press, 1967), pp. 8, 13, 20. Subsequent references, indicated parenthetically, are to this edition.

36. *Religious Studies,* pp. 93-94. In her *Letters to Mothers* (New York: Harper and Bros., 1840), Lydia Sigourney extols maternal love as changeless and "next in patience to that of a Redeemer" such that it fulfills a "sacred mission." The nearly complete "dominion" of mothers over their children allowed Christian mothers to perform an angelic ministry within the household (pp. 49, 53, 16, 10). Elizabeth Ammons ("Stowe's Dream," 158-59), draw-ing in turn on historian Ruth H. Block, points out that a distinctly idealized concept of "feminized parenthood" or "motherhood" did not take hold in America until after the Industrial Revolution.

37. *Religious Studies,* p. 93.

38. *Oldtown Folks* in *Harriet Beecher Stowe: Three Novels* (New York: Library of America, 1982); cf. Captain Kittridge's remark in *Pearl* that "'This 'ere old Bible—why it's just like yer mother,—ye rove and ramble . . . and mebbe think the old woman ain't so fashionable as some; but when sickness and sorrow comes, why, there ain't nothin' else to go back to'" (p. 386).

39. In *Harriet Beecher Stowe* (esp. pp. 127, 140-41), Joan D. Hedrick points out that Stowe suffered not only bereavement but also persistent failure in attempting to raise her children and govern her household in a manner consistent with her professed ideology.

CHAPTER 4

1. On the ethnoreligious impact of immigration during this period, see Sydney E. Ahlstrom, *A Religious History of the American People* (New Haven: Yale University Press, 1972), pp. 735-38, 749-52, 851-52; and Barbara Miller Solomon, "The Anglo-Saxon Cult," in *Intellectual History in America: From Darwin to Niebuhr,* ed. Cushing Strout (New York: Harper & Row, 1968), 2:28-38.

2. Peter Gardella points out the linkage between Marian interest and Romanticism on the part of several of these figures in *Innocent Ecstasy: How Christianity Gave America an Ethic of Sexual Pleasure* (New York: Oxford University Press, 1985), esp. pp. 102-29.

3. Barbara Welter, "The Cult of True Womanhood: 1820-60," *American Quarterly* 18 (1966): 152.

4. Martha Banta, *Imaging American Women: Idea and Ideals in Cultural History* (New York: Columbia University Press, 1987), esp. pp. 45-91. Further description of the New Woman appears in Adele Heller and Lois Rudnick, *1915, The Cultural Moment* (New Brunswick,

N.J.: Rutgers University Press, 1991); and in Lois Banner, *Women in Modern America: A Brief History* (New York: Harcourt Brace Jovanovich, 1974), pp. 1–44.

5. Henry James, "The Madonna of the Future," in *The Tales of Henry James*, ed. Maqbool Aziz (Oxford: Clarendon Press, 1978), 2:232, 210.

6. Banta, *Imaging American Women*, pp. 433, 426.

7. On the further relevance of Frederic's own childhood family associations with Methodism in upstate New York, see Thomas F. O'Donnell and Hoyt C. Franchere, *Harold Frederic* (New York: Twayne, 1961), pp. 24–25, 32–33, 110–12.

8. *The Damnation of Theron Ware or Illumination*, ed. Charlyne Dodge and Stanton Garner, in *The Harold Frederic Edition* (Lincoln: University of Nebraska Press, 1985), 3:27, 97, 207. All subsequent references are to this critical edition; the same text and pagination are used in the 1986 Penguin Classics edition.

9. Larzer Ziff, *The American 1890s: Life and Times of a Lost Generation* (New York: Viking Compass, 1966), p. 214.

10. On the suicide plan as indicated in Frederic's working notes, see Stanton Garner's "History of the Text" in *The Harold Frederic Edition*, 3:372, 380.

11. In *The Faces of Eve: Women in the Nineteenth Century American Novel* (New York: Oxford University Press, 1976), Judith Fryer argues in the course of an otherwise nuanced discussion that "one-dimensional" Celia is "purely a temptress" (62, 57).

12. That Theron never was a good man is likewise the viewpoint set forth by Austin Briggs in *The Novels of Harold Frederic* (Ithaca, N.Y.: Cornell University Press, 1969), pp. 117–20.

13. Such is also the conclusion, with which I concur, articulated by John Henry Raleigh in his Introduction (previously published as "The Damnation of Theron Ware" in *American Literature* 30 [1958]: 210–27) to *The Damnation of Theron Ware* (New York: Holt, Rinehart and Winston, 1960), p. xvii.

14. John W. Crowley, "The Nude and the Madonna in *The Damnation of Theron Ware*" 3 (1973): 379–89. In "Passion, Authority, and Faith in *The Damnation of Theron Ware*" (*American Literature* 58 [1986]), Fritz Oehlschlaeger likewise emphasizes Theron's "inability to accept mature sexuality" and the "effeminization, regression, and adolescent prurience that emerge increasingly in Theron as the novel proceeds" (241, 238–39).

15. Crowley, "The Nude and the Madonna," 381.

16. See also Frederic's short story, "Cordelia and the Moon," reprinted in *The Harold Frederic Edition*, 3:471–87. In this brief precursor to *The Damnation*, a minister named Ware appears, as does a beautiful organist named Cordelia Fenlark, who is linked repeatedly to the winter moon and shares several character traits with Celia.

17. On Frederic's indecision about whether to name the Madden woman Celia or Cecilia, see Garner's "History of the Text" in *The Harold Frederic Edition*, 3:262. Cecilia, a Roman saint commonly pictured at the organ as patron saint of music, would be at once an apt name for Celia and—in view of Cecilia's reputed martyrdom—a somewhat ironic one. See also figure 4.3.

18. Although the Virgin sometimes appears alone without an infant Jesus in Western depictions (unlike Eastern Orthodox icons, where she must be linked to the child), Frederic's preliminary reference and subsequent dialogue both imply that the portrait in question would have presented "the Virgin Mary and the Child," or at least *some* mother and child (p. 191; cf. pp. 258–59).

19. Frederic could have read about Cyril and Hypatia in several of the sources he consulted, including two works by John William Draper, as Garner points out in notes to his critical edition of *The Damnation*. Draper more than once refers to "worship" or "adora-

tion of the Virgin Mary" surpassing mere devotion, as in his *History of the Conflict between Religion and Science* (New York: Appleton and Company, 1875), pp. 55, 71. Celia does appear to confuse the doctrine of virgin birth with that of the immaculate conception, but this error—for which I have not found precedent in Frederic's known sources—is common in popular discourse.

20. Garner identifies these and other relevant sources in the notes attached to his critical edition of *The Damnation,* in *The Harold Frederic Edition,* 3:345–50.

21. *Utica Daily Observer,* May 3, 1880. A reference in O'Donnell and Franchere's *Harold Frederic* (p. 44) gave me a useful lead on this report and on where to track it down. Later in the same year (September 11), report from the foreign press of a "startling" apparition of Mary in Limerick, Ireland, gained front-page billing in Frederic's newspaper.

22. *Utica Daily Observer,* March 19, 1879; June 30, 1879. Frederic reprinted the whole of Terry's "Non-Exclusiveness" sermon of June 30.

23. *Utica Daily Observer,* June 30, 1879; July 14, 1879.

24. According to Stanton Garner (*Harold Frederic Edition,* 3:348 n. 194, 372), Frederic's reading of Matthew Arnold also informed Celia's division of all humanity into Greeks and Jews. Frederic expresses his own relish for Hellenistic culture in a letter he wrote defending a recent suicide in 1893. In the course of praising ancient Greek responses to death, he there laments the "tragic submerging of Greek philosophy and graces under the acrid flood of theocratic Semitism" (*Harold Frederic Edition,* 1:342, letter of August 20, 1893). Such sentiments resembled those Frederic had previously encountered in his reading of Lecky and other scholars.

25. Raleigh, Introduction to *The Damnation,* pp. xiii–xiv; O'Donnell and Franchere, p. 115.

26. Fryer, *The Faces of Eve,* p. 62.

27. *Harold Frederic Edition,* 3:356.

28. The Celia Madden who reappears as a secondary character in Frederic's last novel, *The Market-Place* (1899), offers yet another variant on the New Woman, or perhaps on the New Woman manquée. Bereft of her earlier exuberance, this later Celia admits her disillusionment with the possibilities available to women and laments that she has never quite discovered what to do with her independence: "'Oh, we women all have our walls—our limitations—if it comes to that. . . . The free woman is a fraud—a myth'" (*Harold Frederic Edition,* 2:163). Frances ("Frank") Bailey, a self-supporting London typist and office manager in Frederic's *Gloria Mundi* (1898), also seems to compromise her resolve to remain independent when she ends up marrying a wealthy duke. In notes for this novel (as cited in O'Donnell and Franchere, *Harold Frederic,* p. 129), Frederic describes the new class of professional women as "Hens who won't sit."

29. Crowley, "The Nude and the Madonna," p. 385.

30. For another view of how this novel addresses the problematic, socially constructed character of gender roles and identities, see Lisa Watt MacFarlane's "Resurrecting Man: Desire and *The Damnation of Theron Ware,*" *Studies in American Fiction* 20 (1992): 127–43.

31. *Harold Frederic Edition,* 1:164.

32. In her well-known account of *The Feminization of American Culture* (1977; reprint, New York: Anchor-Doubleday, 1988), Ann Douglas points out the growing sense of alliance in the nineteenth century between sentimental, womanly values and disestablished clergymen.

33. William Edward Hartpole Lecky, *History of European Morals from Augustus to Charlemagne* (1877; reprint, New York: Arno Press, 1975) 2:367–69.

CHAPTER 5

1. Henry Adams, *Novels, Mont Saint Michel, The Education* (New York: Library of America, 1983), p. 1070. All subsequent references to the Adams texts in question are to this edition, with page numbers indicated parenthetically.

2. On the impact in Boston of large-scale Catholic immigration during this era, its encouragement of industrialization through expansion of the labor supply, and the reaction of Boston Brahmins to demographic change, see Oscar Handlin, *Boston's Immigrants: A Study in Acculturation* (New York: Atheneum Press, 1968); and Paula M. Kane, *Separatism and Subculture: Boston Catholicism, 1900–1920* (Chapel Hill: University of North Carolina Press, 1994).

3. Peter Gardella, *Innocent Ecstasy: How Christianity Gave America an Ethic of Sexual Pleasure* (New York: Oxford University Press, 1985), p. 102.

4. For an unusually severe critique of Adams's personal and artistic failings in writings subsequent to the *History of the United States,* see William Dusinberre's *Henry Adams: The Myth of Failure* (Charlottesville: University Press of Virginia, 1980). Dusinberre probably does not exaggerate Adams's personal defects, though to my mind he overstates their damaging effect on works like *Chartres* and *The Education.*

5. See Barbara Welter, "The Cult of True Womanhood: 1820–60," *American Quarterly* 18 (1966): 151–74.

6. Previous commentary on the import and comparative origins of Adams's Mariology can be found in Daniel L. Manheim, "Motives of His Own: Henry Adams and the Genealogy of the Virgin," *New England Quarterly* 63 (1990): 601–23; John Patrick Diggins, "'Who Bore the Failure of the Light': Henry Adams and the Crisis of Authority," *New England Quarterly* 58 (1985): 165–92; and Richard F. Miller, "Henry Adams and the Influence of Woman," *American Literature* 18 (1947): 291–98.

7. Ernest Samuels, *Henry Adams: The Major Phase* (Cambridge: Harvard University Press, 1964) p. 287, 626 n. 44. Samuels presents a useful summary article, drawing on much of the same material, in "Henry Adams' 20th Century Virgin," *The Christian Century* 77 (October 5, 1960): 1143–46. On Adams's interest in Isis, as eventually conflated with his Mariolatry and as heightened by his own travel in Egypt, see Joseph F. Byrnes, *The Virgin of Chartres: An Intellectual and Psychological History of the Work of Henry Adams* (London and Toronto: Associated University Presses, 1981), p. 112.

8. On the relevance of travels in the South Seas to Adams's ongoing search for eternal womanhood, see Kim Moreland, "Henry Adams, The Medieval Lady, and the 'New Woman,'" *CLIO* 18 (1989): 294–96; and William Merrill Decker, *The Literary Vocation of Henry Adams* (Chapel Hill: University of North Carolina Press, 1990), pp. 23–28.

9. See, for instance, Adolf Katzenellenbogen's learned study of *The Sculptural Programs of Chartres Cathedral: Christ, Mary, Ecclesia* (New York: W. W. Norton, 1959), esp. pp. viii, 9–12, 26, 46, 56–61, 65, 101–2. Analyzing in detail the Incarnation cycle of the Royal Portal as well as portals of the transept wings, Katzenellenbogen points out many ways in which representations of Mary complement Christ's "essence" and manifest the inseparable tie between "the Incarnation of Christ" and the "Triumph of Mary-Ecclesia" (10, 65). Adams never specifies where he finds the Trinity—which must be pictorialized obliquely if at all—represented in the art of Chartres. Yet it is worth noticing that at Chartres the Baptism of Jesus, which traditionally implies a Trinitarian reference, fits harmoniously into the same lancet or Incarnation Window that portrays Mary enthroned with two flowered scepters. Beyond my own imprecise memories of Chartres, I have relied on Malcolm Miller's guide-

book, *Chartres Cathedral* (London: Pitkin Pictorials, 1985) to confirm this point. Adams does discuss the Marian image, but not the remainder of the central window, in his chapter "The Twelfth Century Glass" (465).

10. Moreland, "Henry Adams," esp. 292, 304.

11. See Byrnes, *The Virgin of Chartres,* esp. pp. 163–68. Throughout this book, Byrnes offers an extended psychological argument for the influence of Marian Adams and Elizabeth Cameron—particularly for Henry Adams's defensive response to Marian's death—on Adams's literary productions. Others, too, have stressed the way in which Adams's symbolic Virgin reflects a compensatory reaction to Marian's death. Such assessments include that of William Dusinberre in *The Myth of Failure,* pp. 54–85, 188, 212 (with an excellent general account of Marian's character and role); and of Robert Mane in *Henry Adams on the Road to Chartres* (Cambridge: Harvard University Press, 1971), pp. 197–202.

12. Decker, *Literary Vocation,* p. 23.

13. On the perception of these financial woes for the nation and for Adams personally, see Samuels, *Henry Adams,* pp. 168, 411–12.

14. *The Letters of Henry Adams,* ed. J. C. Levenson et al. (Cambridge: Harvard University Press, 1982–88), 3:561.

15. *Letters,* 5:496–97.

16. Critical studies relevant to this point include Decker's commentary (*Literary Vocation,* pp. 204–57) and Millicent Bell's essay on "Adams' *Esther:* The Morality of Taste," *New England Quarterly* 35 (1962): 147–61. Biographical accounts of the novel as roman à clef can be found in several sources, including J. C. Levenson's *The Mind and Art of Henry Adams* (Stanford, Calif.: Stanford University Press, 1957), pp. 115–16, 199–205; and Ernest Samuels's Introduction to *Democracy* and *Esther,* reprinted in *Critical Essays on Henry Adams,* ed. Earl N. Harbert (Boston: G. K. Hall, 1981), pp. 76–83.

17. On Adams's relation to pragmatism, in its William Jamesian as well as its more vulgar forms, see Michael Colacurcio, "*Democracy* and *Esther:* Henry Adams' Flirtation with Pragmatism," *American Quarterly* 19 (1967):53–70.

18. Although *Esther* alludes directly to Hawthorne's character of Esther Dudley, Decker (*Literary Vocation,* 214–17) perceives also certain parallels between Esther and Hester Prynne.

19. On the multiplicity of meanings Niagara inspires for characters in *Esther,* see Elizabeth McKinsey's *Niagara Falls: Icon of the American Sublime* (Cambridge: Cambridge University Press, 1985), pp. 275–77.

20. See Patrick V. McGreevy, *Imagining Niagara: The Meaning and Making of Niagara Falls* (Amherst: University of Massachusetts Press, 1994), p. 110. According to McGreevy, a large hydroelectric plant was in operation by 1896.

21. See Adams's Lowell Institute Lecture of 1876 as reprinted in *The Great Secession Winter of 1860–61 and Other Essays by Henry Adams,* ed. George Hochfield (New York: Sagamore Press, 1958), particularly the passage concerning Egypt on pp. 342–43.

22. Such, for example, is the perspective adopted by Robert Mane (*Henry Adams,* vii–viii), who acknowledges that he is following in the spirit of suggestions made some years ago by Maurice Breton and Oscar Cargill.

23. Michael Colacurcio, "The Dynamo and the Angelic Doctor: The Bias of Henry Adams' Medievalism," *American Quarterly* 17 (1965): 697.

24. On the influence of La Farge and Richardson, see Mane, *Henry Adams,* pp. viii, 62–74; on the influence of Brooks Adams, see pp. 76–82 and 92–99, together with Brooks Adams, *The Law of Civilization and Decay: An Essay on History* (New York: Macmillan, 1895); Mane (pp. 47–61, 86–88, 91) also discusses Adams's ethnic and anti-Semitic attitudes.

25. Robert Mane argues that *Chartres* is "composed like a triptych, with the first three chapters neatly balancing the last three." He proposes that "Adams' vision of eleventh-century art and his interpretation of thirteenth-century scholastic philosophy flank with due Gothic proportions the twelfth-century shrine of the Virgin" (*Henry Adams,* 227).

26. Cited in ibid., p. 107.

27. Ibid., pp. 151–52.

28. Ibid., p. 241.

29. On the question of Adams's relation to fideism, see Colacurcio, "The Dynamo and the Angelic Doctor," 709–12.

30. See Colacurcio ("The Dynamo and the Angelic Doctor," 701–2) and Mane (*Henry Adams,* 219–20) on issues arising from Adams's peculiar translation of the Latin *movens.*

31. In *Exiles from Eden: Religion and the Academic Vocation in America* (New York: Oxford University Press, 1993), Mark R. Schwehn discusses implications of the author's wordplay on his own name. "In the *Education,*" writes Schwehn, "the name Henry Adams has mythic implications of its own, invoking at one and the same time the heroic founding fathers of the American political tradition and the Biblical progenitor of all humankind. . . . By repeating his own name throughout the *Education,* he suggests that the fate of America as well as the larger destiny of humanity can be figured in the fall of one Adams" (104).

32. In "Dynamo and Virgin Reconsidered," *American Quarterly* 27 (1958): 183–94, medievalist Lynn White Jr. argues on historical grounds that the Dynamo and Virgin should not be regarded as "opposing and mutually exclusive energies" (187) despite Adams's motives for portraying them as such.

33. A cultural circumstance that further complicates identification of the new technological age with masculinity is the way in which electricity, electric lights, and communication were commonly represented to the public with female icons. For an informative description of this phenomenon, with illustrative reference to the 1893 Columbian Exposition, see Martha Banta, *Imaging American Women: Idea and Ideals in Cultural History* (New York: Columbia University Press, 1987), pp. 515, 530–32.

34. See Priscilla L. Walton, *The Disruption of the Feminine in Henry James* (Toronto: University of Toronto Press, 1992), pp. 6–33.

35. In curious ways, Adams anticipates here Julia Kristeva's contemporary emphasis on the transverbal force of the Virginal Maternal. See Kristeva's "Stabat Mater" in *Tales of Love,* trans. Leon S. Roudiez (New York: Columbia University Press, 1987), pp. 234–63.

36. On the possible meanings of the Rock Creek Memorial, see R. P. Blackmur's *Henry Adams,* pp. 15, 101, 114, 339–344. Writing on "Henry Adams: His Passage to Asia" (in *Critical Essays on Henry Adams,* ed. Harbert), Margaret J. Brown proposes that Adams came to link the Marian Virgin, with her "unifying power of divine love," to "the mother goddesses of Asia," particularly the Buddhist Kwannon; Kwannon, in turn, "became an important source of ideas for the monument to be placed at the grave of his wife" (p. 248).

37. In "The Dynamo and the Angelic Doctor" (701, 704–5), Colacurcio points out the inherent inadequacy of Adams's trying to explain piety, metaphysics, and love in terms of dynamics, and it is indeed questionable whether "the single concept of force" can account for the entire universe.

38. In *Henry Adams,* ed. Veronica Makowsky (New York: Harcourt Brace Jovanovich, 1980), pp. 149–55, R. P. Blackmur discusses what Adams may have meant in describing himself as "conservative Christian anarchist." "Unitarian mystic" aptly identifies other incongruities in Adams's temperament, though Samuels (in *The Major Phase,* pp. 263, 559,

622 n.7, 647 n.28) seems to have erred in suggesting that Adams described himself this way in correspondence with Elizabeth Cameron dated 16 February 1917. Instead, my investigation reveals that in a letter of this date (unpublished, at the Massachusetts Historical Society), Harriet A. Dillingham uses the term to describe herself in writing to Adams.

39. R. P. Blackmur, *Henry Adams,* pp. 13, 16.

CHAPTER 6

1. T. S. Eliot, "A Sceptical Patrician," Review of *The Education of Henry Adams: An Autobiography, Athenaeum* 4647 (1919): 361. Jewel Spears Brooker proposes the Adams-Prufrock analogy in "Substitutes for Religion in the Early Poetry of T. S. Eliot," *The Placing of T. S. Eliot,* ed. Brooker (Columbia: University of Missouri Press, 1991), pp. 19–20.

2. T. S. Eliot, *The Complete Poems and Plays, 1909–1950* (New York: Harcourt, Brace & World, 1952), p. 38. Subsequent references to the poetry, with pagination given parenthetically, are to this edition.

3. *Selected Prose of T. S. Eliot,* ed. Frank Kermode (New York: Harcourt, Brace Jovanovich, 1975), p. 178.

4. Jewel Spears Brooker, *Mastery and Escape: T. S. Eliot and the Dialectic of Modernism* (Amherst: University of Massachusetts Press, 1994), p. 2.

5. Henry Adams, "The Rule of Phase Applied to History" (1909), in *The Tendency of History* (New York: Book League of America, 1929), p. 172.

6. Concluding with remarks on Edwin Muir and T. S. Eliot, A. M. Allchin considers a range of Anglican responses in *The Joy of All Creation: An Anglican Meditation on the Place of Mary* (Cambridge, Mass.: Cowley, 1984). Allchin's remarks (pp. 17–34) on the Marian implications of nativity sermons by Lancelot Andrewes are particularly salient in view of Eliot's strong interest in Andrewes.

7. William Force Stead, *The Shadow of Mount Carmel: A Pilgrimage* (London: Richard Cobden-Sanderson, 1926), p. 64. American-born Stead, who later became a Roman Catholic, does retain skepticism or ambivalent feelings toward aspects of Marian piety in this book, which Eliot praised in a letter of recommendation dated 9 December 1938 (Osborn Collection, Beinecke Library at Yale).

8. See Joseph Bentley, "Some Notes on Eliot's Gallery of Women," in *Approaches to Teaching Eliot's Poetry and Plays,* ed. Jewel Spears Brooker (New York: Modern Language Association, 1988), pp. 39–45; together with Brooker's reflections on "Tradition and Female Enmity" in *Mastery and Escape* (pp. 213–28); and Lyndall Gordon's more severe assessment in *Eliot's Early Years* (New York: Oxford University Press, 1977 [esp. pp. 25–28]) of how Eliot's personal limitations affected his imaging of women. Philip Sicker analyzes the Belladonna figure at some length in "The Belladonna: Eliot's Female Archetype in *The Waste Land,*" *Twentieth Century Literature* 30 (1984): 420–31.

9. On the Sibyl of Cumae, including her relation to *The Golden Bough,* see Jewel Spears Brooker and Joseph Bentley, *Reading The Waste Land: Modernism and the Limits of Interpretation* (Amherst: University of Massachusetts Press, 1990), pp. 44–48 and 202. Analyzing wording in Eliot's original draft of "What the Thunder Said," Brooker and Bentley argue that "the Sibyl of Cumae was in the poem before Eliot put her in the epigraph" (202).

10. Grover Smith, *T. S. Eliot's Poetry and Plays: A Study in Sources and Meaning,* 2d ed. (Chicago: University of Chicago Press, 1974), p. 99.

11. Jessie Weston, *From Ritual to Romance* (1920; reprint, New York: Peter Smith, 1941), pp. 75, 46–47.

12. Bentley, "Some Notes," p. 41.

13. On the connotations of hyacinth, see Sicker, "The Belladonna," 422; and Grover Smith, *T. S. Eliot's Poetry and Plays,* pp. 74–75. Sicker sees Marie, who "unquestionably anticipates" the hyacinth girl (421), as closely identified with the latter. That Eliot repeats the name "Marie" in conjunction with his prelapsarian woman of promise is worth noting, though the evocative effect may be accidental insofar as the passage in question derives from his reminiscences of Countess Marie Larisch, according to Valerie Eliot in *The Waste Land: A Facsimile and Transcript of the Original Drafts* (New York: Harcourt Brace Jovanovich, 1971), pp. 125–26.

14. Smith, *T. S. Eliot's Poetry and Plays,* p. 74.

15. James G. Frazer, *The Golden Bough: The Roots of Religion and Folklore* (1890; reprint, New York: Crown Publishers, 1981), 1:287. This description appears in the "Adonis" section, one of three Eliot singled out as most useful in his own treatment.

16. Particularly as one looks ahead to "Ash-Wednesday," an ironic linkage between "belladona" and the Virgin Mary may be reinforced by way of allusion to Leonardo da Vinci's painting of *Madonna of the Rocks.* See Grover Smith, "T. S. Eliot's Lady of the Rocks," *Notes and Queries* 194 (1949): 123–25.

17. On these other senses of Belladonna, see Sicker, "The Belladonna," p. 424; and Elizabeth Drew, *T. S. Eliot: The Design of His Poetry* (New York: Charles Scribner's Sons, 1949), p. 72.

18. *Waste Land* facsimile, p. 23; a canceled insertion within this passage (p. 29) reinforces the sense of Fresca as a latter-day mock reincarnation of Venus.

19. Bentley, "Some Notes on Eliot's Gallery of Women," p. 41.

20. Sicker, "The Belladonna," p. 424.

21. "And so I pray you, by that Virtue which leads you to the topmost of the stair—be mindful in due time of my pain." Thus Eliot translates the passage for his essay on "Dante," in *Selected Essays* (1932; reprint, New York: Harcourt Brace, 1950), p. 217.

22. See Eliot's remarks in *Selected Essays,* p. 217.

23. Ibid., pp. 235, 223.

24. *Paradiso* 23:92–93; Dominic Manganiello, *T. S. Eliot and Dante* (New York: St. Martin's Press, 1989), p. 65.

25. Barbara Seward, *The Symbolic Rose* (Dallas: Spring Publications, 1954), p. 22. In addition to tracing the development of rose symbolism through Western literary history with due regard for Marian themes, Seward's book devotes a full chapter to "Eliot and Tradition" (pp. 156–86). In Dante's representation of St. Bernard's prayer in *Paradiso* 23.73, the Virgin is addressed as "the Rose in which the divine Word was made flesh" (trans. John D. Sinclair in *The Divine Comedy of Dante Alighieri, III* [New York: Oxford University Press, 1961], p. 335).

26. Liturgically, the Simeon-Mary association would have seemed all the more inevitable to Eliot insofar as the Magnificat or Song of Mary (from Luke 1.46–55) is the other canticle most commonly sung or said in combination with the Nunc Dimittis at Evening Prayer.

27. The anima implications of Marina have been pointed out by Drew, *T. S. Eliot,* p. 129; and by John H. Timmerman, "T. S. Eliot's 'Marina,'" *Christianity and Literature* 41 (1992): 413.

28. Smith *T. S. Eliot's Poetry and Plays,* p. 132; Timmerman, "T. S. Eliot's 'Marina,'" 417, 413.

29. Neville Braybrooke (in *T. S. Eliot: The Man and His Work,* ed. Allen Tate [New York: Delacorte Press, 1966], p. 383) contends that "some parts of 'Ash-Wednesday' already can be linked with an engraving of Murillo's 'Immaculate Conception' [figure 6.2] which

hung in his parents' bedroom at 2635 Locust Street" in St. Louis; Gordon (*Eliot's Early Years*, p. 4) refers more generally to a painting of the Madonna and Child but attributes its presence there to Eliot's mother, Charlotte Champe Eliot.

30. Louis L. Martz, "Ash-Wednesday: Voices for the Veiled Sister," in *T. S. Eliot, Man and Poet,* ed. Laura Cowan (Orono: National Poetry Foundation, University of Maine, 1990), 1:190. Moreover, in Eliot's day Anglo-Catholics ordinarily supplemented the *Book of Common Prayer* with unofficial liturgical and devotional texts (e.g., the *Anglican Prayer Book*) that display a more "Catholic" orientation.

31. Commentators such as Grover Smith (*T. S. Eliot's Poetry and Plays*, p. 140) have often noted other allusions relevant in this section, particularly those to Shakespeare and Cavalcanti.

32. Smith, *T. S. Eliot's Poetry and Plays,* pp. 143–44.

33. Glen Bush assesses the range of likely possibilities—including "the Virgin Mary, Beatrice, Matilda, or a mythic female symbol"—in his essay on "The Mysterious Holy Lady in T. S. Eliot's 'Ash Wednesday,'" *The Aligarh Critical Miscellany* 1 (1988): 198–215.

34. In *The Golden Bough* (2:29), James Frazer describes European folk rituals of fertility in which bone boiled on Shrove Tuesday was mixed with ashes and later seed corn; other fertility rituals (1:254–60, 2:250–51) enacted a burial of death and symbolic regeneration through the destruction of a straw effigy at Ash Wednesday.

35. Manganiello, *T. S. Eliot and Dante,* p. 69.

36. Eliot was not alone in his verse portrayal of Mary as Lady of Silences. For example, Mary Elise Woellwarth had earlier published in England a collection of *Songs to Our Lady of Silence* (Ditchling, Sussex: S. Dominics Press, 1921) in which she, too, contrasted the reticence of Mary with the discourse of her son: "Beside His perfect Speech Divine / Shall stand the Perfect Silence, Thine" (p. 2).

37. Though these verses about the transformation of desert rock are often thought to allude to Baudelaire, Manganiello (*T. S. Eliot and Dante,* p. 69) suggests a link between Baudelaire's reference to "Cybele, the 'Great Mother'" and Eliot's sense of intercessory influence exercised by "the second Eve, the Virgin Mary."

38. The evident contrast here is with the soul's condition, without "wings to fly," in part 1; likewise in *Paradiso* 33, Dante has St. Bernard insist that those who "would have grace" but do not turn to the Virgin Mary are seeking uselessly to make their desire "fly without wings" (trans. John Sinclair, p. 479).

39. Smith, *T. S. Eliot's Poetry and Plays,* p. 157.

40. Letter of 15 March 1928 to William Force Stead, Osborn Collection, Beinecke Library at Yale.

41. *Selections from Ralph Waldo Emerson,* ed. Stephen E. Whicher (Boston: Houghton Mifflin, 1957), p. 271.

42. *Dante's Paradise,* trans. John Sinclair, p. 335; in this passage Beatrice identifies Mary as "the rose in which the divine Word was made flesh."

43. Manganiello, *T. S. Eliot and Dante,* p. 34.

44. Much though not all subsequent commentary has accepted Grover Smith's schema, which defines Eliot's major subject (formulated in the third movement of each *Quartet*) as follows: "in the first *Quartet*, God the Father as the unmoved Mover; in the second, God the Son as Redeemer; in the third, the Virgin as Intercessor; and in the fourth, God the Holy Ghost as the voice and power of Love" (*T. S. Eliot's Poetry and Plays*, 253).

45. I have previously discussed the interplay between musical metaphors and mystical theology in "Spheric and Silent Music in Eliot's *Four Quartets*," *Renascence* 32 (1980): 195–213.

46. Allchin, *The Joy of All Creation,* p. 145; other worthy reflections on Eliot's response to the Annunciation theme and the Angelus devotion can be found in John Booty, *Meditating on Four Quartets* (Cambridge, Mass.: Cowley Publications, 1983), pp. 34–42; and Harry Blamires, *Word Unheard: A Guide through Eliot's "Four Quartets"* (London: Methuen & Co., 1969), pp. 92, 109–114.

47. In part 3, Eliot's reference to Krishna's teaching in the Bhagavad Gita presents a Hindu parallel to this ideal of detachment from interest in the product of one's actions or in private gain.

48. Allchin, *The Joy of All Creation,* p. 146.

49. Nancy Duvall Hargrove presents a detailed description of this shrine in *Landscape as Symbol in the Poetry of T. S. Eliot* (Jackson: University Press of Mississippi, 1978), p. 165.

50. Helen Gardner, *The Composition of "Four Quartets"* (New York: Oxford University Press, 1978), p. 34. Gardner reports further (p. 141) that the Marian shrine Eliot correctly imagined at Gloucester he had also, according to William T. Levy, brought to mind from observing the Church of Notre Dame de la Gard, which surveys the Mediterranean at Marseilles. It is fascinating to see how Olson himself makes poetic use of the Marian statue at Gloucester in part 2 of "I, Maximus of Gloucester, to You."

51. Gordon, *Eliot's Early Years,* pp. 6–7.

52. Ibid., p. 3; Robert Sencourt, *T. S. Eliot: A Memoir* (New York: Dodd, Mead, 1971), pp. 5, 9; book review cited in Gardner, *Composition,* p. 47.

53. Moreover, the Acts of the Apostles (1.14, with representions in later Christian iconography) confirms Mary's presence at Pentecost, the episode at which tongues of flame appear and which Eliot dramatizes in "Little Gidding."

54. Julian of Norwich, *A Revelation of Love,* ed. Marion Glasscoe (Exeter: University of Exeter Press, 1976), p. 20.

55. Lyndall Gordon, *Eliot's New Life* (New York: Farrar, Straus, and Giroux, 1988), p. 211.

56. Gordon, *Eliot's Early Years,* p. 11, 83, 124; Peter Ackroyd, *T. S. Eliot: A Life* (New York: Simon and Schuster, 1984), p. 91.

57. Evaluating biographical evidence relevant to the case, Lyndall Gordon ends up stressing the role of Emily Hale—"Eliot's muse in *Ash-Wednesday* (p. 15)"—in *Eliot's New Life,* pp. 3, 11–16, 146–240.

58. From a sermon preached in 1948 as cited in Gordon, *Eliot's Early Years,* p. 12.

EPILOGUE

1. Much that Sacvan Bercovitch has written, in seminal books such as *The Puritan Origins of the American Self* (New Haven: Yale University Press, 1975) and *The American Jeremiad* (Madison: University of Wisconsin Press, 1978), must be counted exceptional in this regard. Another instance would be Lawrence Buell's treatment in *New England Literary Culture: From Revolution through Renaissance* (Cambridge and New York: Cambridge University Press, 1986). As Jenny Franchot points out, scholars such as Ann Douglas (*The Feminization of American Culture* [Knopf, 1977; reprint, New York: Anchor Doubleday, 1988]) and Jane Tompkins (*Sensational Designs: The Cultural Work of American Fiction, 1790–1860* [New York: Oxford University Press, 1985]) have also recognized religion's role in imaginative literature, particularly as regards Stowe. A few studies also focus more specifically on American cases of imaginative intersection with Roman Catholic culture. These include Franchot's own account of *Roads to Rome: The Antebellum Encounter with Catholicism* (Ber-

keley: University of California Press, 1994); and Paul Giles's *American Catholic Arts and Fic-tions: Culture, Ideology, Aesthetics* (New York: Cambridge University Press, 1992). Written from outside the standpoint of theistic belief, Camille Paglia's controversial analysis of eroti-cism in Western culture (in *Sexual Personae: Art and Decadence from Nerfertiti to Emily Dickinson* [New Haven: Yale University Press, 1990]) nonetheless recognizes the enduring mythical influence of Mediterranean paganism in conjunction with Catholicism and versions of the goddess mother that had been "banished from Protestantism" (p. 579).

2. Jenny Franchot, "Invisible Domain: Religion and American Literary Studies," *American Literature* 67 (1995): 835; Stephen L. Carter, *The Culture of Disbelief: How American Law and Politics Trivialize Religious Devotion* (New York: Basic Books, 1993).

3. Thomas Moore, *Care of the Soul: A Guide for Cultivating Depth and Sacredness in Ev-eryday Life* (New York: HarperCollins, 1992).

4. See Robert Anthony Orsi, *The Madonna of 115th Street: Faith and Community in Ital-ian Harlem, 1880–1950* (New Haven: Yale University Press, 1985).

5. In *No Place of Grace: Antimodernism and the Transformation of American Culture 1880–1920* (New York: Pantheon, 1981), T. J. Jackson Lears describes more fully the widespread sense of "spiritual homelessness" experienced by nineteenth-century Americans affected by secu-larization and "modern doubt" (p. 42).

INDEX